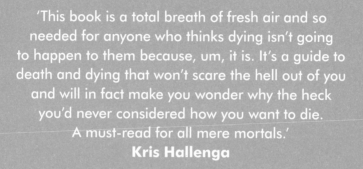
'This book is a total breath of fresh air and so
needed for anyone who thinks dying isn't going
to happen to them because, um, it is. It's a guide to
death and dying that won't scare the hell out of you
and will in fact make you wonder why the heck
you'd never considered how you want to die.
A must-read for all mere mortals.'
Kris Hallenga

'We don't have to think about death and dying
all the time but when we want to – or are forced to –
how wonderful to have a manual to sustain and guide
us through it all. Like a firm but caring hand to hold
our own and steer us along a difficult path.'
Sarah Brown

'*We All Know How This Ends* is a truly compelling
read. A book we can all learn so much from, and a
book that proves why it is so desperately important that
we speak openly about death; of others' and the prospect
of our own. This book will take you on other people's
journeys of loss, shared bravely and beautifully, and
give you a new perspective on what grief and
grieving looks like for so many.'
Elle Wright

'Honest, helpful and healing; the emotionally
intelligent guide to demystifying death so we can
live better lives. Full of the knowledge, compassion
and insight that all of us will need, sooner or later.
I wish I'd read this book in my 20s.'
Rosa Hoskins

@lifedeathwhat

We all
know how
this ends.

GREEN TREE
Bloomsbury Publishing Plc
50 Bedford Square, London, WC1B 3DP, UK
29 Earlsfort Terrace, Dublin 2, Ireland

BLOOMSBURY, GREEN TREE and the Green
Tree logo are trademarks of Bloomsbury
Publishing Plc

First published in Great Britain 2021
This edition published 2021

Bloomsbury Publishing Plc does not have any
control over, or responsibility for, any third-party
websites referred to or in this book. All internet
addresses given in this book were correct at the
time of going to press. The author and publisher
regret any inconvenience caused if addresses
have changed or sites have ceased to exist, but
can accept no responsibility for any such changes

A catalogue record for this book is available
from the British Library

Library of Congress Cataloguing-in-Publication
data has been applied for.

ISBN
HB: 978-1-4729-6681-0
ePub: 978-1-4729-6680-3
ePDF: 978-1-4729-6678-0

2 4 6 8 10 9 7 5 3

Designed by Studio Polka
Printed and bound in Great Britain by CPI Group
(UK) Ltd, Croydon, CR0 4YY

MIX
Paper from
responsible sources
FSC® C020471

To find out more about our authors and
books visit www.bloomsbury.com and sign
up for our newsletters

Lessons about life and living
from working with death and dying

We all know how this ends.

Anna Lyons & Louise Winter

GREEN TREE
LONDON · OXFORD · NEW YORK · NEW DELHI · SYDNEY

Contents

In this book, the word *death* appears 568 times.

The word *life* appears 641 times.

So although this is a book about death,

it's actually a book about life.

Introduction

This book begins at the end

One day you'll eat your very last meal. You'll speak your final words. You'll take your very last breath.

Your heart will stop beating. Your blood will no longer flow.

You will die. You will be dead.

Death is our future, the only future of which we can be truly certain. It's inescapable and unavoidable. Everyone who is born has to die. Life is terminal. There is no cure. Neither life nor death is black and white. We don't come with an expiry date. We might die tomorrow, we might die next week, or we might die in 50 years' time.

Worldwide, 151,600 people die each and every day. That's *one hundred and fifty one thousand and six hundred* people. In the time it takes to watch an episode of *This Is Us* on Amazon Prime, 6316 people have died. If you think about how many other lives each life, and therefore each death, affects, that means countless more have been bereaved and are grieving. Some 105 people have died in the minute it's taken to read these statistics. That's almost two people every second.

Around 600,000 people die in the UK every year. At least one child in every school classroom is bereaved and growing up without a parent. Almost

40 per cent of us will be diagnosed with some form of cancer in our lifetime. Almost 3 million people are currently living with cancer in the UK and, according to Macmillan Cancer Support, this figure will rise to 4 million by 2030. Around 40 per cent of all people over the age of 65 are living with life-limiting long-standing illness. These are stark, sobering statistics and yet we still don't openly talk about death or teach our children how to live with the inevitability of it.

We're Anna Lyons, an end-of-life doula, and Louise Winter, a progressive funeral director, and together we're the team behind Life. Death. Whatever. We joined forces several years ago to find a way to get everyone talking about death, dying, life, living, illness, funerals and grief. Our mission at Life. Death. Whatever. is to help you to have a more empowered approach to whatever you're going through.

As an end-of-life doula, Anna supports people who are living with serious illness, their family and friends, and people living with grief. Her aim is to help people live as good a life as possible until the very end. People who are dying are living right up until their very last breath and she believes it's essential to support people to experience a life they can enjoy for as long as possible.

As a progressive funeral director, Louise has an unconventional approach to her work. Her mission is to encourage everyone to really think about funerals and why we have them. She believes that a good funeral can be transformational in helping us to acknowledge and accept that someone has died.

Anna might be there when your sister finds out that her cancer has a devastating prognosis and support her as she decides how she wants to live with her illness. Louise might be the person you call when your sister has died. She will help you to find a way to say goodbye, in a way that works for you.

Our experiences have shown us that death is a normal part of life and dying is part of living. Acknowledging and accepting that one day we will die is fundamental to living a full life. It's as simple and as complicated as that.

We don't believe death is a taboo, as the media would have us believe. But we do believe that as a society and as a culture, we shy away from it because we don't know what else to do.

However, we can't ignore death and dying. It's not going to go away. Our only hope is to change the way we see it and find a new way of approaching it that's helpful and relevant to the times in which we live.

This book isn't a lament on the loss of life, because we believe that death and dying don't have to be gloomy or taboo subjects. Talking about death and dying can be life-affirming and life-enhancing. That's why we created Life. Death. Whatever. It began life as a groundbreaking festival about death, in partnership with the National Trust's Sutton House, a Tudor house with an eclectic history in Hackney, East London in October 2016. We hosted an art exhibition as well as a line-up of events, installations and workshops, encouraging creative reflection on life, death and everything in between.

We positioned birth, life and death together under one roof and challenged visitors to the house to consider all three as one. We can't have life without birth, and we can't have life without death. These three, intrinsically linked by the mere nature of existence, were spread out across the uneven walls and floors of the Tudor house, encouraging visitors to see the whole rather than just two-thirds. We dared them to imagine that life is finite and encouraged them to consider that ignoring this truth will not make it shrink quietly back into the shadows. We stimulated, provoked, amused, inspired, disgusted and entertained all who came by.

There were interactive installations, coffin ball pits, sculptures, paintings, site-specific sound and mixed-media pieces, photographs and films. We gave visitors the opportunity to add their unspoken words to an ever-evolving piece called Unsaid, and invited them to enjoy afterlife-themed cocktails from a pop-up bar called 'The Waiting Room'.

After the festival, Life. Death. Whatever. developed into an international community of people from many different disciplines, united in a commitment to opening up the conversation about death and making it something we can all live with.

Life. Death. Whatever. then became an approach, a way of working, a common framework and a language, based on principles of empathy, compassion and kindness, underpinned by an awareness of the inevitable. It affected, and then changed, the way we work with death and dying, as well as how we engage with life and living.

In our work, both independently and together, we have unparalleled access to life at its most heightened, vulnerable and fragile. We inhabit the liminal space as people transition between life and death, bearing witness to this once-in-a-lifetime experience. With this comes a wealth of understanding and lessons that teach us so much about how to live, not just how to die.

Throughout this book, we'll talk about the people we've known and worked alongside, the funerals we've facilitated, and the approach we've taken to our work, both together and separately. We'll share our experiences with you, from the ordinary to the extraordinary.

The people we've worked with have had a profound and transformational effect on our own lives. We'll share the heartbreaking, surprising and uplifting stories that have inspired us to live, love and, sometimes, to let go and walk away. We'll reflect on the blessings and tragedies of life, the exquisite agony and ecstasy of being alive, and the fragility of everything and everyone we hold dear.

The work we do doesn't prevent our grief, it simply means we have a better idea of what we need to do when faced with it. When Louise's granny died, and when our friends Jon Underwood, Saima Thompson and Kimberley St John died unexpectedly while we were writing this book, it didn't mean we were immune to grief and pain. It didn't mean that we didn't cry; it simply meant that we knew the most helpful reaction was to let ourselves do whatever we needed to do and feel whatever we needed to feel.

This book is full of stories, conversations, insights and observations about how we deal with the fact that we're all going to die. It's for anyone who wants to know how we can have a more empowered approach to all matters related to our mortality. We'll talk openly and honestly about dying, death, living, life, illness, funerals and grief. It might be an emotional journey but we hope you'll stay with us for the ride.

You'll also hear from people in the Life. Death. Whatever. community who have been generous enough to share their experiences and reflections with us in the form of 'Five Things'. This project started quite by accident in Anna's kitchen on a Saturday night when we were reflecting on how amazed we were by the profound stories of love and loss people were sharing with us. We wanted to find a way for everyone to be able to tell their stories, and for others to be able to read, and learn from, other people's experiences.

Five Things has since grown into an international online campaign where everyone is invited to share what they've learned about whatever they've been through or are going through. We've shared Five Things about what it's like to be diagnosed with cancer in your 20s, what it's like to lose almost your entire family in a tragic accident, what healthcare professionals would like you to know about the reality of CPR, what it's like to hear that a family member has suddenly died from COVID-19, what grief really feels like, and many more experiences besides. We've printed some of them in this book. Whatever you're going through, we hope there'll be a Five Things that will resonate with you.

We hope that these pages are filled with compassion, love and kindness alongside a bold honesty you don't usually find when reading about death. We don't shirk away from our subject matter, and we don't use euphemisms. In our work, no one passes away, they die. No one is at rest, they've died. We use the actual words, even when it's difficult to hear them. Because we believe that by owning what's happening, we're better equipped to deal with the reality of what's going on.

We've written about what we can all do to make our lives and the lives of those around us easier and better, right up until the very end. It's about how generosity, love, honesty and kindness with ourselves and others can change the way we grieve. If we can acknowledge the inevitability of our deaths, it can make a fundamental difference to how we live our lives.

We believe it's possible to embrace a lifetime of love, adventure, curiosity and wonder, acknowledging and accepting the inevitability of having to experience grief, loss and death.

Because we all know how this ends.

It ends.

Anna & Louise

P.S. This book is inspired by our experiences. If you recognise a fragment of yourself in our writing, know that you were of consequence to our work and to our lives. To those who have allowed us to share your journeys through life and living, death and dying, we wrote this book in your honour.

P.P.S. We've made it easy for you to understand whose words you're reading by using a key – [A] for Anna, [L] for Louise and [A + L] when we've written a section together.

FIVE THINGS YOU NEED TO KNOW BEFORE YOU READ THIS BOOK

by Anna Lyons and Louise Winter

1.

We work in death and dying but that doesn't make us experts. We can't tell you when or how you're going to die. We don't know if there's an afterlife or what's going to happen next. Instead, we'll share our reflections and insights based on the many people who have shared their journey with us, and how they've profoundly affected our own approach to living our lives. In doing so, we've tried to find a way to turn death and dying into something we can all live well with.

2.

Take what you need and leave the rest. We've written this book so you can choose what's relevant to you. You might be curious. You might have been wanting to think about and discuss this subject for a while but haven't found a way. You might have just got married and made a decision to discuss the future. You might be facing the end of your life. Perhaps someone significant to you has just died. Whatever it is, there's a section for you. This book is for everyone.

3.

This isn't a dirge on death but it isn't a celebration of life either. We won't gloss over difficult things. It's about life as much as it's about death. We won't disregard grief or anything else gritty and uncomfortable. We'll even talk about the reality of what happens when someone dies, warts and all.

4.

We won't talk in euphemisms. Although we'll always do it gently and sensitively, we'll say things as they are. Hopefully, by the time you reach the end of the book, you'll understand why.

5.

We've written about the people we've accompanied and supported, although we've disguised most of their identities. We've also shared some of our personal experiences of grief, loss and heartbreak because they've taught us the most important lessons about life. We've written about how something happened for us, our truth and our interpretation of events. We know it might have felt differently to you.

We really need to talk about death and dying

[A + L]

'Society has lost sight of the fact that we are all mortal and at some point we are all going to die. We've just got to accept that this is a normal part of life and make it as easy as possible for people to talk about it, think about it and plan ahead.'
DR OLLIE MINTON, CONSULTANT IN PALLIATIVE MEDICINE

There are three basic things we can rely on in this life of ours:

1. We'll be born.
2. We'll live.
3. And we'll die.

These three events are fundamental to our existence, and can sum up our finite lives. Birth, life and death are a messy business, but death is the only one we try to avoid altogether.

We might talk about our fears of giving birth to our children, our concerns as parents, our frustrations with work and relationships, and the struggles we face in life, but rarely do we volunteer to talk about death and dying, especially our own.

Birth is the beginning of the unpredictable adventure we call life. Death is the end. When someone dies, it leaves an irreplaceable hole in our lives. It hurts. We have no control over it. We don't want to imagine that it will happen to us or anyone we know. We might not be able to imagine a world without us, or them, in it. No wonder we don't want to talk about it.

But how can we truly live a good life if we never properly acknowledge that one day it's going to end and the people we know and love will die? Avoiding it won't prevent it from happening. It is going to happen to all of us.

How many of us would jump headfirst into marriage without truly thinking about the implications and consequences? Do we give birth with no thought as to how and where? Have you ever bought a house without stepping inside it first? Yet we tend to hurtle towards the end of our lives mostly without thinking about it, discussing it or really believing it's going to happen.

Death will happen, no matter how much we're loved, how accomplished we are, how many Prada handbags we own, how many supplements we take, or how much money we have in our bank accounts. It might be 80 years from now or it might be tomorrow. Death is life's great unknown.

As a society, we hide death and dying behind closed doors, squirrelled away in metropolis-sized hospitals, nursing homes, hospices and suffocatingly warm makeshift bedrooms hastily moved to the ground floor of someone's home. We talk in hushed tones about someone's life-limiting diagnosis. We play hide-and-seek with our feelings and push our heartbreak far beneath the surface so we can outwardly maintain the guise that we're coping.

A recent report by the British Medical Association concluded that doctors continue to treat people who are dying when active treatment is no longer of any benefit. The report stated they do this because of pressure from patients and their families. Many doctors we have spoken to also feel that by acknowledging there's nothing more that can be done, they themselves are admitting defeat and have failed.

Death is not a failure. It's a natural and normal part of life. If we view it as such, we might be able to approach it in a different way. If we discussed end-of-life issues regularly we wouldn't find them so tricky to broach when we're in a hospital bed talking about what might happen next.

Doctors are not superhuman and we are not immortal. Things happen to us – we're involved in accidents, we become unwell and our lives come to an end, sometimes sooner than we'd like or had imagined. The inability of a doctor to save our life is rarely a failure on their part.

One member of the Life. Death. Whatever. community is a doctor who works in hospitals in London, specialising in emergency medicine. She talks about how the doctors she works with go outside to smoke a cigarette with their colleagues after a patient has died, often after aggressive and unnecessary attempts to keep them alive. Smoking a cigarette is their coping mechanism. It's a paltry three minutes of therapy, before they're back on the wards dealing with another emergency.

Doctors, more than anyone, need to understand that our death is not their failure. If this were acknowledged and understood there might be less unnecessary, ineffective and aggressive treatment at end of life.

We are all responsible for lack of good communication. Doctors can be hesitant and reticent, often because they haven't been taught how to communicate; patients, families and friends can be understandably unwilling to hear the reality of a situation.

When people are dying, we usually take gentle and loving care of them. Then as soon as they've died, we sometimes push them away, fearful of the reality of them being dead. Most hospitals don't even have signposts to the mortuary, as though its very existence needs to be hidden away and denied.

When someone dies in a nursing home, most require that they are immediately 'removed' by the funeral directors, who arrive at 3 a.m., dressed in black. They use the back doors and don't tell the other residents what's happened, leaving everyone wondering what happened to lovely Doris in room 23. Families rush to the nursing home to find their person has already been taken away, leaving them with no time or space to say goodbye.

Why don't we build nursing homes with adequate facilities for taking care of people after they've died? Why are the residents 'removed' from the community after death, as though they're now something contaminated and unsavoury? Even hospices are often built without adequate facilities for caring for people after they've died. The simple addition of a chilled room could allow families, friends and the community the opportunity to come together to acknowledge what's happened and say goodbye. Rather than hiding death away, so as not to distress the other residents, why not acknowledge it?

These changes are simple, but could make a remarkable difference to our grief and our ongoing lives – it just requires a shift in the way we think about death, both as professionals and as members of the public, too.

When someone dies, even if it's expected, many of us panic and call the first funeral director we can think of on our high street. We rarely ask questions and just accept whatever we're told. We pay huge sums of money for a funeral that might not serve our needs, fitting into the bronze, silver, gold or platinum package, defined by the number of limousines following the hearse. At a time of overwhelming grief, we might not know there's any other way.

We may have spent a lifetime going to funerals that didn't honour the life of the person who has died. Far too often, we squeeze everything into a 20-minute service at the crematorium, strictly patrolled by funeral professionals who treat it as business as usual, seemingly forgetting that we're there because a person has died.

For over 100 years, our funeral directors have protected us from our dead. They mostly hide behind dusty net curtains in shabby funeral homes and use archaic language, distancing themselves, and us, from the reality of their work. Most have terrible websites and won't put their prices online. They tell us that the person who has died needs to be embalmed because we couldn't possibly cope with the reality of seeing them dead. They use language like 'conveyance of the deceased', rather than using simple language we can all understand.

No wonder some of us have dismissed funerals, opting for a direct disposal service instead. A member of the Life. Death. Whatever. community who is a funeral director talks openly about the queue of coffins waiting to be unloaded from vans at her local crematorium. Is this what we want for our dead? Do we want to live in a society that doesn't properly acknowledge and commemorate its members as individuals who deserve to be recognised, both in life and in death?

Yet we *can* do death differently. Funerals can serve us in our loss, our suffering and our grief. They can be done well. They need to be done well. *Our funerals really matter.*

After the funeral, we don't know how to support each other in our grief. We cross the road to avoid awkward encounters. We stop talking about the person who has died, scared that someone will cry or show how they *really* feel. We leave people alone with their grief. We don't show up for others when they need it the most, because we just don't know how.

We all need to take responsibility for our approach to dying, death, illness, funerals and grief. Let's talk about it openly, embracing whatever comes up – our fears, anxieties, difficulties and upset. It's hard to discuss the end of life at the end of life. It's hard to make a good decision about a funeral if we've never thought about it before. It's much easier to talk about all of it while we're living a healthy life.

Let's encourage our teachers to talk about death and dying with our children, openly and honestly. Let's include it as part of the curriculum. Rather than worrying that our children won't be able to cope with it, let's give them the opportunity to ask questions and decide for themselves. We might find these death-aware children are the more open-minded, resilient and emotionally switched-on adults of the future.

If we spend our final days in a hospice in the UK, we're lucky. Partly thanks to Dame Cicely Saunders, the founder of the hospice movement, the UK is considered to be the best in the world for end-of-life care. But we can still improve. Being the best in the world doesn't mean we are good enough. Dying well is a basic human right. Dying with care, dignity and respect is the very least we should be able to offer ourselves and each other, whether we die at home, in hospital, in a nursing home or a hospice.

If end-of-life issues were a part of our everyday conversation and chat, we'd find these subjects so much easier to broach. As children, we discuss our hopes and dreams for the future. We describe how we want our lives to look and feel but we don't think about the end of our lives. We hear stories of our introduction to the world but rarely do we imagine stories of what it will be like at the end.

What would our society and culture look like if we embraced death and dying as part of life and living? Would we be kinder and more compassionate individuals? Would we teach children about all the facts of life, rather than just some of them? Would we include our elderly in our lives rather than hiding them away in nursing homes? Would we equip our doctors with the right language and training and give them the support they need to support people at the end of their lives? Would we find a way for our society to properly acknowledge, and say goodbye to our dead? Would we build facilities that adequately cater for our needs when someone has died? Would our funeral profession employ individuals with the required qualities of emotional intelligence, gentleness and sensitivity? Would we have funeral homes that were run for the greater good of the community rather than to serve the bank accounts of shareholders? Would we be able to be there for each other in our grief, our sorrow and our pain?

It's time to end the deathly silence. Let's talk about it and find out.

Why we really don't want to talk about it

[A + L]

'When we avoid difficult conversations, we trade short term discomfort for long term dysfunction.'
PETER BROMBERG, WELL-KNOWN SPEAKER AND PHILANTHROPIST

For as long as we've lived, we've died. Religions, belief systems, faiths, rituals and traditions have all contributed to how we handle this simple fact of life.

Historically, we were so much better at talking about death and dying. For example, the Victorians may have been reluctant to discuss sex, but they talked about death as part of daily life. Disease was prevalent, so living with death and dying was perfectly normal. Everyone was exposed to it from the moment they were born.

No one was exempt from an early death in the Victorian era, no matter how privileged or wealthy they were. Only 40 per cent of babies born in the 1850s would reach their 60th birthday. Less than 10 per cent made it to their 80th. That meant that the Victorians saw a lot of dead people and attended a lot of funerals.

As medicine's abilities have improved, life expectancy has increased. Today, we may well be in our 20s, 30s or 40s without ever having to confront the reality of our mortality, see a dead person or attend a funeral. We now *expect* medicine to be able to prolong our lives.

Over the last 110 years, we've witnessed death on a major scale with two world wars and a major flu epidemic. During the wars, millions of people left home and never returned. Everyone knew someone who had died, yet no one was taught how to grieve or deal with the difficulty and complexity of their emotions. The severity of the trauma was minimised. Society was taught to keep calm and carry on because, in order to survive, there was no other choice. In the face of such adversity, the British became known for their unwavering fortitude – the stiff upper lip.

Today, we're getting better at dealing with how we feel. As a society, we're beginning to embrace sobriety, appoint therapists and willingly work on the quality of our lives. We go to yoga, we meditate, we eat consciously and we talk about our mental health. Life used to be about surviving, now it's about thriving. We want to live happy, contented, purposeful and meaningful lives.

Talking about death and dying is hard because it brings up so many difficult emotions, which most of us don't know how to manage. At school, we're not taught how to cope with the way we feel, the complexity of our emotions and our reactions to difficult situations. We're getting better at it but we're not there yet.

Avoiding talking about death won't prevent it from happening. By changing the way we deal with our emotions, we can transform the way we approach death and dying, and perhaps live fuller and more satisfying lives.

The key isn't to wait until we reach the end. It's to deal with how we feel today.

The Life. Death. Whatever. manifesto

[A + L]

We believe that our relationship with death and dying can be re-imagined. Over the last few years, we've been working to redesign the dialogue around death and dying, to open it up and to find new approaches to this important subject. Our work, and the rest of this book, is based on seven core beliefs that influence everything we do:

1. **Death is a natural and normal part of life**
   Death isn't separate to life. It might be sad, scary, moving, difficult, messy and profound, but it's still a natural and normal part of life.

   We all face 'death' in some form on a regular basis – whether it's the end of a relationship, a job change, the loss of a friendship or the death of someone we love death is an essential part of our lives.

2. **Death is not the last taboo**
   Just because it can be emotive, difficult and controversial doesn't mean it's taboo. Death is everywhere; it's all around us. It's on our TV screens, in cinemas and on the news. Funeral homes are on our high streets with mortuaries hidden in plain sight between the Post Office and the dry cleaners. We get married in churches surrounded by graves (containing real dead people!). We walk through cemeteries on our way home from work.

   If we say things often enough, we will believe them. So let's stop saying that death is taboo; let's say that death is a natural and normal part of life. Perhaps if we say it loudly and frequently, it will become the norm.

3. **Death is about dealing with difficult emotions**
   It's hard to have conversations about difficult subjects – relationships, sex, money, mental health for example – but death really is the ultimate. It's the subject that brings everything to the forefront, revealing our deepest, most emotional inner selves and all the fault lines in the dynamics of our relationships.

   We need an emotional toolkit that supports us in dealing with difficult emotions so we can have tricky conversations. If we can handle the emotions we experience in life, we'll be better equipped to deal with the emotions we experience around death.

4. **Death is not a failure**

Death is not a test. We don't succeed or fail at it. If we die because we haven't survived an illness, that doesn't mean we've failed. Death is generally not a failure of medicine either.

No one loses their battle. Using combative language like this implies that a person didn't try hard enough to live. Waging war on a disease like cancer isn't any kind of a fair fight. People die because their treatment didn't work, not because they didn't fight hard enough to stay alive.

5. **Our use of language around death and dying needs to change**

Euphemisms aren't helpful. No one has passed away, is late, sleeping or at rest. *We're dying. We die. We're dead.*

Euphemisms prevent true understanding, rather than softening the blow. Saying that someone has 'passed away' rather than they've died doesn't make the reality of their death any less difficult to bear.

Owning and acknowledging the reality of what has happened helps us to really show up for ourselves and for others. We can use the real words and tell the story as it is. By doing so we invite everyone else to do the same.

6. **We need to create links between communities involved in end-of-life and after-death care**

Death and dying aren't separate. Yet after someone has died, the care team step back, handing over to another set of professionals.

We need a common framework that includes everyone who works at the end of life – hospices, nursing homes, carers, hospitals, coroners, funeral directors, cemetery and crematorium staff, therapists and counsellors. We need to work together to create an emotionally intelligent, flexible and more holistic system that better serves and supports everyone.

7. **Talking about death and dying can be life-affirming and life-enhancing**

Death isn't something to be avoided, but to be acknowledged, considered and explored. By doing so, we can live our lives with an awareness that we're not going to be here forever, so can make the best possible use of today.

By talking about death and dying, we believe we can live fuller, richer, kinder, more purposeful and meaningful lives.

What is Five Things?

[A + L]

We've written a lot about what we've learned from working with dying, death and grief, but all of our words and work are underpinned by other people's experiences. Five Things evolved from this. Everyone experiences life and death differently and walking alongside so many incredible individuals has allowed us an insight into the most closely guarded aspects of our existence.

Sharing our stories is not only helpful for people going through something similar, but it can be healing in itself. Our pain being acknowledged, our experience being 'seen' and our voice being heard is cathartic. Knowing that we are not alone, knowing that someone else is living through something similar, understanding that there are a multitude of ways to cope, finding out that you're not the only person in the world who is struggling, resonating with someone else's experience – all these shared experiences help.

Five Things brings together hundreds of people's experiences. Through the project, we've been able to share their lessons and their words of wisdom; lessons born from their lives, their jobs, their loves, their illness, their imminent death or the death of someone intrinsic to their life, their grief. In their own words and on their own terms, they have collaborated with us to create an ever-growing social resource of information, advice, musings, reflections and learnings. Five Things belongs to you, it's for you and it's about you.

Weaved throughout the book are just a few of the Five Things we've received. If you look up #FiveThings and #lifedeathwhatever on social media you'll find many more. There's a permanent home for them on our website and we are always looking for people to send us theirs. Please do get in touch with us via the Life. Death. Whatever. website if you'd like to contribute.

www.lifedeathwhatever.com

What is Unsaid?

[A + L]

It's often said that everyone has a book inside them, one that they ought to write. We all walk around with conversations we never had, emotions we were unable to express, unarticulated fury and disappointment, moments we wish we could take back, actions and reactions and inactions that we'd do differently given half the chance, whirring inside our minds. Words sound different in our heads to how they sound tumbling from our mouths. We may later act out old scenarios, reworking them for an audience that will only ever be ourselves. There's no arbitrator, no one to offer a measured reply or gentle advice when we keep these words locked tight inside our skulls. Words left unspoken can disrupt and damage, they can become bigger and more troublesome as silent intruders in our minds. We need to find a way to release them, to say them or to write them.

We created Unsaid to do just that. It's an anonymous (unless you choose otherwise) interactive installation that allows people to express all the things they've been unable to say. It's a collection of cathartic postcards that we take care of for you. We share your words, your burden, your sorrow, your secrets and your sadness without judgement or comment. We give those words a physical presence, we give them space outside of your thoughts and we bear witness to your experience. We've shared some of them throughout this book.

What words have you left unsaid?

Death & dying

[A]

We can live through the unimaginable: with help and support, we can live well with dying, death and grief. We just need to help people do it. We often get end-of-life care just right, when we refer people to the right places and they have the right resources available to them. However, according to research carried out by Independent Age, more than 100,000 people die each year in the UK with no end-of-life care in place and that's just not good enough. We need to provide extra support for people living with life-limiting illness. Perhaps one way we can do this is by introducing the role of an end-of-life doula into the mainstream, and into the NHS. End-of-life care cannot be exclusive to those who can afford it. Everyone dies and everyone deserves proper care. Everyone. How can we ensure we get the care we need? What care are we all entitled to and what are the questions we should be asking? Read on to find out more. In this section, we'll learn:

1. What end-of-life doulas do and how to become one.
2. All about getting diagnosed, and living with illness.
3. How various types of care differ, from hospitals to hospices.
4. What dying actually looks like.
5. Getting your needs met.
6. How to prepare for your own death by putting your affairs in order.
7. How to help someone who is dying.
8. What happens when a child dies.
9. The undeniable beauty in the impermanence of life.

Can doulas be part of the future of end-of-life care?

[A]

Winter was finally turning to spring and the promise of warmth hung in the late-afternoon air. My phone rang but I put it on silent, choosing to finish my work rather than chat so I could get outside to feel the breeze on my skin before the sun set and the cold clambered back out of the darkness. Moments after the deliberately missed call, my phone glowed to life with a message that simply read, 'She is dead'.

Guilt, panic, sorrow, disbelief, despair, fear, numbness all whizzed around in my head. I called back. No reply. I called back. Engaged. I called back. He answered.

Even expected death can shock when the moment actually comes. This was one of those times. We'd been on high alert for two years but had somehow become lulled into complacency by the passing time – more time than we'd anticipated. She'd carried on long past consultants' predictions, and statistical averages. I'd stopped grabbing for the phone every time he called. But now she was dead. And I was heartbroken.

'I know she was a relative but shouldn't you be used to this by now?' asked one of my friends when my uncontrollable sobs receded. 'You work with people who are dying. Doesn't that make it easier?' Both his clumsy questions had a single, resounding answer: 'No'.

As an end-of-life doula I support people who are dying, their family and their friends. Sometimes, I'll work with people who are grieving. My aim is to help people live as good a life as possible right up until the very end. Someone who is dying – *right now* – is still alive. It's essential to help them keep living a life they love, enjoy, even – for as long as possible. I don't help people have a 'good death'. I'm not even sure that's possible. Death is loss. The actual act, and moment, of death can never be seen as 'good'. What all of us can do, however, is to make life as good as possible.

But the answer to my friend's question is still, and will always be, no. Working with death and dying doesn't make these things easier when it's someone I love. What it *has* done is teach me about life and living.

THE BEGINNING AND THE END OF LIFE

I've always loved the idea of pregnancy. Not so much the reality of it – morning sickness, cramps and the inability to be comfortable – but the idea of it. We *grow* a *human*. We grow a human! Inside us! While we're doing other things! I have no idea about the complexity of the human nervous system, but I made three of them without even trying!

The rhetoric of fertility and the birthing goddess is not so far from the truth. We are life-givers, in the truest sense of the words. And at the end of this miraculous gestation, our babies are welcomed into this world excitedly with a pure celebration of life.

When our newborns whimper they are soothed and fussed, fed and changed. When they reach a milestone, however small, we record it proudly; those babbling sounds that become our first real words, the clumsy crawl that becomes our first real steps. It's right that we do this. It's good that we do.

Here's something that people don't like to think about, even though we all know it to be true: every one of those vulnerable 'firsts' after birth is mirrored in vulnerable 'lasts' before we die. We find it so difficult to offer the same protection and care for the fragility of people who are unwell or elderly. We are terrified of those *final* words, and those *final* steps. It shows. We do not offer the same deference at the end of life as we do at its beginning. We need to change this. Life's final moments should be treated with the same importance as those at the start. We need to embrace the end as we did the beginning. The end-of-life process marks the final time we'll be able to do things for the people we love, and for them to feel the things we've done for them.

THE ROLE OF THE END-OF-LIFE DOULA

The profession of end-of-life doula is still very new. The reason for this is very, *very* old: we fear death, and these days we don't like to talk about it. The problem is that we *need* to talk about it. I've been doing this job long enough to know that people *want* to talk about it. They just don't know how.

End-of-life doulas talk about death with the living and people who are dying. Just as a birth doula provides support and guidance to mothers and mothers-to-be at the start of life, as an end-of-life doula I provide support and guidance for people who are living with dying, their family and their friends.

Some of it is prosaic. I'll take children to the park. I'll walk the dog. I'll help keep the house clean and cook comforting food; I know it's the last thing anyone will be thinking about but everyone will need it. Some of it is emotional. I'll help answer questions. I'll help create memory boxes. I spend time with the person who is dying. I facilitate those difficult and necessary conversations that everyone has spent their lives avoiding.

Some of it is practical. I'll work on Advanced Care Planning and Directives (more on these later on), and when the moment of death comes and goes, I am there to support people in their grief. I can help with funeral arrangements and plans for the wake. If you want to keep the person who has died at home, I can help you to do this too.

Some of it is intermediary. I'll be there to liaise with the medical team and help translate medical jargon. I'll ask doctors the questions that get forgotten in those overwhelming medical meetings. I'll interact with care agencies and hospices. I'll make notes during medical consultations and keep a record for you of what was said.

Sometimes, I'm tasked with delivering news to waiting family members. One day a client received news that she felt unable to share with her family. She asked me to talk to her mother about her results. I usually try to empower people to take charge and support them to have these conversations themselves, but on this occasion the right thing to do was just what she wanted. I encouraged her to come with me and we sat together to deliver her news. I supported my client and her mother, by ensuring they did not feel alone. I wasn't able to change the news or its terrible consequences, but I was able to make sure they had all the information in layman's terms and they understood not only what was happening, but what their next steps could be.

I cannot fix breaking bodies but I can help to support the person inside. Every time I step into the role, I need to change my approach. The hardest part of this is that no matter how I adapt to a new client, I very rarely get to deliver something that isn't bad news. No matter how resigned someone is, no matter how accepting a family is, there's usually always a part of them that hopes for a miracle or a leap in medical science that will suddenly become available to save them. This hope is the blessing and the curse of our species. Everyone hopes that they will be the exception.

It does happen: a man I worked with many years ago had been given a maximum of six months to live, 20 years before. He was the exception to the rule. It remains, to this day, the only time I've ever seen it happen. This outcome didn't come without difficulties, though. He'd resigned himself to an early death, he'd put his affairs in order and said his goodbyes. He'd left his job. He was ready for the end, and it took a very long time to come. He sometimes spoke of feeling that his prognosis had haunted him throughout his life. He'd never felt able to relax and enjoy the time he had. He was always looking over his shoulder, waiting for the Grim Reaper. He'd carried on smoking because he didn't see the point in giving up with so little time left. Over the years his breathing had become so difficult he'd needed a constant supply of oxygen. He lost confidence in his body; he stopped leaving the house. He became depressed and isolated from his friends and family. At times, he spoke of feeling like the boy who cried wolf and was worried others saw him as a phoney. He was grateful for the extra years he'd had, but on some bleak days he wondered if he'd squandered the gift of this extra time.

The end-of-life doula role is flexible, centred around people and tailored to individuals. I won't ever push my own ideas or impose my way of thinking. I will discuss their needs – your needs – and my ability to meet them. I will find out what is important to my clients. I will ask, 'What matters to you?' and, 'What do you want and need?' Sometimes, I will only work with the person who is dying. Other times, I will only work with their family and friends. A few years ago, on a beautiful summer evening, I sat in a garden in Crouch End and listened to stories of love and friendship. Earlier that day, one of the integral members of their friendship group had died. I'd never met her but I'd spent many months supporting her friends. I felt some vicarious affinity to her through photographs and stories. I'd first been asked to come and help when she received her life-limiting diagnosis and her friends had felt at a loss as to how to cope.

Living well until the end is, then, at the very heart of what an end-of-life doula hopes to help people achieve. In the end, being a doula isn't about any of the big things. In fact, grand gestures can be entirely out of place. It's the simplicity of people who care reaching out to people in need. It's the trust to remain in the process until the end. It's that warm smile, that sharing of a silence or a favourite song. All of these small things can help forge a path to finding acceptance of the life ebbing away and can offer strength and fortitude for the necessary quiet letting go. Doulas walk alongside you and bear witness to the experience. We'll never tell you what to do at the end of your life; we're only there to help you live it.

Today, I sat in a large London teaching hospital with one of my clients. We were waiting for test results. These results would change the course of his life. We did the crossword and we chatted about the weather. I'd learned from spending time with him that he likes to be distracted during the final moments before we go in to see his consultant. We'd already talked through possible outcomes, hopes, fears and concerns for the future. These last minutes, in a frantic waiting room, filled with faded NHS-blue wipeable chairs, are neither the time nor the place for those important discussions. They're for calm and gentle distractions, for creating a sense of normal among the horrible abnormality of the situation. They weren't the results he'd hoped for. They weren't the results he'd expected. There were no words that could change their outcome. But I was there, sitting beside him, for as long as he needed me.

Why I became an end-of-life doula

[A]

People find it strange that I've dedicated a large part of my life to working in this field, but I cannot emphasise enough what a privilege it is. I'm sure there are many reasons why I set off on this path, some perhaps even I don't fully understand, but the driving force was a boy, my best friend, and a friendship that will last a lifetime – even though he's now been dead for longer than he was alive.

Many years ago I flew across an ocean to say goodbye to my best friend. As he lay dying in a hospital bed, I sat on an aeroplane, staring out into the cotton-wool clouds in the brilliant blue end-of-summer sky, internally bargaining with all the forces of the universe to get there in time to say goodbye.

I didn't.

Feeling the grief and failing to understand it or know what to do with it is a huge part of why I decided on a career in end-of-life care.

Love and friendship do not end when someone dies. There's a saying that a person dies twice: once when their heart stops beating and again the last time someone speaks their name. He is a vital part of the history of my formative years, but he's also a part of my present. He'll always be a part of my future. His name is spoken by my children and will, I hope, be spoken by theirs. He's as influential to me in his death as he was in life, and I will always be grateful for the time we shared.

I can't remember if it was 1989 or 1990, but I do remember it was the year he was working on a stall in a department store. It was the year I stole his favourite corduroy jacket. He had a lump on his forehead, which he thought was a boil. He gave it a name, too. I want to say he called it 'Simon', but it's been a long time. We laughed at how big it was. They decided to cut the lump out, but more appeared. He stopped naming them, and we stopped laughing. One by one, the doctors removed them.

Results, they said each time, were inconclusive.

In the summer of 1991, he took me to see *Dying Young*. Twice. We both sobbed during the film and then complained afterwards about how shamelessly manipulative it was.

The next year, when the sun had just about warmed the sea enough to swim in, we sat in the garden while his mum made burnt grilled tomatoes and mashed potato. We loved swimming; it was our thing. He didn't reply when I suggested we could go to the beach after lunch. His mum and I tried to pretend we couldn't hear him being sick. I took him water and we sat back down outside. I asked him, straight out, if he was going to die.

'They wouldn't be doing all of this if they didn't think I'd be alright,' he said.

Four weeks later he was dead.

His life – and his death – shaped me. In the weeks following the funeral, I found out that he had melanoma. I found out that he had known that he was going to die. Worst of all, I found out that he hadn't told anyone.

He'd refused hospice care. He'd opted for active treatment at every point, even after he'd been told there was nothing more they could do to save his life. He hadn't really talked about any of it. To anyone.

We found drawings he'd made, chronicling his illness, and a poem he'd written about his death; the death that robbed me of my best friend. He'd sought solace and understanding in writing and drawing, but never in the people around him.

It was his denial that hit me the hardest. I'll never know exactly how he felt. His silence had ensured that. I imagine it was a bleak and despairing loneliness at having to carry this burden alone. I questioned our friendship. How could he not share such a terrible, significant, truth? We shared everything. So I thought.

Just moments after his heart's final beat, I decided – an exact moment that I can recall with perfect clarity – that I wanted to stop this from happening to anyone else. Nobody should have to die such a lonely death. I wanted to change the way we die. Whether, in that moment of confusion and grief, I wanted revenge against death, or to redeem myself for my inability to be there for him isn't clear to me. But what it amounted to – what it meant, for this optimistic, arrogant, ambitious and grieving 17-year-old girl – was a new determination to try to create a new life's ending. A better one. I wanted to find a way to turn dying into something we could, if you'll forgive the contradiction, live with. Something that we can live through.

I wanted, for myself and everyone who'd ever suffered a loss, to have the opportunity to look back on death with a certain knowledge that everything had been done to make those last months, weeks, days, hours and minutes as good as they could possibly be; for people who are dying, and for the living.

I was naive. Hindsight and a good many years' reflection have made me understand just how naive I was. But today, in my role as an end-of-life doula, I can sometimes come close to achieving a small part of that inexperienced girl's wish. If I'm able to make a difference to the end of someone's life, I feel overwhelming gratitude, privilege and, occasionally, peace.

Getting to this position has been to follow a long path; with the obstacles and diversions that life presents slowing me down. It was a path that stemmed from my total lack of emotional preparation and readiness for his death, and for a life without him. I became an end-of-life doula to help prepare and support people through this part of their lives, in the hope that the people I work with might be able to have a better end of life than the one that shaped my life.

I've written this story in many different forms now, but for the first time I've been able to see it in a different light. Perhaps his death and his end of life were how he wanted them to be. Maybe his final act of love to us all was to do what he believed was protecting us. His two decades had perhaps not afforded him the experience to grasp our desperate need to be there for him. With no control over the disease that was killing him, this could have been his last rebellion; his last chance to do something exactly how he wanted. But what it also did was remove our ability to say a proper goodbye. He and I were always awful at goodbyes. I still am. Perhaps this was his way of not having to do it for the last time.

My best friend's death led me into working at end of life but it was my nana's, and later, grandfather's death that fundamentally showed me how to be a doula. And how not to be.

My grandfather was a bugger. I say that with a huge amount of love and affection but the reality was that he was often very difficult and not especially pleasant. He told incredible stories – he *held court* – over dinner to rapt audiences as he regaled us with his misdemeanours and misadventures. We listened to his exploits wide-eyed and open-mouthed, and he most definitely taught me a lot about the world, some of which I'm not sure I ever needed to know. It was beautiful in many ways, and unfortunate in others: the story of how he lost his virginity in Canada is something I'll never be able to unhear.

He was a creature of habit. He ate the same lunch every single day for almost his entire adult life; home-made vegetable soup with a Golden Delicious apple and some Cheddar cheese. He chewed each mouthful 30 times. He drank an inordinate amount of gin. When he was 80 he gave up his hand-rolled cigarettes, smoked through a patent black cigarette holder that made a clinking noise when it knocked against his false teeth. He'd mostly lived alone since my grandmother had been moved into a nursing home after her devastating diagnosis of progressive supranuclear palsy. She was one of the first people to be diagnosed with the condition in the UK, and as a result, little was known about it. Her death, 30-something years ago, was prolonged, and awful, and a different story for a different time.

When we were young, my grandfather spoke articulately about how he would end his life himself if he were ever unable to live well, and independently. I was sure his stance was in part due to the way my grandmother's illness had progressed, robbing her of who she was. She'd lost her ability to manage the most basic human functions, such as swallowing or walking. She couldn't even cry.

He was vocal and determined about what he wanted and told anyone who cared to listen. He was, however, unable to follow through with these wishes. After several bouts of illness, he ended his days in a nursing home unable to communicate or care for himself. He had to be fed and washed and dressed, always refusing to use the communication boards so we could ensure we were doing the right things for him. I cannot remember how long this lasted, but I do know that he'd have said that one hour would have been too long for him. To be stuck in a cramped room on the ground floor of a nursing home, with no view of his beloved sea, in this intolerable state of persistent life-and-death limbo, was everything I knew he'd wanted to avoid.

When he did die, I was with him. It was the middle of the night and he had been given a syringe driver that was slowly and steadily delivering medication to relieve his suffering and keep him calm. I rubbed his hands and talked to him about the fairy sandcastles he used to build with us on the beach near his house. They were architectural masterpieces, with sand steps leading up to the top. Adorned with shells and seaweed, three-year-old me thought of them as iconic sculptures and still, to this day, I try (and fail) to recreate them with my children on that very same beach.

I was sad he'd lived through such an appalling end of life and unashamedly relieved when he died – finally no longer suffering. I was grateful for the kindness he was shown by the staff, but I also felt we'd let him down by allowing his life to continue well beyond the point he could bear. Nature had taken its course, and that course had been long, difficult and involved relentless suffering. There were, perhaps, some fleeting, bearable moments, but there were certainly no good days.

My eldest daughter was five and she insisted on seeing him after he died. I drove her back to the nursing home, without knowing if I was doing the right thing. She marched into his room and said with the matter-of-fact assuredness of the young, 'He doesn't look like he's sleeping, he just looks dead.' She was right. I stood by the window to give her the space to do what she needed. She kissed his forehead and wished him well and then took my hand and asked for ice cream.

The two of us painted his coffin his favourite blue and we chose his favourite plants, (not flowers, he hated cut flowers) to put on top. We made vats of his own vegetable soup for the wake and served large, cheering glasses of gin. We all talked about his cantankerous nature and which of his inappropriate stories we found the most difficult to hear. He was cremated that day and his ashes were delivered to the house mid-wake. We walked him from the home where he'd spent almost 50 years, to the beach where he'd spent a lifetime swimming, and we scattered his ashes far and wide into the cool blue waters he sought solace bathing in almost every day of the year.

His end of life hadn't been at all what he'd wanted, but we'd returned him to the place he loved best and we'd done it with a huge amount of love. His life, his death and his funeral taught me so much; even if sometimes they weren't lessons, like some of his stories, I felt I wanted to learn. His death – like all the others in my life – informed how I work as a doula. It's one lesson of many and his death is a constant reminder that quantity of life is considerably less important than quality.

Sadly, my work is often most radically shaped and improved by the mistakes I've witnessed – or been part of. There are no do-overs, but we can, and should, learn from our mistakes and make sure we don't make the same ones twice.

We are all mortal, but this is because we are human. I cannot tell you that I will certainly change your life for the better at its end but I can reassure you that I'll make it as close to the way you want it to be as possible.

Everyone dies. Let's always make it the best life and the best death we can.

BERNARD'S VEGETABLE SOUP

(My version; I'm sure everyone else in my family makes it slightly differently)

Serves 4

2 x onions or shallots, finely chopped

3 x leeks, thinly sliced

1 x heart of celery thinly sliced, you can add the leaves too.

1 x swede or any combination of root vegetables, chopped into medium-sized chunks

4 x carrots, cut into chunks

3 x potatoes, cut into chunks

1 tsp vegetable oil

1 litre of vegetable stock

generous pinch each of salt and lots of ground black pepper

a handful of green peas or some shredded cabbage, if you like

To serve:

Good bread and butter, 1 Golden Delicious apple, a square of mature Cheddar cheese

- Prepare and rinse all the vegetables, then chop them into even-sized pieces.
- Sauté the onions in the vegetable oil in a large pan until translucent and soft. Add the celery and leeks and cook down until soft.
- Put in the swede, carrots and potatoes and add enough vegetable stock to cover the vegetables by about 5cm (2in). Season well with salt and pepper.
- Bring to the boil (my grandfather would always cook his in a pressure cooker) and then turn down to a simmer and cook until all the vegetables are done. This usually takes about 15–20 minutes.
- If using, add in the peas and cabbage towards the end of the cooking time.
- Serve steaming hot with plenty of good bread and butter, accompanied by wedges of apple and cheese. It's even more delicious the next day.

How to become an end-of-life doula

I get lots of correspondence each week asking me how to become an end-of-life doula. I've put together a list of things you could do if you'd like to be one.

Do you have any end-of-life training or experience?

If the answer is no, I'd suggest these steps are a really good place to start:
1. Volunteer at your local hospice.
2. Apply for a job as a healthcare assistant at your local hospital, hospice or care home.
3. Run a regular Death Cafe for your local community. See www.deathcafe.com for details of how to set one up.
4. Read: Atul Gawande's *Being Mortal*, Paul Kalanithi's *When Breath Becomes Air*, Kathryn Mannix's *With the End in Mind* and Ruth Picardie's *Before I Say Goodbye*. There are lots more great books out there but these are a good start.
5. Watch: B.J. Miller's TED talk *What Really Matters At The End of Life* on YouTube. Emily Hayward and PeeWeeToms both documented their end of life honestly and openly on YouTube. Look them up.
6. Listen: Atul Gawande's *Reith Lectures*, *Griefcast*, and *You, Me and the Big C*.
7. Follow Kris Hallenga on Twitter. She's one of the many inspiring people documenting their experiences with illness online. It will give a real insight into what is going on for an individual. Also look up Saima Thompson on Instagram. Saima documented the ups and downs of cancer treatment and showed the realities of living with incurable lung cancer in a candid way.
8. Have some therapy. Think about your own relationship with death and dying. Think about why you want to do this work. Explore how you'll sustain yourself emotionally. Figure out how you feel about it all first. It's impossible to support others at the end of their lives if you haven't got a handle on your own thoughts and feelings about it.
9. Hone your listening skills. Actively listen. Listening is the most important aspect of the doula role. Listen without judgement, without interruption, listen to every word.
10. Once you've done all these things and more, follow the answer for yes.

If the answer is yes:

There are a good few training courses worldwide now, which is great as there's a lot more choice out there. There is no regulatory body for end-of-life doulas and no official government certification or registration, no matter what any of the trainers may tell you. Anyone can be a doula but I think it's really essential to do some of the training even if you have end-of-life care experience. Some of the courses are online, some are taught.

Each course has a different emphasis: some are more academic, others more spiritual. The prices of the courses and their length vary greatly and depending on how much end-of-life or social/healthcare experience you already have, you might feel that doing a shorter course is enough. Call them up. Chat to them and ask lots of questions about their training. If you have considerable experience in end-of-life care already, you may find that a short foundation course might be enough. If this is all new to you, one of the longer, more involved courses would probably be better. Do your research. Find the right course for you. Once you've trained, find a good supervisor. You can only do this work well if you're well supported. It's a must.

FIVE THINGS I'VE LEARNED WHILE TRAINING AS AN END-OF-LIFE DOULA

by Emma Dixon

1.
Death is a normal and natural part of life.

2.
Dying is still living.

3.
Death is a transition.

4.
You can plan your own death...

5.
...but it may not go according to plan!

What does a good doula look like?

1. They listen to you. You feel heard.
2. They ask questions and they listen to the answers. They take notes. They remember what you've told them.
3. They make you feel safe and secure. They ensure you feel comfortable with them. They build your trust and maintain it.
4. They have good and strong professional boundaries. They do regular CPD (continuing professional development) and they go to supervision.
5. They don't try to be your friend.
6. They do what they say they are going to do.
7. They maintain your confidentiality.
8. They work flexibly depending on your changing needs. They check in on your progress and they alter according to need.
9. They treat you with respect and dignity. At all times.
10. They treat your family and friends with respect and dignity too.
11. You feel happy to have them in your home.
12. You feel comfortable sitting in silence with them.
13. You're able to say 'no' to them. To tell them that you don't like something or don't want them to do something.
14. They do not foist their beliefs, ideas or agenda on to you.
15. They never judge you.
16. They know that this experience is all about you and nothing about them.
17. They offer person-centred individualised care.
18. They ask you what matters to you.
19. They are honest and open about what they can and cannot do for you.
20. They refer you to someone else if they know they are not the right doula to fit your needs and requirements.
21. You like them. You feel that having time with them is time well spent. They make you laugh. They don't shy away from difficult conversations but they back off when they know you need space.
22. They don't crowd you or take over. They ask the questions you forget to ask in consultant meetings but they always check with you first. They advocate, not talk, for you.
23. They have an up-to-date DBS check.
24. They have exemplary testimonials and references. No matter how much you like them at the first meeting, make sure you check these thoroughly before you engage their services.
25. They make an excellent cup of tea.

From doula to patient and back again

[A]

How many of us take our health and well-being for granted? Illness is the kind of thing that only happens to other people, right?

I used to pride myself on being empathetic and compassionate. Then I became unwell. Really, properly unwell. And I finally, truly understood what it meant to be a patient. Going through this ordeal fundamentally changed the way I work and provided an unwelcome but worthwhile and ultimately positive insight into how it feels to be ill. It was a hard-fought lesson and not one I'd have volunteered to learn, but I now understand a little bit more about how my clients feel. I am a much better doula because of it.

Several years ago I was a relatively fit woman in her 30s. I was more concerned with potty training my youngest and the endless cycle of nits and snotty noses than the state of my health.

Then I collapsed – quite dramatically – in the midst of a chaotic joint birthday celebration for my three daughters. I was filling party bags and worrying that the cakes I'd ordered hadn't arrived. I'd been feeling strange for a couple of days, but had put it down to doing too much and sleeping too little.

I ended up being 'blue-lighted' to a large teaching hospital after the local A&E pronounced me too unwell for their facilities. I lost my entire left side – my dominant side – and my speech.

I always thought I'd be verbose if I were very ill, that I'd be endlessly telling everyone how much they meant to me and about all the things I wanted and needed. It never occurred to me that my speech and my capacity to write would be taken from me. Without my ability to communicate, I couldn't explain myself. Things were being done to me over which I had no control. I didn't understand them, and I was powerless to ask for explanations.

Not being able to communicate is a terrifying isolation. You can't ask the doctors what they're doing and why they're doing it. You can't call your friends to catch up. And you can't contribute to a conversation anyway, so what's the point in being around anyone? I was lost and vulnerable, useless and without purpose. I couldn't be a mother. I couldn't work. I couldn't be a friend. Nothing of me was left. I didn't look like me. I didn't feel like me, and I had no idea if I would ever be me again. I shut people out and I pushed people away. Some people held me tight, some people disappeared.

It felt like everything had been taken away from me and I had no idea how to start to reclaim it. I couldn't bear anyone to see what I'd become. I was used to being a carer, and being cared for was so alien and uncomfortable that I fought it every step of the way.

My experience has changed every aspect of my life. Some things are much harder these days but I'm better now at doing the job I love because I truly understand what it is like to be a patient.

I understand the isolation, the loneliness and the fear that illness brings. I know how it feels to be treated as a 'case' and as an 'illness' rather than as a human being. I understand the frustrations of the endless and too often fruitless hamster-wheel hospital appointments and tests and treatments. The grim waiting rooms with their uncomfortable blue plastic chairs. I know how precious life is and how quickly it can all be taken away. For the first time in my career, I'm not just imagining how you feel about being unwell, I actually really understand. It's shit. Sometimes it's the shittest thing in the entire world. Sometimes it's absolutely unbearable.

It has also made me more determined than ever to be defined by things I can control. To make positive choices, to find ways to let my work define me. I want my kids to define me. I want my ability to make an excellent cheesecake to define me. I want my inability to remember song lyrics to define me. My disabilities won't. Not then, not now, not ever.

There were things I needed when I was very unwell that I couldn't ask for. There were things I wanted and things I really didn't want. I wish there had been a list I could have shown people. I wish I'd had a resource to turn to, to help me explain what I wanted and needed. I've devised one. Some of it might relate to you and some might not. The most important thing on the list is to be guided by the person who is unwell, to ask them, to involve them, and to keep showing up for them, long after the initial 'novelty' of their illness has worn off and the stream of well-wishers and helpers have retreated back into the normal of their everyday lives.

THE THINGS I WISH PEOPLE HAD DONE
(BUT DIDN'T FEEL ABLE TO ASK)

1. I wanted people to treat me like me.
2. I wanted people to assume I *could* do things as opposed to assuming I couldn't.
3. I wanted and needed my friends and family to tell me their news. To send me snippets of what was going on in their lives. I wanted to feel like I was still a part of their lives, but for some reason they stopped telling me about their fun or about their sadness. Just because I'm going through something awful doesn't stop me from wanting to be there for you, too. I want to hear all your news, the good and the bad. I want to listen! Listening was one of the only things I could do in the beginning and I really honed my skills. It's amazing how good you can get at listening when you don't have the ability to talk. *Talk to people when they're ill. Don't hide your life from them. Be normal! Ask their advice. Tell them your worries and your problems. Share yourself with them still. It's important It matters.*
4. I needed people to stop asking, 'How are you?' or sending me text messages that were only ever inquiring about my health or the results of the latest round of tests. If there was an update I wanted to share, I would. *Let people tell you when they're ready. Let them know you want to hear all about it but also that you want it to be on their terms and at their own pace. It's exhausting telling 20 people the same piece of information. Let people do things in their own time. Show interest but not morbid fascination. If someone is living with a serious illness, chances are that when you send your, 'How are you feeling?' text that they'll be feeling like crap. There's only so many times you want to reply, 'Not great'. I wanted acknowledgement of what was going on but mostly I wanted distraction.*
5. I needed people to not try to finish my sentences or assume they knew what I was trying to say.
6. I needed everyone to keep inviting me to places even though I most probably couldn't go.
7. There was the most incredible deluge of well-wishing and thinking of you loveliness (I'm so grateful – thank you!) during the first week or so and after the first operation and then it all stopped. I needed people to acknowledge that the fifth operation was just as scary and daunting as the first. I needed people to not forget that I still needed people.
8. I found conversation impossible and frustrating. What I really wanted was for someone to sit in silence with me, to watch a film, to read me a story, to tell me something. It was so lonely but I also couldn't cope with too much stimulation or too many people at once. I needed little and often. I wanted someone to hold my hand. I wanted to be looked after without it seeming like I was being looked after. I needed some invisible 'care'.

9. Go to appointments with people. Keep going. Scanxiety is very real and it doesn't get any easier just because you're an old hand at having scans and tests. People came to the first few outpatient appointments and then they stopped. I didn't like to ask. I didn't know how to ask. I needed people to be a bit pushier, to insist no matter how much I proclaimed to be FINE all by myself. I wasn't fine, I just didn't know how to tell people.
    Remember, people might not be used to asking for and accepting help. Be pushy without being pushy. Make it seem like they're actually doing you the favour by letting them accompany you to your appointment.

10. Rest doesn't mean get into bed and never get out again. When people are told to rest, it doesn't mean don't move. It doesn't mean be disenfranchised by everyone rushing around you to take over and 'do' everything. It means not overdoing it. It means listening to your body and stopping when your body tells you to. It means walking a bit slower or taking the shortcut home if you get too tired. Resting is about finding ways of living your life to the full while being mindful of your body's needs. I wanted to cook but I was endlessly ushered out of the kitchen when what I really wanted was for someone to cook with me, to take over when I needed to sit down, to finish up if I couldn't do any more.
    Help people do the things they want to do, the things that make them feel like themselves, the things that make them feel alive. Help them be themselves. Help, don't disenfranchise. Support don't stifle. Co-create rather than taking over. Rest is essential but so is feeling alive. Being ill makes you want to feel more alive than ever. Help people feel alive. Help them live their lives. Don't allow your need to 'do' and support to stop them living.

11. Exercise can really help. Help people do what they can. Encourage, don't discourage. Go for a walk with them. Offer to take them swimming. Whatever it is that they want to do. Support but don't cheerlead. And don't ever patronise. I wanted to swing for people who clapped when I managed to walk a couple of steps. Everyone is different. Some people might love the clapping and the cheering, I did not! Know your audience.

12. Don't ever underestimate the emotional distress of going from being 'able' to being seen as 'disabled'. Don't try to play it down and don't try to say you understand. No one can possibly imagine what it's like to lose the ability to move, to speak, to drive, to be the person you were. I had actual arguments with people because I didn't want to register myself as 'disabled' even though I was advised to. I wasn't ready. I wanted to see how far I could get in my recovery before I did that.
    Allow people to go at their own pace. DO NOT project what you'd do or what you think they should do on to them. I'd have rather they'd grumbled about my decisions behind my back than actively challenged me on them.

13. Listen without judgement.
14. Illness can last for years. It sometimes lasts a lifetime. Keep being there. The emotional toil of illness lasts even longer than the physical impact.
15. Having a lot of surgical procedures doesn't necessarily make you blasé about them. Just because someone has had several operations doesn't mean they're not scared or apprehensive and it certainly doesn't mean that because it's a regular occurrence they don't need support. They do. They really do.
16. Grand gestures aren't necessary. It's the small, everyday kindnesses that really make a difference. Being there doesn't have to be all-encompassing or time-consuming. It can be the simple act of sending a ridiculous meme every few days. Making an extra portion when you're cooking for your own family. Sending a handwritten note. Regaling them with stories from the outside world. Sitting in a hospital waiting room and pretending to do the crossword that someone else discarded. Checking in. Watching a film. It's more about keeping the person who is unwell involved in everyday life. Keeping their place. Making them feel that they still belong.

TEN THINGS I LEARNED FROM BEING ILL

1. Do practical things. Ask what would be the most helpful. Do not presume. Never presume. Things like arranging to have someone clean the house regularly and making sure the washing is done and the kids' uniform is ready. One of my brilliant friends arranged an email thread with all the parents in one of my daughter's year groups at school to organise meals for my family. This lasted for many months. They asked my eldest daughter what her favourite things were to eat and, miraculously, delicious and sustaining meals appeared on the doorstep every day. Another school mum gave freshly made smoothies to my childminder most days. I couldn't eat, only drink things through a straw, so these were a lifesaver. Other friends made soup. Soup that fitted through a straw. Delicious soup that sustained me for many, many months. That carrot soup. So good. So necessary.

   The key thing was that they all asked each other what they were doing so we weren't overwhelmed with things that we didn't want or couldn't fit in the freezer. People helped in a really helpful way. And one person coordinated it so I wasn't overwhelmed. It's controversial to say it, but some help just isn't that helpful. It's not ingratitude, it's just that there's only a certain number of lasagnes someone can fit in their freezer and when no one in the household actually likes lasagne it's such a waste of food and of help. Ask what people want. If you can't ask the person directly, ask someone who is in their inner circle and who knows. Your help matters and it can make such a difference. But make sure the help you are offering and giving is the right kind.

2. Illness impacts the entire family, not just the person who is ill. I was so grateful when people took my kids out to do fun stuff or invited them over. I can't tell you how much it meant to me to know they were having a good time. And it was so lovely hearing their stories about what they'd done when they got home. Thank you to everyone who did this. You know who you are. I can never express just how grateful I am.

3. Involve the school if you have kids. My girls' nursery and primary school were remarkably supportive. The secondary, not so much. The teachers came to visit and bought flowers. The nursery put together a book for me of all the things my youngest was doing while she was there. Young children need lots of support but so do older children. My eldest was 16 and really needed support at school. She didn't get it. We all too often forget how much support older children require. Don't forget. Don't assume that because they're older that they don't need help. They do.

4. Some people don't know how to be there. They don't know how to show up. Forgive them. As the old saying goes, it says more about them than it does

about you. If you're one of those friends who don't know how to be there, who really can't be there, say, 'I'm so sorry, I'm out of my depth, I don't know what to do and I don't know what to say.' Honesty is so much better than disappearing without a trace.

5. Illness is boring. Not being able to do all the things you want to do is infuriating. Watching TV all day and sitting alone in bed is incredibly dull. The novelty of having so much 'free' time wears off pretty quickly. Try to find nice things to help relieve the boredom.

6. What can you offer? One incredible lady, one of my nearest and dearest, gave the gift of her magical needles and over many nights, over many months, she came and sat and treated me. It's very special having a close friend who is also an amazing acupuncturist and her skills went a long way to helping me heal, but it was her kindness and generosity that I will hold on to forever. If your friend is sick and you can offer help, do it. Giving isn't a one-way transaction. Trust me.

7. Show up. Being poorly showed me how to show up for someone. To really be there. It taught me that being there really isn't about doing, it's about presence and it's about a willingness to bear the weight of the unbearable load, to show that it can be borne, it can be held. That despite illness robbing you of your very essence, that you are worth showing up for. That you matter. You really, truly matter.

8. What else did I learn? Do more exercise, lose those few pounds, drink less and eat your five a day? I could tell you those are the lessons I learned from all this but I'd be lying. According to all the doctors there was absolutely nothing I could have done to prevent my collapse. That was the only thing they had actually agreed on. Those sensible, taking-care-of-us things? We should do them regardless. That's not the lesson, that's common sense. The lesson is that there's nothing special about me at all. I'm just normal. Spectacularly average, in fact – but it happened to me, and if it happened to me then it can happen to anyone.

9. Live your life. I remember lying in A&E and regretting all the hurt I'd caused people, wishing I'd had a lot more sex, wishing I'd been bolder and braver. Wishing I'd put my mobile phone away when I was with my kids more, wishing I'd walked at their pace more often, wishing I'd spent many more hours playing with them rather than trying to cook them endlessly complicated healthy meals that they'd almost always reject, wishing I'd put that swimming costume on despite my brain shouting at me not to, wishing I didn't drive that bloody awful 'mum-car' and still had my VW camper van.

It's a cliché because it's true: we only get one chance at life and we've got to grab it by the balls and make it the very best it can be. Take those chances. Eat that cake. Take your baby swimming weeks after you've given birth and don't give a crap about how you look. You've just grown a human! Don't let anyone, including yourself, give you shit about it.

10. Embrace yourself and all your flaws. If you can't embrace your flaws, change them. Or at least change the way you think about them. Our biology may give us a template, our childhood may give us insecurities, our experiences may form us, but we are responsible for our futures. We have the opportunity to create a good life, despite our difficulties, to design a beautiful, *brilliant* life – for ourselves and the people we love.

Do this. Take control. Because believe me – you don't know when it'll all be taken away.

When you're first diagnosed

[A]

'It's possible to grieve for yourself, even though you're still alive. You grieve for the person you were, for the life you had and what could have been.'
ALICE-MAY PURKISS, DIAGNOSED WITH BREAST CANCER
AT THE AGE OF 26

Even if you have an inkling or all the evidence points to you being very unwell, an actual diagnosis, a confirmation that the issues you'd been having were very real, is still shocking. It can feel like you've been run over by a bus, it can feel utterly overwhelming, it can feel like it's not happening to you and that you're living out somebody else's worst nightmare. People are emotionally vulnerable when they're first diagnosed because it's all so new and so alien. One day you're fretting that your tomatoes were a bit squashed in the grocery delivery and the next you're being asked to make what can feel like life-or-death decisions. A serious-illness diagnosis is terrifying and we need to make sure everyone is well supported through this tumultuous and uncertain time.

1. There's no right or wrong reaction to being told you are living with a serious illness. You will most probably be in shock. You will definitely need time to process the news. You unquestionably will not be able to take in all the information you're being given about your diagnosis. I write later in this section about the importance of noting everything down and taking someone along to appointments with you. It's impossible for us to process a lot of information after we've just been given distressing and life-changing news.

2. Take your time. Ask for help. Ask the healthcare professionals to repeat the information as much as you need to in order to fully understand what's going on. Ask to have a named person and a direct number to call for more information.

3. If you don't feel able to call someone, ask one of the medical team to call a friend or relative to come and be there with you. If you don't feel able to explain to them what's going on, ask someone in your care team to explain for you.

4. Try not to google too much. It's hard to resist but it's important to remember your illness is different to everyone else's even if they have a similar diagnosis.

5. Keep notes of questions you want to ask as they come to mind.

6. Don't isolate yourself. You might feel that you want to hide away from the world but it will feel more manageable if you let people in and don't shut the world out.

7. Telling people individually can feel like an ordeal in itself. Ask someone else to tell everyone if you don't feel you want to. Don't feel it's imperative you tell everyone immediately; you might want to sit with the news to help it settle a bit before you tell everyone, but also don't leave it too long before you tell your nearest and dearest (*see* point six).

8. Your illness is nothing to be ashamed of. This might seem like a strange thing to say but the amount of shame that goes hand in hand with a serious illness diagnosis is vast.

9. Don't be put off talking or telling people by some people's reactions. Human beings tend not to be adept at hiding their feelings and often what they're thinking is written all over their faces. People will say and do ill-judged things. Some will undoubtedly compare your diagnosis to the time their next-door neighbour was diagnosed with something similar and didn't live until her next birthday, they will tell you they know exactly how you feel because 'only last week I was told by the doctor that my cholesterol is too high' and they will shift uncomfortably from foot to foot, unable to make eye contact and then run off. Some people don't know what to do and they don't know what to say. Your diagnosis may well be triggering for them and they might not be able to be around to support you. You might feel that people are looking at you, pitying your situation, and they may well be. It isn't helpful but I would say that pity is a natural reaction to knowing that someone is in pain and is going through a very difficult time. We do not equip people well enough or give them the tools to respond helpfully and appropriately when faced with tricky news. If you can, let people know their reaction wasn't what you wanted or needed. If you can't, that's OK too, it's really not your job to manage their reactions but sometimes you'll need to let them know what you need from them as they might not get it right without direction. It can be exhausting managing

others' reactions to your news and it's absolutely fine for you to not bother. These people are most probably not your people; they are certainly not the people who you will want and need by your side every step of the way. The people who do step up will often surprise you. The people in your life who you might expect to be understanding and supportive might not be able to be. It's them, it's not you.

10. Ask your medical care team if there are any support groups for people living with a similar diagnosis. If there are, go along. And if there aren't, start one. Seek online support. There's a huge supportive community on Twitter, Instagram and many of the other social media channels. Anything you can do to make yourself feel less alone and not so overwhelmed will help.

11. Be really gentle with yourself. Take one minute at a time. Allow yourself to feel everything. Allow yourself to vent. Allow yourself to cry and rage.

12. Find a really good therapist. Ask your GP to refer you or ask others for recommendations.

— Emma's Experience

'In mid-January I went to see the doc. I felt lousy but I didn't look too bad. I'm young, I looked healthy, therefore, I must be OK, is what the doctor thought.

I explained my symptoms and the doc wasn't concerned, said he would do some tests, and he prescribed me with some IBS medicine, which obviously did zilch. My blood tests came back fine, it was only when my stool sample tests came back they realised that something was wrong. It basically showed that my bowel was attacking itself. I'd already had to repeat those stool sample tests because of the strikes. I very nearly didn't repeat them because I felt like I was wasting people's time. I don't blame the doctor and I remember him saying, "I don't know how you are walking around, you look so healthy."

Doctors are only human and they only have a short time to come up with a diagnosis. If I was going again now this is what I would do differently:

- I would keep a diary, detailing how often I was going to the toilet and if there is any blood etc.
- I would also take photos. Yes, I appreciate that's grim but when I showed them a photo during my second visit, they suddenly got that I wasn't being a drama queen.
- I would also make notes of any other possible symptoms. Do I feel tired, am I losing weight?

If you have any concerns that you have bowel cancer, please don't wait. Get yourself to the docs but go prepared. You can also find a great symptom checker on the Bowel Cancer UK website.'

Emma Critchley lives in Jersey with her husband and children and writes about her experience of being diagnosed with bowel cancer at www.islandliving365.com

FIVE TERMINAL ILLNESS PERKS NO ONE TELLS YOU THE DAY YOU'RE DIAGNOSED

by Kris Hallenga

The charity CoppaFeel! was founded in 2009 by Kris and her twin sister Maren after Kris was diagnosed with secondary breast cancer at the age of 23. Although Kris will always live with cancer, she wants to let everyone know that catching cancer early means you have a higher chance of surviving and recovering.

1.
You get out of social engagements with no questions asked.

2.
A blue badge means you can park wherever the F you like!

3.
Discounted public transport and FREE 'carer' passes at the cinema – I mean, GET IN.

4.
Life can become way more meaningful.

5.
You will laugh again.

A SHORT PROGNOSIS

Lois Tonkin was a highly regarded lecturer, researcher, counsellor and writer about loss and grief. Her work with grieving people, and with the other professionals who support them, reflects her understanding that grief is not only about our responses when someone dies, but about losing anything that is important to us. Lois created the 'growing around grief' model of grief that is widely regarded as one of the most up-to-date and relevant models in current practice. Lois died in July 2019.

People have described their diagnosis and illness as being like a huge magnifying glass, augmenting what matters most and sometimes allowing them to let go of things they realise don't really matter. Others have described to me the lucidity that can come with a short prognosis, how things taste and look different when you know you'll only ever get to eat or see them a few more times. Of course, this isn't always the case, and depression can go hand in hand with being physically unwell. When Lois received an unwelcome diagnosis with a short prognosis she wrote a Five Things for us about what took her by surprise.

FIVE THINGS I DIDN'T EXPECT WHEN I WAS TOLD I HAVE A LIFE-LIMITING ILLNESS WITH A SHORT PROGNOSIS

by Lois Tonkin

1.
Envy
Along with sadness, denial and all those expected emotions, I didn't expect envy – envy of people with rounded limbs, and a presumption of a future. Living life without an expectation of it going on for much longer is so radically different, and hits me hard at the strangest moments.

2.
It's nothing like I thought it would be
Turns out this is like most things in life – totally different to what I'd expected. It's surprised me with how happy I feel a lot of the time, and what can make me feel terrible. I can't accurately anticipate how things will be, ever, and that's a good thing to remember when I feel overwhelmed by horrific thoughts of dying, or being dead. Whatever I think (and fear) it will be like, it probably won't.

3.
I'm still me
Suddenly, my body acts and feels different; I don't go to work, I don't eat or feel the same, and so many people in my life start treating me like 'a cancer patient' instead of Lois, who has cancer. It's hard to hold on to a sense of still being me; someone that has the courage, creativity and skills to deal with this huge challenge in my life. I need to limit my time with people who only want to hear about my pain levels or the cancer, and cherish time with those who remind me I am strong and capable, and can do this.

4.
It's important to have a project
It's too easy for life to get taken up with managing pain and drugs and medical issues. It's been important for me to have something that matters to me to structure my days and give me a continuing sense of myself and a purpose for my life.

5.
I get to see some of the fruits of my life
I've always known people are kind and generous, but I've been overwhelmed by how many people have taken time to tell me how I have touched their life and inspired or helped them. It's made me realise how important it is for me to do the same, and tell people what a difference they have made to my life, and how glad I am to have crossed paths with them.

A DEMENTIA DIAGNOSIS

Dementia is not a disease. The word dementia describes a collection of symptoms related to memory loss and thought impairment that impact someone's ability to manage and reduces their ability to carry out all their tasks of actual daily living.

Statistics show that there are roughly 50 million people living with dementia worldwide. The World Health Organization predicts that by 2030 82 million people will be living with the syndrome and by 2050 there'll be around 152 million. Dementia is not a normal aspect of ageing even though it generally impacts older people.

Dementia affects everybody involved. It is the root cause of dependence and disability in older people and it cannot be ignored. With no cure or effective treatments, dementia has been recognised as a public health priority. However, with early diagnosis, much can be done to help people, their carers and family, live well with dementia.

FIVE THINGS I'VE LEARNED AFTER BEING DIAGNOSED WITH DEMENTIA AT THE AGE OF 58

by Wendy Mitchell

Wendy lives with young onset dementia. Post diagnosis, she was shocked by the lack of awareness, both in the community and the clinical world. She now spends her time travelling around the country raising awareness and encouraging others to speak out in order to reduce the stigma associated with dementia. She's the author of *The Sunday Times* bestseller, *Somebody I Used to Know*.

1.

Enjoy today. Each moment spent with regrets is a moment of joy lost. And if today is a bad day, tomorrow might be better.

2.

Talk. How do those closest to you know how to help if you don't talk? But this has to be two-way: those closest to you must talk about their struggles, too. When the two are brought together, it's amazing how each can help the other.

3.

Complete a Lasting Power of Attorney – yes it's difficult, but it would be strange if it weren't. Then everyone knows your wishes while you're still able to communicate. They then won't have to make those difficult emotional decisions, which often split families, at a time when they're least capable of making them.

4.

Once you've completed the above, don't dwell on the future. Our end is inevitable, so why dwell on something over which you have no control. Instead, carry on enjoying things that bring you pleasure, albeit differently or with support, but still a joy.

5.

Dementia may be terminal but then so is life, so grasp every opportunity that comes your way. Never give up on yourself as you never know what you CAN still achieve, no matter how small or how great. Celebrate each one.

FIVE THINGS I'VE DISCOVERED ABOUT THE REALITY OF LIVING WITH PARKINSON'S DISEASE, AFTER BEING DIAGNOSED AT THE AGE OF 29

by Ellie Finch Hulme

Having been diagnosed with Parkinson's disease in 2013 at the age of 29, Ellie writes about her experiences of parenting and Parkinson's in her blog, PD Mama.

1.

Parkinson's is incurable, not terminal: you die *with* Parkinson's, not *from* it. It is a common misconception that Parkinson's kills.

2.

Parkinson's is life-changing, not life-ending: I've given birth to two beautiful, bright, healthy children since being diagnosed and I'm confident that I'm just as competent and loving a mother as I would have been without PD. You can still achieve things if you adapt around your symptoms and identify what motivates you and makes you happy.

3.

Parkinson's is different every day. Talking to others or writing about your unique experience of the condition – when you're ready – can be helpful when it comes to accepting what is happening to you, but don't benchmark; everyone experiences PD differently, and will progress differently.

4.

Parkinson's takes all the little things you ever took for granted and waves them in your face, laughing at you as it watches you struggle.

5.

In doing point four, Parkinson's dares you to live. And I don't know about you, but I'm not one for passing up a dare.

— Saima's Experience

'I first "came out" online in June this year (2018) after letting the words "stage 4 cancer" sink in for about six weeks. My colourful and passionate world totally shattered; it cut me deep, like a bad relationship break-up with myself.

A mixture of messages poured in of love and also total and utter fear. People exclaimed, "Sorry for you", "Sorry YOU are going through this", almost separating and isolating my condition from themselves.

The messages I was particularly drawn to, which brought me great comfort, were of empathy, hope and encouragement, not empty pity.'

Saima Thompson founded the Masala Wala Cafe in London in 2015 and wrote about her experiences of living with stage 4 lung cancer. She died on 27 June 2020 at the age of 31.

FIVE THINGS YOU NEED TO KNOW WHEN YOUR WIFE IS DIAGNOSED WITH CANCER

by Chris Willis-Baugh

'Mills and I got married in June last year. Just before Christmas, we found out that she had stage 3 bowel cancer. I'd just left the British Army where I'd served as a captain in the Infantry for eight years. I had to delay starting my new job so I could care for Mills. This has given me a great insight into the first-hand care of someone with cancer and all the complications that go with it.'

1.

It's OK to not have a clue what to do at the start, you'll work it out. Just being there, supporting your wife, will have more of an effect than you'll understand.

2.

It's totally fine to feel; you're human. Just because you're a man doesn't mean that it won't get to you and when it does, it's OK to break down (even if you do it behind a curtain).

3.

It's all about perspective. You will have days darker than you think you can deal with, but you WILL come out the other side. You'll be stronger for it as a person and as a couple.

4.

Take time for yourself: go to the gym, to the cinema, to the pub or just go for a walk. It's not selfish to need some 'you time'. Make sure to keep yourself healthy; part of that is your own mental health. You're no good to her if you're not good to go.

5.

You aren't alone. There are, and will be, many more like you who have to do this. The situation isn't a choice, but you can choose not to take it all on alone. Reach out, speak to someone and seek the answers to help you be the best support you can, not just for her, but for you as well.

Debunking the myths of palliative care and hospices

'Death is a big word'

Long and *lingering* are small words.
Kind is a small word, wishing it was a big word.
Cancer is a big word, one of the biggest,
but not as big as *death*.

Medicine is a small word.
Treatment is a tiny word, wishing it was a big word.
Hopeless, painful, these are small words.
You always and *you never*
are combinations of small words
which become big when used too often
and said with sufficient force.
See also *I love you* and *please don't go*.

If only and *too late* are small words
that become big words, when said in a certain way.
Never is a big word. *Love* is a very big word
that will become small when used too often
and said without sufficient force.

Goodbye is a small word,
except when used as a last word.

ANN ALEXANDER

PALLIATIVE CARE

[A]

I frequently get messages via Twitter, Instagram and over email from perfect strangers saying an approximation of, 'I've been referred to the palliative care team, does this mean they think I'm going to die tomorrow?'

People are terrified of the idea of palliative care and they assume they are being sent to their death. The irony is that palliative care is the antithesis of terrifying. Palliative care is not end-of-life care. Palliative care is 'comfort' care.

It focuses on quality of life and works holistically to try to make people as comfortable and as 'able' as possible for the duration of their illness. Palliative care centres around pain control while also offering emotional, physical and spiritual support for you and your family. It can also help with physiotherapy or tasks of actual daily living.

You can have palliative care alongside active treatments such as chemotherapy and radiotherapy. People are not necessarily referred to the palliative care team because they are dying imminently.

Palliative care is a truly brilliant thing. It's all about allowing you to live a much better life. Don't be scared of it and if you've been referred for it, don't think you're being written off; you can receive palliative care for years. In fact, recent research revealed that people who are given palliative care early on in their treatment actually live longer.

HOSPICES

When we hear the word 'hospice' we often automatically assume that they are places where people go to die, and to some extent that is true. Hospice inpatient units do look after people right at the end of their life, but inpatient units also admit people for short stays to get on top of pain and for assessment. This is sometimes called respite care. It gives carers at home a chance to have a bit of a rest, too.

Technically, hospice is the term for a type of 'care' as opposed to a physical place. The emphasis of hospice care is on actually 'caring for' someone as opposed to 'curing' them. People will often opt to have 'hospice at home', whereby they are visited by the palliative care and hospice team and looked after with the help of family and friends.

You may be referred to a hospice to access their other services. They run day centres filled with a wide-ranging list of activities, from art and craft to music and literature. They almost always have a cafe and a beautiful accessible garden. They have complementary therapies and support groups and therapists who all work to support people holistically.

Finding someone who you can relate to and talk to about what's happening, meeting other people who are also living with life-limiting illness, can make such a difference. It helps to share experiences, discuss common symptoms and treatment side effects, understand you are not alone in this and that you are not the only person suffering. Illness is isolating. Hospices help people to not feel so alone.

Hospices are full of love, friendships, laughter, and medical and support staff who are trained to care for you in the best possible way. Hospices are not just for dying. They are full of life. Full of living.

DOCTORS ARE *NOT* GOD AND THAT'S OK

I always wanted to be a doctor. I once even got as far as applying to do a pre-med. Medicine is an incredible, invaluable science. However, how can we expect our medical professionals to be good at things that we don't teach them? How can we expect them to be experts in something to which their medical degrees give little or no emphasis? By not including a great deal of communication training, are we really saying that how we talk to people doesn't matter? And are we expecting too much of doctors and their ability to communicate with us?

I work with medics all the time. I understand medical jargon. I ask questions and I take notes yet still, after a recent operation, I was left unapprised of the information I needed in order to make a sound decision about my choices for my care. I thought I was having the procedure to 'be better' and to get rid of the problem. I had asked all the questions. I had done the research. I had made what I truly believed to be the most informed and educated decision. I had the operation. Then at the second post-op check I asked why I was still experiencing the same difficulties as I had pre op. The reply was not the answer I had expected or hoped for: I was told that the operation was a way to 'attempt' to improve my symptoms but that they could not get rid of the issues I was having. They weren't making me better at all.

This experience raised so many questions for me. Why was this not the first thing I was told before the operation? Would I have gone ahead with yet another general anaesthetic and a long recovery if I'd known? Why are we not taking the time to give people all of the information?

Doctors need to be better at effective communication. Give us the facts and let us make decisions based on those facts. Give us all the information. Explain things several times if needed. Give us the opportunity to make sound decisions about our care. Be really honest about the likelihood of something working.

Even with my experience I still don't always ask the right questions or make the right decisions for my own care, but there are ways to ensure you get the most from your consultations and have all the information you need to make the decisions that are right for you. Being unwell is gruelling. Hospital appointments feel endless. Being ill is a full-time job – a rubbish one you never applied for. It's easy to feel completely overwhelmed but there are ways to make it feel more manageable.

Preparation empowers us. A doctor's clear, thorough and realistic communications will allow us to get a lot more from our consultations and feel less confused about what's going on.

FIVE THINGS MEDICAL PROFESSIONALS CAN DO TO GET TO KNOW THEIR PATIENTS

by Associate Professor Leeroy William

Leeroy is a Palliative Medicine Specialist and is President of the Australia and New Zealand Society of Palliative Medicine. He's passionate about individualising end-of-life care, communication skills and supporting compassionate practice.

1.
Be curious about who your patient is. Explore their heritage, culture and family. How do they make decisions about their health? Curiosity stops you from making assumptions and prevents unconscious bias.

2.
Allow your patient to tell the story of their life before they became unwell. What were their hopes, fears and expectations? What were the highs and lows in their life, and how did they deal with them? Their narrative gives an insight into the meaning they attach to their life and how they will deal with their future.

3.
Try to uncover how they have dealt with the changes from their past health to their current condition. Knowing their ability to adjust and accept these changes can help us support their future care. Remember that people need time to process, if they can, that they may be dying from their illness, rather than just living with it.

4.
Ask the family of an unconscious person to help you understand the person and their life. Do they like to be in control? Have they been a worrier? Family appreciate a chance to talk about their loved one. Including them involves them as part of the team and shows how interested you are in caring for the person.

5.
Listen to the different perspectives people will have about the person. Do they all see the person the way you do? People will trust us in differing amounts. The best insights into a person come from an amalgamation of these views and clarifying the differences.

Getting the most from your consultations with your doctor and specialist

[A]

1. Think about the questions you want to ask *before* your appointment and write them down.
2. Take someone else to the consultation with you. Always take someone even if you think you're going for something as simple as a check-up. It's always better to have support. If you do go alone you can ask to have a chaperone and the hospital will provide someone.
3. Take really methodical notes, or ask the person you're with to do it for you. Repeat what the consultant has said to you back to them to make sure you've understood it properly. 'Are you saying I need to have..?', 'What I understand from this is…'
4. Check you have asked all the questions you had written down. It's easy to get caught up in the stress of the consultation and forget.
5. Try to build a good relationship with your medical team. Ask them their names. Make sure they give you theirs. Thanks to Dr Kate Granger, they all should introduce themselves with, 'Hello my name is…'

— Kate's Experience

'I made the stark observation that many staff looking after me did not introduce themselves before delivering my care. It felt incredibly wrong that such a basic step in communication was missing. After ranting at my husband during one evening visiting time he encouraged me to "stop whinging and do something!"

We decided to start a campaign, primarily using social media initially, to encourage and remind healthcare staff about the importance of introductions in health care. I firmly believe it is not just about common courtesy, but it runs much deeper. Introductions are about making a human connection between one human being who is suffering and vulnerable, and another human being who wishes to help. They begin therapeutic relationships and can instantly build trust in difficult circumstances.'

Dr Kate Granger on why she started the #hellomynameis campaign.

6. You certainly don't need to be upbeat, but being polite and friendly goes a long way.
7. Ask the consultant to spell the names of drugs, treatments or illnesses. They're often tricky to remember and it's important you know what you're taking.
8. Never worry that you are taking up too much time. Believe me, if a consultant needs to hurry you along, they will!
9. Ask to see them again if you still feel unsure.
10. Ask about side effects of the treatments they're offering. Ask for the effectiveness statistics. Ask why they want to perform a particular procedure and what they hope the outcome from it will be. Ask about expected recovery times from operations and find out if you'll need a general or local anaesthetic.
11. Don't make decisions on the spot. Give yourself time to process the information you've been given.
12. If you genuinely feel you are not being looked after well enough, ask for a second opinion.
13. Don't ask questions if you are not prepared to hear the answer. You might not be ready to hear the truth of the overall picture – and there's nothing wrong with that – but build a relationship with your doctor so you can control the spread of information. I have clients who work with their consultants on a need-to-know basis. It's what they asked for. I have clients who want to know every survival statistic and will ask directly, 'How long do I have left to live?' Don't expect a doctor to give you an exact time. It's an impossible question to answer. Instead, they might give you statistics and let you know that other people with a similar diagnosis lived, on average, for X number of months.
14. If you've been diagnosed with a life-limiting illness and you haven't been referred to the palliative care team, ask for a referral. Palliative care really does make everything better.
15. You may well be seen by more than one medical team and, where possible, ask them to cc all the other teams into their correspondence. Having the whole picture can really help with your care.
16. Empower yourself. Walk with your notes. Have a list of medications. Write a brief overview of your condition, treatments, list of procedures etc. Doing this means that if you ever end up in hospital somewhere else or seeing someone who doesn't know the full picture, you've got a lot of the information they need. It'll save you so much trouble and will stop you having to explain yourself a million times.

17. Don't be afraid to acknowledge that you don't understand medical jargon or something someone has said. Ask them to explain in layman's terms. Ask them to explain again and again until you do understand.

18. Don't ever apologise for googling your illness but also don't believe everything you read on the internet either. If you find some information that rings true or that interests you, ask your consultant about it.

19. Be really honest about how you're feeling. Don't underplay your symptoms or your pain. Doctors can only help you properly if you give them all the facts. There's no gain in pretending to be in less pain than you really are. We have a strange fascination with pretending to be capable of enduring everything. You don't need to do this. Your life will be so much better if you are receiving the best possible care and treatment and doctors need you to communicate exactly how things are for you in order to be able to do this.

20. Don't be afraid to show your vulnerability.

21. Don't be afraid to question something you're not sure about or feel isn't right for you.

22. Don't let symptoms get really bad before you ask for help.

23. Remember, you know your body better than anyone. You are the expert of your body, of how it feels, what's changed, what's working and what isn't. Listen to yourself and trust your instincts. Always get changes checked out. Never ever worry that you're being a hypochondriac. It's better to rule something out or catch something in the early stages than miss something important because you were worried about making a fuss.

24. Doctors have seen a million bums before. They really have. I know it doesn't stop it from being excruciatingly embarrassing but it can help to know that yours won't be the first or the last they've seen. They probably have another one to see before they go home. Just because they've seen a thousand bums before doesn't mean that yours shouldn't be treated with dignity and respect, though. If you feel you need one, ask to have a chaperone. Take someone you know and trust into the room with you. Make sure they cover you up as much as is possible. Ask for an extra blanket if you feel exposed. Don't feel you can't ask. Make it as tolerable as possible.

25. Never ever forget that you are in control. Your body belongs to you. Do what's right for you. Don't feel pressured into anything and don't go along with something if you know it isn't right for you or it's not what you want.

26. You may well feel that your life is in the hands of the medical team, and you'd be mostly right, but having autonomy over your treatment and care, being in control and gleaning all the information so you can make

educated choices means that you are in a partnership with the medical team. Working as a team with them, working alongside them as an equal, is a much better place to be.

27. Living with illness isn't just about treating the physical symptoms. Living well with illness requires holistic care – looking after your physical, emotional and spiritual needs. You might not feel like you need emotional support but you will and you do. If you feel OK about the world, if you feel emotionally strong, if you have a safe space where you can talk over your fears and worries, you will be better altogether. Don't underestimate how important looking after your mental health is. It's essential.

Sex and intimacy are still just as important when you're unwell

[A]

Sex and intimacy are fundamental and essential parts of a relationship. They are also fundamental parts of life and, as we've talked about before, someone who is living with dying is still very much living. Therefore, sex and intimacy can be just as important as they were prior to diagnosis and treatment.

When you receive a diagnosis, it throws your trust in your body off kilter. You feel like your body is being disloyal, has cheated and tricked you, and all that you understood about the way it worked is gone. It's hard to love a body that's doing its level best to kill you. It's hard to respect a body that is letting you down in such a spectacular fashion.

When you are so disenchanted by your body it's incredibly difficult to understand why someone else would want to touch it, want to explore it, want to love it. I'm often asked by people who are unwell: 'Am I still loveable? Am I still sexy?'. They want to know if it's possible to maintain or even start intimate relationships. They want to be seen as vibrant and alluring even when it's the last thing they feel like. Sex and intimacy may well change with illness but they don't need to disappear.

Partners might be afraid of hurting their unwell lover and unwell lovers may fear being seen as unlovable and unsexy, but all those issues can be fixed by sharing concerns with one another, by talking and by keeping talking. It might need to be gentler or different, but that doesn't mean it's any less enjoyable. Communication is even more important: let your partner know what works and what doesn't, what hurts and what doesn't. Talk to each other. Reassure one another. Hold one another. Talk to your consultant about how medications may be impacting your sex drive or making it harder to have sex. Find other ways, seek professional help, learn to love your broken body, embrace all its flaws. Remember, the people who love you will still love you no matter how many scars you have or how broken you feel. How you see and feel about yourself isn't how others see you and feel about you.

A different approach may be required, but having a healthy sexual relationship while unwell is perfectly possible.

SEX AFTER DEATH (AND NO WE'RE NOT TALKING ABOUT NECROPHILIA)

Having sex, being intimate with someone else after the death of a partner can be really strange. It can also be wonderful and cathartic and being able to be close with someone else can be a really positive step in the grieving process.

There's no right or wrong time to start exploring and pursuing other relationships and only you will know when it's the right time. People may well judge but that says more about them than it does about you and you can and should embark on a new relationship whenever you feel ready. However, honesty and open dialogue with your new partner is essential. Don't try to replace the person who has died. It'll never work. They are irreplaceable, but that doesn't mean you can't have a really wonderful and fulfilling relationship with someone else one day, and really great sex. You can. You should. And it's OK.

Dying doesn't look like it does in the movies

[A]

Have you ever been with someone who has died? If you have, you'll already know that normal dying tends not to look like it does in the movies. In order to normalise death and dying and to begin to remove the fear from it, it's essential to understand what it actually looks like. I'll caveat this by saying that everyone's end of life is different. There are always going to be exceptions to the rule; not everyone will have access to good end-of-life care and palliative care, which champions 'normal dying' and strives towards everyone having a death with as little pain and suffering as possible. Some people will die traumatically and dramatically, but most of us won't.

It's important to remember that people are living right up until the point of death. The 'dying' phase is often very short in comparison to the 'living with an illness' phase. Do not write people off. Do not assume a life-limiting prognosis is automatically the immediate end. Allow them to live. Help them to live a brilliant life.

People can often feel reassured and less frightened if they understand what usually happens, especially during the last phase of life.

I'm asked all the time whether someone is near the end. In my experience there are signs that life is becoming more difficult to sustain that we can look out for but it's often impossible to tell exactly when the end will come. These are not exhaustive and will not all necessarily occur but are a general overview of what might happen. It's also always best to ask the medical team, the doctors, nurses and healthcare assistants. If you're noticing that the person you're caring for is exhibiting some of these, talk to the medical team, ask them what they think might be happening and let them know how you think the person is. As a carer, you will have unparalleled access to your person, you'll know how they are better than anyone. Share what you've noticed and they'll be able to give you a more accurate picture of where things are at. Don't feel you're being silly or asking unnecessary questions. That's what they are there for.

THE FINAL FEW MONTHS

I think it's hard to know if some behaviours are part of the dying process or if they are a result of knowing your life is ebbing away and the emotional toll that it can take. However, it's widely acknowledged that in the final few months some people can become withdrawn and may seem to be holding back emotionally. They may engage less and talk less. It can feel like they are letting go of the life you have with them and some people have suggested it's a way of beginning to acknowledge the inevitable. It could also be interpreted as them unconsciously or consciously allowing you to start finding ways of re-imagining and creating a life without them. Interestingly, in contrast to adults, it has been reported that towards the end of their lives children tend to talk more.

People tend to be less interested in eating and drinking. We have created such a culture of feeding people up during illness and often family, friends and carers find someone's lack of consumption very distressing. Food and drink are what sustains our life force, but it's normal to decrease what we consume when we are unwell. Don't ever try to force people to eat and drink. Medications, treatments and pain relief can also cause nausea and can make food and drink unappetising. It's also worth remembering that people's tastes may change when they're unwell. Give people what they fancy and what they ask for. Always have food and drink available and in easy reach, but do not insist or push it on them. Have fresh water next to them, with a straw so it's easier to drink. If you're caring for someone, make sure you eat and drink regularly and well.

THE FINAL FEW WEEKS

As the body begins the process of shutting down, people usually begin to feel more tired and they may sleep more.

An increase in pain is not uncommon, therefore increasing the need for more pain relief, which can make people drowsy and less communicative.

Some people experience confusion.

They'll be less likely to be eating and drinking a lot. They may be losing weight and it might be harder to get comfortable. They'll probably wee and poo less and may find it hard to control their bladder and bowels.

You might find they're more irritable than usual.

Don't be surprised by changes in their heart rate, blood pressure and breathing. Breathing can become congested and begin to sound laboured.

There may be changes in body temperature, feeling very hot and then very cold.

THE FINAL FEW DAYS

The last few days are always difficult for everyone and it would be a huge disservice to deny it. It can seem like you're sitting waiting for someone to die. You are conflicted because you may feel you want them to no longer be in pain but you also don't want to say goodbye for the final time. It is hard to watch somebody die – it's distressing to see their deterioration, and watching someone vivacious and full of life become weak and diminished is, without question, incredibly painful.

It's not unusual for people to lose their appetite altogether. The body's usual functions will slow or cease as a result. This is all perfectly normal.

Don't be alarmed if people report having hallucinations and visions.

This phase can be distressing and it's important to monitor their comfort levels so their medication can be adjusted accordingly. Talk to the medical team caring for them. Let them know if you feel their pain is not under control.

Time spent asleep will be greater than time spent awake. Eventually, they'll spend almost all of their time asleep and will become less and less responsive. Their body temperature will drop and their extremities will begin to turn a dark blue/purple. Their pulse will become much fainter and their eyes may begin to glaze over if they are open at all.

Some people may become agitated and restless. There are medications that can help with this but holding someone's hand, talking to them and letting them know they're not alone can help too.

Ultimately, they'll fall unconscious. We believe people are still able to hear and feel, so touch should always be gentle and respectful. Procedures should always be explained clearly: 'We are going to roll you gently on to your side,' or 'We are just going to re-dress the wound on your right leg.' Always keep talking to the person as if they are there and comprehending every word and action. Never talk over them.

Breathing can be noisy. The infamous and unpleasantly titled 'death rattle' is caused by saliva and bronchial secretions accumulating at the back of the throat and in the upper chest. During active dying, people can lose their ability to swallow and this exacerbates the build-up of secretions and saliva. The noise that this can produce can be frightening for carers, family and friends. It is normal. Sometimes drugs can be given to help dry out some of the secretions and minimise the noise. Sometimes repositioning someone can help, too. Remember to let the person know you're going to move them before you do it. It is thought that the person is generally unaware and not distressed by their noisy breathing. Sometimes suction is used to help get rid of the saliva.

Breathing will eventually become more and more intermittent until they exhale for the final time.

The actual end of a life can take a while longer than you'd imagine; sometimes it'll feel like an eternity, sometimes you'll feel it was too fast, and there wasn't enough time. But is there ever enough time with someone who means the world to you? Minutes when sitting by the bedside of someone who is dying seem to move much more slowly, each breath takes a little longer to inhale and exhale. You wait impatiently for the next inhale. Hopeful it will come, hopeful it won't: the paradox of being with people who are dying.

Letting someone go, letting them die, is not defeatist. Acceptance of the reality of our mortality is not to give up on hope, on love, on life. Acceptance allows for a peaceful letting go. Let them go with your love. Let them go with your blessing. Let them go knowing you'll be OK. You didn't give up. They didn't give up. Nature did her job.

FIVE THINGS I'VE OBSERVED AT DEATHBEDS

by Dr Kathryn Mannix

Kathryn has spent her medical career working with people who have incurable, advanced illnesses. Her first book *With the End in Mind* was published in 2017 to critical acclaim. Shortlisted for the Wellcome Prize in 2018, it has become a widely recognised text for aiding our understanding of death.

1.
The sequence of physical changes leading up to death is similar from person to person: a recognisable process, yet a unique experience – just in the same way as pregnancy, labour and birth. Like labour, it's a good idea to plan ahead.

2.
The dying process only causes two symptoms: increasing weariness and gradual, fluctuating loss of consciousness. Any other symptoms are caused by the underlying illness – so it's a good idea to get those sorted out early.

3.
Most people's last breath is an out breath. It usually happens while they are deeply unconscious. Those 'last words' death scenes in TV and cinema are very unlikely; don't wait for that last moment if you have something important to say.

4.
Most dying people are comforted by knowing what to expect. Families who understand the process feel calmer, despite their sadness.

5.
Nobody ever says, 'I wish we'd never talked about dying.' I've lost count of the people who say, 'I wish we'd talked more.'

Conversely, we felt it was essential to represent dying in different or difficult circumstances. Our friend, Anne Bedi, wrote a raw and deeply personal account of her father's death after he died in hospital on Christmas Eve at the age of 67.

FIVE THINGS NOBODY TELLS YOU WHEN AN UNCONSCIOUS PERSON IS GOING TO DIE

by Anne Bedi

1.
They often won't die straight away. It can take many many many many days.

2.
It's not peaceful, it's noisy. They may gurgle and gasp and choke, and drown and seem to howl. You are watching their body fight to live even though their brain cannot.

3.
It will be so harrowing and take so long that you'll wish they would die faster. And then you'll regret those thoughts when they die and you never get to see them again.

4.
Your day and the long nights will be made or broken by the expertise and kindness of the medical staff. Critical care will make you, down in the hell of the wards will break you.

5.
After keeping vigil for days by their bedside scared to leave for a second, devastatingly one of you will probably be out of the room when they die. For my family, that was me.

How to be there for someone when they are dying

[A]

There are many things you can do, but the most important thing is to ask. What you imagine someone might need and want may well be the absolute antithesis of what's right for them. Don't be afraid to ask. Don't be afraid to say you want to help but don't know how. Find out what matters most to them. Find out what they want and need. Do those things. Don't assume or take over with your ideas and ideals of what you think would be nice or what you think you'd like.

HELP THEM TO MAKE AN END-OF-LIFE PLAN

An end-of-life plan is a bit like a birth plan: it allows you to share your wishes and to communicate what is important to you. It might seem like a really difficult thing to do but having those conversations about what someone who is dying wants and doesn't want before they are unable to communicate their wishes really does help.

An end-of-life plan not only empowers the person who is unwell but it also allows those caring for them to deliver the care they actually want, rather than having to second-guess.

One lady I worked with was worried she'd be too unwell to pluck her own eyebrows and stray hairs. She made sure her daughter was on the case. She didn't want anyone who came to kiss her goodbye to be greeted with a coarse hair in their face. It might not matter to you but it really mattered to her.

How to create an end-of-life plan

'In my experience, telling people you know how they feel is not a good strategy. Asking them is.'
DR PATRICIA BRAYDEN, MEDICAL DIRECTOR AT ST CATHERINE'S HOSPICE

It's essential to remember that with dying, as with birthing, needs and wants change – many times, in fact. Something someone thought might be really soothing can suddenly become the most infuriating thing in the world. It's crucial to be flexible and to not stick rigidly to anything if it's not working. Sometimes, too, something might not work for you as the carer, the friend, the family member, and it's OK to say: 'I can't do that.'

These are some of the questions you could ask when you create the end-of-life plan:

1. Where do you want to be? Where do you want to die?
2. How do you want the room? Natural light? Candles? Bright or ambient? Curtains open or closed?
3. Do you think you'll want any scents in the room? Some people really do and some people find scented candles or incense can make them feel nauseous.
4. Who do you want to visit you? Do you want any music? If you do, what music?
5. Do you want massages? Feet? Hands? Head?
6. Do you want lots of people or shall we ask people to come alone? Do you want people to hold your hand?
7. What do you think will help you feel more comfortable?
8. Shall I bring the dog in? Would you like her to be here with you?
9. What matters most to you?
10. Do you have a bucket list? What can we do to help you achieve those things on it?
11. What can we help you to do?
12. Is there anyone you want us to call who doesn't already know what's happening?
13. Is there anyone you definitely do not want to see?
14. What food or drink (if any) do you think you'd like?
15. Is there something you really don't want?
16. What does a good day look like? How can we make that happen?
17. If COVID-19 restrictions are in place, think about what's important to you. How can your family, friends and support system work to make the most of the situation given the constraints?

Listen carefully to the answers, and write it all down.

GRIEVING SOMEONE WHO IS STILL ALIVE

Anticipatory grief is what we feel before someone has died. It can be felt by the person living with a life-limiting illness and by their family, friends and carers. We can also grieve like this for relationships, jobs, friendships and for people who are not currently living with illness. We can experience it for both loss that is cemented in reality and fearful loss – loss that we worry might happen regardless.

Sometimes anticipatory grief is called 'pre-death grief'. It can afford us the opportunity to begin to face the reality and start to process what is happening. It can spur us on and help us to make the most of the time left, such as tying up loose ends, planning funerals, writing Advance Directives, appointing an LPA, signing a DNAR (*see* p. 69), and making plans for what matters to us and how we want things to be. It can help us to take control. But that's the positive side of it. It can also cause fatigue and upset, impact our memory, have a derogatory impact on our emotional and physical well-being, and trigger mental health issues. What we must do is talk about how we are feeling, and explore our thoughts and emotions. We must get support. Given the right support, anticipatory grief can encourage us to communicate better, to acknowledge the reality of a situation and give us the resources to take control.

THINGS TO REMEMBER RIGHT AT THE END
(THESE ARE NOT ALWAYS POSSIBLE AND IT'S ESSENTIAL
TO REMEMBER IT'S OK IF THEY'RE NOT)

1. Try to let people go. Tell them everything will be OK even if you're not feeling like it will be.
2. Consider what you're projecting. They will be needing to feel safe and it helps if you're not projecting too much fear.
3. Right at the end is not really the time to start trying to have full-on conversations about your relationship, about what you wish you'd done and hadn't done. Have those conversations before this point is reached.
4. Try to be calm and if you can't, take yourself away for a few minutes to catch your breath.
5. Hearing is thought to be the final sense to falter so always talk 'to' the person. Never talk over them or about them.
6. Say the goodbye you want to say. You'll never get the chance again.

STRAIGHT AFTER DEATH

In the moments after someone has died there's no rush to do anything. It may seem obvious but there's nothing that can be done now. What matters is that you give yourself time and take the next steps at your own pace. There's no need to call the funeral director straight away, unless that's what you want.

— Kate's Experience

When Jenny died at five in the morning, Kate and her siblings didn't feel ready to say goodbye to her physical form. Instead, they called for the doctor to certify her death and let the funeral director know they'd contact him in the morning when they were ready. They filled Jenny's room with candles and put on her favourite radio station. The nurse, who had been with their mum right until the end, helped them to gently close her eyes and mouth. They carefully bathed her with warm water and lavender oil, then laid her favourite blanket over her. Her son, Charles, didn't feel able to help so instead he made cups of tea and bacon sandwiches. As their mum lay in her bedroom, the whole family gathered around to eat breakfast and just be together. Later that morning, the funeral directors came to take Jenny into their care. As she was taken out of the front door, Kate laid a flower from the garden on her chest.

The reality of death doesn't have to be horrifying. If we give ourselves the time and space to do what we need to do, being with the person immediately after they have died can be a cathartic experience.

We'll talk more about what to do after someone has died in the chapter about funerals.

Preparing for death: doing your death admin

[A]

One of the greatest gifts you can give to your family and the people closest to you is to put your affairs in order, or do your death admin as some people call it. It's what we should all do regardless, since it will make everyone's life easier. It's not fun – it tends not to feature on people's bucket lists – but if you do anything, do these five tasks:

1. **Advance Directive – fill one in**
   An Advance Directive or Advance Decision (sometimes also known as a Living Will) is a legal document setting out someone's specific wishes for medical treatment if their health deteriorates and they're unable to explain their wishes at the time. It allows people to state their desire to refuse certain treatments such as CPR (cardiopulmonary resuscitation). An Advance Statement is not legally binding but in a similar way to a birth plan, it allows you to communicate your wishes and express your preferences for care and treatment.
2. **DNAR – sign one**
   DNAR stands for Do Not Attempt Resuscitation. It's a form, signed by a doctor, alerting your medical team that you do not want them to give you CPR.
   It is not a legally binding document but medics do use it as a guide to your wishes. If you do not have a DNAR in place, the medical team will *always* give you CPR if you go into cardiac arrest. Even if you have the form in place it only covers CPR so you will receive other treatments. Your wishes are much more likely to be adhered to if you also have an Advance Directive stating that you do not want CPR.

WHAT IS CPR AND WHY WOULD YOU WANT TO REFUSE IT?

Cardiopulmonary resuscitation or CPR is an emergency procedure that attempts to restart someone's heart if it stops. It consists of chest compressions, inflating the lungs, and defibrillation, which delivers an electric charge to the heart in order to allow restoration of the normal heart rhythm. CPR in real life is nothing like it is in the movies. Even if people do survive CPR they do not necessarily regain any meaningful quality of life. Here are a few, often surprising, facts:

- Only 3 per cent of people over the age of 80 will survive CPR.
- 1.9 per cent of people with secondary cancer will survive CPR.
- Around 40 per cent of people who receive CPR will survive immediately after resuscitation. However, as few as 10 per cent of those people will ever be well enough to be discharged and go home.
- A study of 827 patients who had been resuscitated concluded that three months on from their cardiac arrest, just 12 per cent of the people were still alive.

3. **Will – write one**
   A will is a document that sets out what you want to happen to your property, possessions and money after you die. To make it legally valid it needs to be formally witnessed. You can write your will yourself but a lawyer can also help you. If you die and you haven't written a will, there are rules that dictate who will get what from your estate and this may be in contrast to what you wish to happen. If you have children, it's essential to set out provision for who will look after them in the event of your death. Talk to a lawyer. Google options. Talk to the Citizens Advice Bureau. They can all help.

4. **Lasting Power of Attorney – instruct one**
   A Lasting Power of Attorney is someone who is legally allowed to make decisions on your behalf about your welfare and care if you're ever unable to make them for yourself. While you're able, appointing someone you know and trust to act as an LPA for you can give you peace of mind that your needs and best interests will always be looked after. There's lots of online advice about appointing an LPA, and you can appoint more than one. However, if you appoint multiple LPAs, you need to decide if you want them to make joint decisions for you or if they'll be deciding on different aspects of your care and welfare separately. An LPA must be over 18 and have the ability to make their own decisions, also known as mental capacity. You can appoint a family member, your partner, a friend, or you can opt for a professional. The most important thing to consider when appointing one is to choose someone reliable and someone you wholeheartedly trust.

5. **Digital legacy – plan it**
   Put your digital affairs in order so you have control over what happens to your online life after you've died (*see* Five Things on p. 72 for more information).

FIVE THINGS THIS HEALTHCARE PROFESSIONAL WOULD REALLY LIKE YOU TO KNOW ABOUT MODERN RESUSCITATION

by Dr Mark Taubert

Mark is a palliative care doctor and senior lecturer.

1.

Cardiopulmonary resuscitation (CPR) has many success stories, especially in younger patients with heart conditions. For those with multiple long-term conditions and palliative patients, however, it is hardly ever successful and often not indicated at all.

2.

Cardiopulmonary resuscitation can work in cardiac arrest situations, when, for instance, a nonsensical heart rhythm (that makes the heart ineffective) may be reversed by giving an electric shock. However, the cardiac rhythms involved in less acute 'natural dying' situations are not reversible, so cardiopulmonary resuscitation actually has no chance of success.

3.

We should aim for people with serious life-limiting illnesses to have advance and future care planning documents, clearly outlining decisions on CPR before any deterioration. This paradoxically might mean talking to people about it when they are actually feeling rather well. But we need to find better ways to reach out more, and the only way is through patient empowerment. So resources like www.TalkCPR. com and the Second Conversation Project need to be shared widely.

4.

Blanket guidance to administer CPR no matter what, whenever a Do Not Attempt Resuscitation (DNAR) or advance care planning form is not in place at the scene, is likely to mean that many people will be denied a peaceful death and will receive traumatic interventions that are either not indicated at all, or very unlikely to lead to survival. The UK's Nursing and Midwifery Council should urgently rethink their guidance to their nurses on this issue and give them the respect they deserve to make such calls.

5.

The values we are currently using to dictate necessary measures when someone is close to death and dying, or actually dead, are biased towards defensive medicine practices. They are aggressive and often based on fallacious logic sequences. We can do better.

FIVE THINGS TO REMEMBER ABOUT DEATH AND THE DIGITAL

by Elaine Kasket

Elaine is a speaker, psychologist and the author of *All the Ghosts in the Machine*.

1.

Much of your personal information will stick around online for a while after you die, and there are virtually no laws or systems governing what happens to it, so you can't make assumptions about who will – or will not – be able to access your data after you're gone. Record your preferences and have conversations with loved ones about your wishes for your digital information.

2.

Grief is a highly individual phenomenon, online and off, and what's painful to one person is precious to another. Social media accounts are tailor-made for continuing bonds with the dead, but that comforts some and unnerves others. Facebook recently announced that they'll now be using AI to prevent people from receiving birthday reminders for dead people, but for every bereaved person who's upset by these reminders, there's another mourner who *wants* them. There's no rulebook for grief.

3.

Email accounts and social media profiles of deceased persons can be hacked by criminals for nefarious purposes, but even well-meaning people can cause emotional distress by accessing those accounts. If you are 'managing' or otherwise operating from within a deceased person's accounts, remember that your activity may result in 'voice from beyond the grave' phenomena. Put yourself in other people's shoes.

4.

Throughout your life, be an unapologetic curator. Tidy up your digital house frequently. If our accumulated digital material were like our physical possessions, we'd all be considered extreme hoarders. When you die, your loved ones will have your digital estate to sort out. Will it be stacked to the rafters with an undifferentiated mass of digital stuff, leaving them unable to see the wood for the trees?

5.

Your online information is *not* forever. Ancient Egyptian papyrus scrolls are still around, but hardware, software, coding and the internet are constantly changing. Your digitally stored information may be non-existent, inaccessible or unreadable within just a few years. Don't trust the cloud or digital legacy websites with the sole care of your most precious memories. Go old school and back them up in material format.

Making funeral arrangements in advance

[A + L]

IF YOU'RE LIVING WITH A LIFE-LIMITING ILLNESS

Sometimes a person who is unwell may want to contact a funeral director to begin the process of planning their own funeral. It's not weird, maudlin or 'tempting fate'; in fact it can be an empowering experience. It can be helpful to contact a few funeral directors to find one you really like. Ask them to meet you and talk about what you want. A good funeral director will be more than happy to facilitate this.

When you feel you have so little control over the illness that is wreaking havoc on your body and is cutting short a life you love living, taking control of what you can is vital. Making decisions about what happens to you after you've died, choosing who you want to care for you and who you want to conduct your funeral can give you a sense of self-government. When everything is being done *to* you, this is one way to take charge and assert your design.

IF YOU'RE CARING FOR SOMEONE AT THE END OF THEIR LIFE

— Jacob's Experience

Jacob called Louise late one Friday night. He talked about how his husband Ben had been diagnosed with cancer and was now in intensive care. The doctors said he was unlikely to make it through the weekend. He wanted to know what would happen after Ben died. He'd never arranged a funeral before and was nervous about what would happen and when. He wanted to make enquiries and empower himself with all the information he needed. Yet he felt enormously guilty. 'I'm outside in the corridor,' he told Louise. 'I don't want Ben or the rest of the family to hear what I'm saying. It feels awful to be talking about his funeral when he's not even dead yet.'

We might feel unable to speak the direct words and say that we are mentally (and organisationally, in the case of Jacob) preparing for someone's death, but that's in effect what anticipatory grief can do. The process of considering what will happen, contemplating it, seeing how it plays out in our minds, can help prepare us.

Don't feel guilty about pre-empting someone's death because you call a funeral director to discuss next steps before they've died. Sometimes it's an important part of the process. Putting things in place for when someone dies will not instigate their death, acknowledging the reality of a situation will not cause it to happen, it just means that you'll know what to do when the time comes.

Ben didn't die over the weekend, he died in the early hours of Tuesday morning. Jacob called Louise to let her know, feeling reassured that he already knew who would be on the other end of the phone and what the next steps would be.

Different places to die

[A]

Research reveals that some 70 per cent of people would choose to die at home. In reality, just over 50 per cent of people die in hospital. Why are we in a situation where hospitals are being pushed to treat people who are dying, who actually want to die in the comfort of their own home?

The answer is that we are all responsible for the lack of good communication at the end of life: doctors can be reticent and clumsy, and patients can be unwilling or unable to accept hard truths. Our fear of dying as a culture, or fear of discussing death and dying, can prevent us from making sound decisions about end-of-life care.

Doctors' cautiousness to be upfront and honest about how successful a treatment will be, or about the gravity of the illness, compounds the issue. People choose to continue active treatment because they believe (and hope) they 'might' get better. Why do they believe this? Because no one is telling them they're dying in a language they're able to process and understand.

Then there's the issue of why people feel compelled to go into hospital or turn up at A&E during their dying process in the first place. The answer is panic. They panic because they can't breathe properly or the pain is too great. They panic because they are going through something they've never experienced before and unless they've been given enough information, it can be terrifying.

We often compare birth and death. When we are expecting a baby, we can think and feel like we've gone into labour several times before it actually happens. We turn up at the maternity unit with our overnight bag crammed full of swaddling blankets and newborn nappies only to be sent away and told that our eagerly awaited arrival won't be putting in an appearance just yet. We go because our bodies feel alien and are doing strange things. We've got pains we've never felt before and we don't know what to expect. This also applies to end of life: if we don't let people know exactly what's going to happen and how it will probably feel and look, they will panic and come into hospital. And dying alone on a ward in a busy hospital is no way for anyone to die.

It doesn't have to be this way. We used to die at home. We used to accept death as a normal part of life. Medical advances and our ability to keep people alive for longer have meant that we now routinely over-medicalise death. If we acknowledge and 'treat' someone for the death they are going to die, we will be able to ensure they're comfortable, well-informed and accessing the end of life they have chosen, in the place they want to be, remaining in charge of their own lives all the way up until the end.

— Max's Experience

Max's diagnosis with stage 4 cancer came very late in his illness yet he was given the option of active treatment to 'potentially' give him more time. The hope of this extra time was impossible to resist and he agreed. He died during the treatment – heartbreakingly, as a direct result of it. He died a painful and difficult death, desperately trying to live a life that his body was unable to sustain.

Had Max's medical team been more honest, had he been given more time to process and talk through his options, had his family had the courage to accept his prognosis, Max's death could have been very different.

HOW TO MAKE DYING AT HOME MORE COMFORTABLE

1. Strive to develop compassionate communities: groups that come together to provide support at end of life. Their aim is to provide integrated care with the medical teams, the family and the community all working together to enable all 70 per cent of people wanting to die at home the chance to fulfil their end-of-life wishes.
2. We need to maintain a structure of person-centred care based on compassion and communication.
3. We must allow patients and their carers to be the 'experts' of their illness. We need to listen to patients and their carers, and keep listening.
4. If we teach doctors and nurses to communicate with patients and their families well – clearly and carefully – we can get people home to die.
5. Doctors need regular supervision and support. It's an emotionally difficult job to work with people who are dying and we need to make sure our medical professionals' mental health is well looked after.
6. Involve patients and carers in clinical decisions and in their care. Work collectively and as a team.

7. Involve everyone to make sure all their needs are catered for:
   - Ask the occupational therapist to come to the home to see if any adaptations are needed so they can access as much of the house as possible. For instance, can they safely use the bathroom and potentially go up the stairs?; could they make their own cup of tea if they wanted to and felt up to it?
   - Ask the physio to come and do a home assessment so they can create a movement plan to help keep someone as mobile as possible.
   - Ask someone from the spiritual or pastoral care team to come and do a home visit.
   - See if there's a regular ambulance pick-up service so they can access the therapies and activities at the hospice.
   - Make a rota for friends and family so there's always someone there, even if they are in a different room. Factor rest and time out when designing the rota – everyone, no matter how close they are to the person, will need a break. EVERYONE.
8. If you're not coping, ask for help!
9. Make sure you have telephone numbers for the hospice, the ward, your GP, a named nurse and all key players in the medical care team stored in your phone and to hand. It's awful having to scrabble around for telephone numbers if you're in a panic.
10. Engage the services of a doula!
11. Hospice at Home allows you to access excellent end-of-life care in your own home. Get a referral to it.

HOW TO MAKE DYING IN HOSPITAL MORE COMFORTABLE

Sometimes we have no choice about where we die. Sometimes there's no time. Sometimes hospital is where someone feels safe. Some people *do* want to die in hospital. Whatever the reason, if someone you love is dying in hospital there are ways to make the experience warmer, less clinical, more peaceful, even.

1. Engaging the services of a good end-of-life doula can really help make dying in hospital a better experience for both the person who is dying and their family and friends. Supporting people who are dying and empowering them to make informed choices and decisions about their care changes the way people die for the better, and doulas can and do help exponentially in this process.
2. Bring in a blanket from home. A pillow too. Something familiar and cosy. Something that reminds them of home.

3. Wearing your own clothes and pyjamas and not the horrible hospital gowns and paper pants makes everything better.

4. Bring in photos and small meaningful things. Sadly, most hospitals discourage anything large or valuables coming in as they cannot guarantee they won't get stolen, but having hand-made cards and photographs of familiar and well-loved faces around the bedside can bring a lot of joy.

5. If they haven't already been referred to the palliative care team, insist this happens as soon as possible.

6. Ask if there's a side room available. This is a single room off the ward that will afford you and your family and friends some privacy. Dying feels like something that deserves this privacy but sometimes you do have to ask to get it. There will, however, be occasions when a single room cannot be found. If this happens, close the curtains around the bed, and ask if they can be moved to a bed on the ward by the window – there's often a bit more space around these bays and being able to see the sky can be a lovely thing.

7. If they are still wanting to and able to eat, bring in their favourite home-cooked food. Doing this also means you can sit and eat with them so you'll be well nourished, too.

8. Candles are problematic because of health and safety rules and regulations but you could bring in a diffuser with some essential oils if that's the kind of thing they'd like. In a ward this might be harder because of the other patients. Ask the ward staff – the worst they can do is say no.

9. If you want to and if your person wants you to, there's lots of general care you can do. The nurses and healthcare assistants will thank you for carving a chunk off their enormous workload and it can make you feel like you're doing something to help. Tasks could include washing, helping with meals and toilet visits. Ask the nurse or healthcare assistant to show you how to do things like mouth care. When someone has voluntarily stopped drinking their mouths can become dry and uncomfortable. To combat this, the care team use little pink sponges on sticks that can be put in water and gently used to lubricate the mouth. Applying a little smear of petroleum jelly to their lips can help, too. These small things make a huge difference. Remember, though, that it's also absolutely fine to step back and allow the staff to do it.

10. If you do have a single room, you can bring in a radio or play music quietly. It's very difficult to do this on a ward as there are other people to consider but quietly in a side room is almost always OK.

11. Build a good rapport with the ward staff. They're much more likely to go over and above the call of duty if they're invested in your person. Kindness

and generosity go a long way, too. No one will expect it but delicious biscuits and a basket of fruit will brighten up the most tired and overworked nurses' and healthcare assistants' day. Please and thank you goes a long way too; you'd be surprised how often staff don't get spoken to politely.

12. If there's something like reflexology that your person enjoys you can arrange for the practitioner to come to the hospital to treat them. Again, ask permission. The hospital might even have their own complementary therapist who is able to give a treatment.

13. If you feel there's something wrong, if you know your person is in pain, alert the ward staff immediately. Don't worry that you're being difficult and demanding.

14. There's no going back at the end of life. We have one chance to get it right so never hesitate to ask to do something or to request something. If your person wants to go into the garden, do all you can to make it happen. If they have a well-loved pet they want to see again, do everything you can to make it happen. If you build a good relationship with the ward staff you'll find they are considerably more accommodating.

15. National Institute for Health and Care Excellence (NICE) end-of-life guidelines state that the spiritual needs of someone who is dying must be attended to. All hospitals will have a spiritual or pastoral care team, so if you'd like to see someone, ask.

16. If you want to stay overnight with your person, ask. There is provision for this but hospitals tend not to advertise it and will often actively discourage it. Don't be discouraged if you know it's the right thing for you and your person. Stay. Get a friend to bring in blankets and pillows if the staff say they don't have any spare.

17. It's one of the only times when being a bit of a pain is entirely justified. I have had to very sternly say the words, 'I am not leaving,' several times. You might not want to be so forthright but occasionally you might need to be.

18. Don't forget about your needs. Sleep when you can. Eat when you can. Get up and walk around. Go outside for a few moments when you can.

19. If you're on a ward, be considerate of all the other patients – don't talk too loudly, don't have hundreds of visitors crowding the ward all at once. If you're considerate of others, they'll be considerate of you. There can be a real sense of camaraderie on an acute ward. Support one another. Give one another a hug. Check in. It helps.

20. It's a popular myth that you can get access to the best drugs in hospital. In reality, it's the hospices that have the greater jurisdiction for pain relief. If there's time, if your person isn't dying imminently, you can ask for a referral to a hospice.

21. Your person is still your person even though they have been admitted to hospital. Don't allow the medical team to disenfranchise them, you or your relationship.

22. After your person dies, make sure you have the time with them that you want and need. Do not be rushed by anyone. If you want to be involved in their after-death care, let the team know you want to help. Some hospitals and most hospices have a 'family room' in which your person and you can go for as long as you need. Ask if this is an option. You can also take your person home after they've died and spend time with them there. There's more on this in the section about funerals.

23. Take your time to make decisions about what's next. Don't be swayed to contact a particular funeral director – sometimes hospitals will steer you towards someone in particular – try not to let yourself be steered if that's not what you want.

24. Don't forget that this is your life and this is your person's death. Assert yourself to make it as close to what they want it to be as possible.

25. Hospital staff need to remember that family and carers are absolutely not 'visitors' but they are a vital and essential part of the medical care team and must be treated as such.

THE NEED TO FEEL NEEDED

Death and dying aren't solely about the person who is dying; they're about everyone who is involved. Someone who needs help to do things isn't just receiving help and care; they are allowing the people around them and their carers to give it to them. It's a gift from both sides. In allowing people to 'serve' them, those living with a life-limiting illness are helping to mould and shape their bereavement and grief experiences. I've heard countless stories of how comforted those left behind feel when they recall all the things their 'person' allowed them to do at the end. Are people who are dying unconsciously allowing their loved ones to feel helpful? Feeling helpful makes us feel wanted and cements our position as someone special and important. Feeling and being helpful is therefore essential.

FIVE THINGS I'VE LEARNED SINCE MY YOUNGER BROTHER DIED FROM CANCER AT THE AGE OF 21

by Alice Miller

Alice lost her brother, Elliott, to a rare form of cancer at the age of 21 in March 2016. He died within six months of diagnosis, after the tumour in his jaw spread to his lungs and he essentially suffocated to death.

1.

Waiting for someone to die is worse than the moment they actually do. There is almost relief when they finally die, because the anxiety from waiting goes away.

2.

People grieve in different ways, just because someone's way of grieving doesn't match yours, doesn't mean they aren't grieving.

3.

Smoothies are great when you don't feel like eating much. Friends who cut up and individually bag smoothie ingredients to keep in the freezer are even better.

4.

Slow down and be selfish. I was so hyper aware of everyone's attention on me – I'm the girl whose brother died – that I put way too much energy into worrying about how I would be perceived. When Elliott died at 4 a.m. the first thing I did was write a post letting all my friends know. I went back to work after a week and walked into the office smiling. I didn't want people to think I couldn't cope with what was being thrown at me. I wish I'd taken a little more time at the very beginning just to slow down and look after myself.

5.

When you're ready, take on new challenges that will make you feel accomplished. I've tried to take on a new physical challenge every year to raise money for charity. So far I've done two half marathons, an ocean swim and a corporate boxing event. I do these things because he can't, and he is always the one pushing me through if I am doubting myself. Accomplishing something you never thought you'd be able to do helps bring meaning into your life when it's crashing down around you, is a way to pay tribute to your lost one, and in some instances an amazing way to raise money to help fight back against the causes of their death.

FIVE THINGS I LEARNED ABOUT DEATH AND DYING WHEN MY SISTER DIED FROM BREAST CANCER AT 44

by Louise Head

Louise's sister Gemma died from breast cancer in October 2018
at the age of 44. She had just got married and had a four-year-old son,
and worked as an actor and writer.

1.

The loss of a young person changes a family irrevocably. There is a
paradigm shift and it takes time to adjust to the new normal.

2.

Bereavement is inequitable. There is no such thing as a fair share when
it comes to loss. Accept that it's just timing; sooner or later everyone will
experience it.

3.

It is a test of friendships. Notice the ones who never shied away, no matter
how dark it got, who were brave enough to try to make you laugh when you
didn't think you had a smile left in you – they are the real keepers.

4.

Children are stronger than we give them credit for. Don't spend all your time trying
to protect them or you'll run the risk of denying them their chance to say goodbye.

5.

There is no greater privilege than to share the last weeks of the life of
someone you love. Don't be distracted by anything else. It will all still be
there at the end, but you only get one go at this.

COVID-19: A pandemic in our lifetime

[A]

It will be many years before we fully come to understand the far-reaching consequences that COVID-19 has had on end-of-life care, on medical treatments, on cancer treatments and screenings, on mental health and mental health services, on grief, on funerals, on everything.

It is not an exaggeration to say that coronavirus has changed all our lives. It has turned our entire world upside down and inside out. Our fundamental sense of stability has been thrown off-kilter and nothing looks or feels the same. We are all struggling to find a way to express our feelings. I don't think I've had a single conversation during this period of our lives that hasn't been in some way dominated by COVID – our thoughts about it, our emotional reaction, the surreal sense of living through the kind of event that history books will discuss at length. And each of our experiences has been different. Some of us have been to socially distanced funerals and lost people we love, others have been touched in different ways. But we've all been affected by it to some degree.

One of the most troubling aspects of all of this for me, as an end-of-life practitioner, is that because of the pandemic and the procedures that have had to be put in place to alleviate as much risk of infection as possible, people have been dying alone. We are living and dying in a way we have never experienced and its impact is profound. Hospitals have *often* had to refuse to allow visitors to anyone, whether they have been admitted because of COVID-19 or not. People have died without anyone by their side. In an attempt to help people say goodbye, members of overstretched medical teams have been holding up mobile phones and video-calling so that people can say their goodbyes.

WHAT CAN WE DO IF WE CAN'T BE THERE AT THE END OF LIFE?

1. Build a good relationship with the medical team. Ask them to keep you informed and ask them to help you keep lines of communication open via a mobile phone or an iPad.
2. Be really kind to yourself. Allow yourself to not be OK. Ask for help and support. Create space just for you. Some people find putting together an 'altar' helpful. It can have photos, letters, any reminders of your person and perhaps a candle. Take time out to process what's happening. Allow yourself to grieve. Take all the time you need.

3. Write down all the things you want to say. Put them in a voice note. Say them aloud. Call your person and even if they're unable to respond tell them all you need to say. Express how you're feeling. Talk about it. Talk about them. Allow yourself to be vulnerable. Allow others to be there for you.
4. Find a ritual that works for you. Only you will know what that might be, but perhaps it's walking the walks you used to walk together, talking about your person with others, sharing stories or cooking their favourite dinner.
5. Sometimes we have to try to let go of how we want things to be and embrace the unknown. There's beauty in the unknown and sometimes all we can do is surrender to it.

In the end, the most vital and fundamental thing we can do is just love our people. Through all of this, the thing I've come to understand with more clarity than ever before is that there is nothing more important than love. Nothing matters more.

FIVE THINGS I'VE LEARNED AFTER LOSING MY DAD TO COVID-19 AND GRIEVING IN LOCKDOWN

by Helen Smith

'On 9 March 2020, my dad Ian received a clean bill of health from his GP. On 10 March he started to feel a bit unwell. This was the last day I ever saw him. By 11 March he was bedridden, where he stayed for two weeks except for a visit to the GP where they ruled out COVID-19. On the afternoon of 23 March, he was blue-lighted to hospital and, by the evening, he was one heart attack down, on a ventilator and in an induced coma. He never regained consciousness, and died on Sunday 12 April 2020 with me, my mum and my brother by his side (albeit in full PPE).'

1.
Losing your dad to a virus that didn't even exist six months prior is near-impossible to get your head round. It makes you feel completely alone. Remember, though, that you never are, even if grieving in lockdown convinces you otherwise. Modern technology is a lifeline, and there can still be so much support found through social media, online resources, and even video or telephone calls with friends. Although it's never a substitute for a physical hug, there are still always people there for you.

2.

Grieving in lockdown can be extra tough, because you are limited with how you can distract yourself. It gives you more of an excuse to spend all day in bed, for days on end. It's therefore important for your mental health to make sure that even if you aren't going anywhere, you still get out of bed, shower and put on fresh clothes, even if it's to just go and sit and cry on the sofa. It makes a difference.

3.

COVID-19 robbed us of so many things – kissing my dad goodbye, being able to see him in the Chapel of Rest, hugs from family and friends, and having a 'normal' funeral. Do the best you can with the restrictions that are in place. On the day of Dad's funeral, friends lined up down the street, socially distanced, dressed in his favourite colours, to meet his hearse and pay their respects that way. We then organised a 'virtual toast' to Dad, where friends and family from all over the world raised a glass at the same time from the safety of their homes, and sent us the photos.

4.

Find ways to distract yourself at home that still allow you to grieve and honour your loved one. I am currently on furlough, isolated at home with no obvious light at the end of the tunnel. I've therefore taken to sharing my grief journey on Instagram as a cathartic release, writing poetry, talking to friends, baking, looking at photos of Dad, scrapbooking, gardening, going on walks, and reading books about grief. Creating a bit of routine when there's no real routine has helped.

5.

My mantra is 'one step at a time.' Every tiny step is an achievement, and it's OK to take no steps at all sometimes. Cry when you need to cry, ignore people when you don't feel like speaking, blast music and go on a run when you need to clear your mind, have a nap when you're tired. Just one step at a time and all in your own time.

'Out of order' death

You are about to read a sentence that nobody ever wants to write and certainly nobody ever wants to digest:

Babies and children die.

This is often described as 'out of order' death because it disrupts the natural order of life, it seems to defy and go against nature. It's so unimaginably awful that we don't talk about it. What words are adequate when trying to console a parent whose child has died? There are none. So, people often say and do nothing, paralysed by tragedy.

We often work with out of order death. We don't have a different vocabulary, we are no stronger or more hard hearted than anyone else, we just choose to sit with the discomfort because our words, no matter how inadequate, matter. Our acknowledgement of this short life makes a difference. We know that being there for parents at this impossible time makes a difference to their grief and ultimately their lives.

When a baby dies *in utero*, saying hello is also saying goodbye. What we do is help those parents be parents. Reading stories, singing lullabies, dressing and bringing their silent newborn home. For the first and the last time.

The death of new and fledgling life elicits a pain so unbearable, so life-altering and so fundamental that to attempt to describe it would be to do it a heinous injustice. It is indescribable, but it is essential to find a way to bear witness to it, to recognise and acknowledge it.

FIVE THINGS I'VE LEARNED FROM FACING THE END OF LIFE WITH ESSIE, MY LIFE-LIMITED TRIPLET DAUGHTER

by Lorna Cobbett

Lorna is mum to triplets, Roman, Essie and Eva. Essie was diagnosed as life-limited at 11 days old and died aged 18 months.

1.
End of life is only end of life if the child decides it is

Doctors might tell you that they cannot do anything more and your 13-month-old baby daughter is going to be transferred to her children's hospice for her end of life, but that will only happen if your child decides it is so. Essie entered her end-of-life phase on 25 March 2017. I expected her to die. And quickly. I didn't expect her to come home at the end of April 2017. I was confused and didn't understand. But when we went through another end-of-life episode, and another one, and another one and then the fifth one that ultimately was too much for Essie and she died, I got it. Doctors aren't in control. I was not in control. Essie was in control. That's why Essie will forever be my inspiration. She should have died the day she was born, given the nature of the brain injury she suffered at birth. But Essie never did anything that was expected. Rules are there to be broken, especially by children.

2.
Your child can die at home and you won't want to put the house on the market immediately

Essie was diagnosed as life-limited at 11 days old while in NICU at St George's and we knew that she would not live beyond childhood. We were 100 per cent adamant that she was not going to die at home. We thought that this would be the worst thing that could happen to us. We were wrong. Knowing your baby is going to die is the worst thing, that feeling of the air being sucked out of your body, and your throat having a permanent lump is the worst thing. When Essie went through her third end-of-life episode at Chestnut Tree House and came home, we realised what she wanted. Essie wanted to stay at home until she died. We moved her care to our house – at night, she had a nurse; by day, she had a carer and the community team on standby to help us when needed. Essie flew away to be a shooting star on Sunday 13 August 2017 at 2.12 a.m. and it was peaceful. It felt right to have her in our home.

3.
A children's hospice is a home and a place full of life

Ignore the fact that hospice sounds like hospital, it isn't. They are very different places. Chestnut Tree House became our second home. It is a place where smiles, laughter, memories and life come first. If you have never been to a children's hospice, go and visit one and be surprised. These are very underfunded places and don't get the level of funding that adult hospices do. I honestly believe that Chestnut Tree House saved us, individually and as a family. Don't fear a hospice and know that they can help anyone who has faced the death of a baby or child. They will give you time, which is so precious and priceless. Time to grieve and time to make memories.

4.
Being life-limited isn't the same as having a terminal illness

Due to the catastrophic brain injury that caused Essie to have a long list of disabilities, no one could tell us when the end would be. Life-limited means that every day you wake up and your child could die. It doesn't mean they are getting worse each day, but the risk that they could die is always there. Some days Essie was alert, her epilepsy would be under control and she'd tolerate her feeds. Other days, Essie would struggle. But life-limited doesn't mean that every day you're losing a part of your child you'll never get back. You will have good days and you will have bad days. We always tried to find the light and laughter, and took as many photos and videos of Essie as possible.

5.
Life goes on and you will be OK

There will be new routines and new ways of keeping your baby's memory alive. I speak Essie's name freely and will try to correct people who don't speak it for fear of upsetting us. We also write Essie's name (or a little star) in cards. We buy her a birthday card and Essie has her own birthday cake. Don't get me wrong, I will be grieving forever and cry when I need to, but life is precious and I need to smile and laugh. There will be ways you find to make the child who is no longer in your arms part of your daily life – we say goodnight to Essie every day and turn fairy lights of little stars on in the bedroom where her pot of ashes are when we put Roman and Eva to bed.

I am always going to be a mummy to triplets. The world might see twins now, but I correct anyone who calls Roman and Eva twins. This is not who they are, and I will never apologise for telling it how it is. Death is a stigma. Baby loss is a stigma. Child disability is a stigma. Grief is a stigma. But it's time to end the stigma and to talk about death.

Baby Amy

[A]

My phone rings and it's not a number I recognise. It's almost Christmas and I am out shopping trying to cross off a few things on what feels like a never-ending to-do list. I'd normally let it go to answerphone and call back when I'm less distracted, but something makes me pick up.

'My baby has died.'

I find a quiet place away from the hustle of the high street and I listen. It is one of the saddest stories I have ever heard. I am struck by the bravery of this woman, a first-time mother, telling me, to all intents and purposes a perfect stranger, about her beautiful baby girl, the life she lived and the death that ended it.

She grew her, she gave birth to her, she survived purely on milk from her breast, in her short life she'd never been more than a few feet away from her, she'd tended to her every need and loved her with a love she'd never experienced before. A love so ferocious, so deep and fundamental that she'd have given her own life to swap places with her now. She wanted to hold Amy again. She wanted to have time with her. She wanted to be a mother to her again.

I tell her that, no matter what, she will always be Amy's mother. That nothing can change that. She tells me she is a mother with empty arms and a broken heart. A mother without her child. We arranged for her to have time with Amy. Every day for five days she came, and every day I gently lifted Amy into her arms and she sat with her, cradling her, reading her all the stories she hadn't had the chance to read her, telling her all about the life she'd imagined for her, and telling her how much she loves her.

On the day before her funeral she swaddled Amy in the blanket in which she had brought her home from the hospital on the day she was born. She placed her in her tiny coffin surrounded by mementos of her love and her life, she kissed her and she closed the lid. She was the first person to see Amy and she'd also be the last.

We took Amy home the night before her funeral and she stayed in her nursery, embraced by the accoutrements of her too-short childhood. Her mummy lit a candle and she sat with Amy's coffin on her lap, rocking her in the feeding chair she's slept more hours in since Amy's birth than her bed. She had one last night with her baby.

Amy's funeral service was filled with life, with love and with tears. At the end, Amy was placed in my arms and I carried her in her coffin to the cremator. I tenderly laid her down and my hand rested on the engraved nameplate. I traced her name with my finger, I thanked her for allowing me, in her death, to be a part of her life and I wished her a safe journey. Her family asked me to stay until the very end and I said goodbye as I watched her embark on her final journey into the flames.

A tiny life making the biggest of impacts.

SUPPORTING PARENTS AT THIS IMPOSSIBLE TIME

1. To the medical team and funeral professionals: give parents the time and space to say the goodbye they need to say. Never rush them. Let them control what happens and when. Never let them feel that you are taking their child away from them; allow them to give their child to you, in their own time and on their own terms.
2. In death, your child is still your child. Do what you need to do. You can still hold and hug your child. Don't let anyone tell you otherwise.
3. Never assume that a parent is no longer a parent because their child has died.
4. Each parent's grief will be different. Amy's mum is grieving differently to Amy's dad. They both need different things. Neither is right or wrong. Find ways of honouring your needs and your grief without trampling on the other person's. Accept and acknowledge the differences even if you don't understand why someone needs to do something in particular. Amy's dad didn't see her after she died. He didn't want to, but he understood that it was important to her mum. He came with her every day. He sat in a different room and he supported his partner while also looking after his needs. We all grieve differently. We grieve the same person differently. Grief is a shapeshifter and something that we want and need today may well be something we really don't need or want tomorrow. If someone alters what they need, what they're asking for in their grief, do everything you can to accommodate it.
5. When a baby dies their appearance tends to change quite quickly. Often, we hear of funeral professionals advising that it would be better for all concerned if the parents did not see their child. Over the years I've come to realise that it's not for us to make those decisions, it's for the parents. They gaze upon their child with pure and unconditional love and to them, regardless of the changes that death has brought, all they see is the beautiful and perfect human they created.
6. Don't just ask dad how mum is doing. It's important to remember that he's grieving and needs support, too. Ask how *he's* doing. Give him a huge hug.
7. Talk about them. Keep talking. Parents want and need their children to be remembered. Listen. Keep listening. Love. Keep loving. Hold. Keep holding. Be there. Keep being there.

FIVE THINGS I'VE LEARNED FROM LOSING MY TWO SONS AT BIRTH

by Mark Shepherd

Mark and his wife Desiree have experienced the death of two of their children –
the first through premature birth and the second through stillbirth. In 2019, Mark
established Bonded, a once-a-month support group for grieving dads based in Surrey.

1.
Be with your baby

Hours before our first baby was to be born prematurely, and knowing that he
would die shortly after birth, a midwife asked us if we would like to see him
once he had been born or if we wanted him to be taken away. Through all the
emotion and confusion we immediately agreed that he should just be taken
away out of sight. Fortunately, the midwives had the wisdom to keep him in a
cot in the room next door, and I went and held his hand for about 45 minutes
while his heart was still beating. After that I took him through to my wife.
Losing a child at birth is the most painful and joyful experience I've ever felt,
both emotions happening at the same time. If it happens to you, do everything
you can to maximise the joy of the child's birth through all of the pain. When
we lost a second baby, we were more prepared. We had him in a basket on the
bed with us for about an hour after he was born, just enjoying his company.

2.
Have photos taken

This will be one of the last things on the minds of parents who are experiencing
a premature or stillbirth, but having photos of the baby is priceless. Charities
like Remember My Baby offer a free professional-grade photographic service
for situations like this. Having a word with the midwives as soon as possible
about the options for remembrance photography will improve the chances of
securing the services of a photographer in time.

3.
Brace yourself for people avoiding you

My wife and I both noticed how people deliberately avoided us once we returned to daily life, especially men. This is probably true in many situations of bereavement, but it was pronounced with the loss of a child. Friends and colleagues simply didn't know what to say and so avoided contact. A smile, a little hug, a touch on the arm or perhaps a simple card is all that's needed in most cases to acknowledge someone like a colleague in a situation like this. Avoiding the issue is not a solution.

4.
Brace yourself for well-meant but hurtful comments

Comments or advice like, 'It was probably God's will', 'At least it wasn't a proper baby yet', 'So and so had it much worse than you did, their baby died a few months after it had been born', and 'You need to move on and forget about it now' are likely to be fed to you from colleagues, friends and even family members. You'll never forget these comments, but do your best to forgive the ignorance of those who made them.

5.
Connect with others

When we lost our first son, I struggled to go in to work for about six months. I just wanted to lie in bed all day. I tried to get some help, but couldn't find any, let alone something specific for fathers. Since then, things have improved in the UK and there are charities and organisations that can genuinely help. It's unlikely that anyone's grief will be 'fixed' through counselling, but connecting and sharing with others in a similar situation brings much relief in the midst of pain, even many years later.

FIVE THINGS I LEARNED ABOUT BABY LOSS AFTER MY FOURTH CHILD, MILES, WAS STILLBORN

by Annabel Bower

Annabel is the proud mother of four children, three who are physically with her and one who lives on in her heart.

1.

People don't always know what to say. Perceived silver linings may be pointed out or nothing said at all. People are often terrified of mentioning your baby for fear of upsetting you, but the reality is that you are always thinking of your child so acknowledging them will not remind you. Conversely, it will bring comfort and show that others also remember and love your baby.

2.

Baby loss is often misunderstood and its impact belittled with statements such as, 'At least it was early', 'It's very common', 'You can have another one' or 'Be thankful for the child(ren) you already have.' What people need to know is that each baby is a precious individual; future or existing children will never replace or make up for the one who has been lost.

3.

The loss of a child goes against the natural order of life. It is an event in which grief and trauma collide as the death of your baby occurs within your own body. This is incredibly confronting and heartbreaking both physically and emotionally. It is a loss which stays with you forever.

4.

Men and women often grieve very differently after miscarriage and stillbirth. I felt like my world had stopped turning and found it hard to function; my husband was able to resume normal activities long before I could even contemplate them. We were just as devastated as each other, but it looked very different on the outside.

5.

What I miss most about Miles is all of the memories we will never get to make together. His first smile, first words, first day at school. We will never have the moments I dreamed of and hoped for. This lasts a lifetime as I will always wonder who he would have become and grown to look like. I will always feel like someone is missing from my family.

The toll illness can take on relationships

[A]

Relationships can be tough to negotiate at the best of times and when we throw illness, dying, death and grief into the mix, the tough gets even tougher. Being entirely together and 'at one' with someone emotionally, physically and spiritually can feel like the holy grail even when the going is good. The reality is that it's an unattainable goal that we exhaust and frustrate ourselves attempting to reach. Life never works like that, no matter how much we wish it did.

What happens if your partner has a life-limiting diagnosis and you're not on the same emotional page as them? What happens if you're grieving differently to your partner? What can you do when your needs are the complete antithesis of those closest to you?

A statement I hear all too often is: 'My partner has a life-limiting diagnosis but we are so far apart in our understanding of what's going on and we seem to be coming at it from totally different perspectives.'

My reply is always: 'Everyone is coming at it from a different perspective. Everyone. It's just that no one really talks about it openly.'

They say: 'We disagree so much – the things I need, she doesn't need and vice versa. I want to talk, he doesn't. I need to cry, she doesn't. We're not processing what's going on emotionally at the same rate. It's causing friction and distance. I don't understand his needs, she doesn't understand mine. She feels me asserting my needs are a direct rejection of hers. I don't understand why she doesn't understand...'

Illness can be divisive, really and unhelpfully divisive. There's no doubt about that. Illness doesn't just impact the life of the person who is ill, everyone in the family and beyond will be impacted, too. Everybody manages differently and needs different things at different times.

— Gemma's Experience

Gemma is unwell. She wants to know everything about what's happening to her. She wants all the information. She wants to make plans and preparations for her young family after she's died. She needs to talk and be open about what's happening and what is going to happen. She wants reassurance from her partner that he'll do certain things after she's died. She wants to discuss him meeting someone else and loving again. She wants to discuss their children's future and imagine with him what their lives will look like without her. He cannot. He will not. Facing her imminent death is not the page he is on. He is traumatised. In shock. Living in a nightmare he still cannot believe is true. He will not discuss their future.

He won't talk about death and dying or help her put preparations in place. It's not because he doesn't love her. It's not because he doesn't want to please her or support her, it's because he's in a different place. He's processing her illness and the devastating far-reaching impact at a different pace. She needs him to hurry up. The more she pushes the more he retreats. The more he retreats the less loved and supported she feels.

— Frank & Imogen's Experience

Frank and Imogen have been together for 10 years. They have two sons and their youngest, Alfie, has died. He was three years old. Frank wants to spend as much time as possible with Alfie before the funeral but Imogen finds it too traumatic. Frank wants to sit and hold his son and read him stories, Imogen feels she's said her goodbye. Imogen feels pressured into having time with Alfie because Frank encourages her to come along and be in the same room, even if she's not seeing him or holding him. On each of their visits I take Imogen into another room and we sit and she talks about why she finds it so difficult to be with her dead son. She talks of feeling she's letting everyone down by not doing what Frank is doing but she says she's reached a point where she cannot emotionally do it. On his last visit, Frank arrives alone. He has some time with his son and then we talk. He feels it's his job to encourage Imogen to be with Alfie, to have as much time as possible with him before the cremation. He thinks she'll regret it if she doesn't. I encourage them both to acknowledge and accept that they had a different relationship with their son in life and they'll continue to have a different relationship with him in death. Frank says that if Alfie fell over it was always him who he screamed for but that his mum was the only person that Alfie would allow to tuck him up at night. He always wanted Imogen to be the last person he saw before the lights went out. Once they began to recognise the differences in their roles and in their own individual relationship with their son, their need to do different things didn't feel so troubling. We talked about giving each other space to honour their individual relationship with Alfie and how needing and wanting things was perfectly normal and right.

HOW CAN WE BRIDGE THE DIVIDE?

If someone doesn't want to talk it's almost impossible to make them. If someone doesn't want to acknowledge the end of their life or make plans for it, there's nothing you can do to make them. Perhaps you shouldn't – maybe it is their way of coping with the unimaginable.

However, what you can do is gently remind someone that illness is bigger than just them. That the consequences of their illness extend far beyond them. What you can do is explain how something is feeling for you. You can acknowledge one another's thoughts and feelings and where each other is at without being there too. It's OK to be on a different page. It's OK to have different needs. It's OK to disagree but it's also essential to respect where each other is at. There's no right or wrong place to be. There's no should or must.

TEN THINGS TO TRY TO HELP BRING YOU TOGETHER

1. Listen without judgement.
2. Allow someone else to be in a different place.
3. Talk about where you are both at and let the other one know that it's OK to not be in the same place.
4. Agree to disagree.
5. Find a point in the middle perhaps, a way of working towards each other as opposed to further away.
6. Find someone (a therapist) to talk to, perhaps together or apart.
7. With time being limited it's important to find a resolution or to accept the other's stance.
8. Find a compromise.
9. Find a group of other people in a similar situation. Carer groups can be hugely helpful.
10. Remember your relationship, your family, your love, is bigger than the illness that's driving you apart.

HO'OPONOPONO

Ho'oponopono is a practice of forgiveness and reconciliation from Hawaii. Some describe it as a prayer but in my work I use it as a tool for self-care and self-love. The idea is that you repeat the four lines over and over: 'I'm sorry. Please forgive me. Thank you. I love you.'

Many people I work with find it hard to love their breaking bodies and this 'mantra' can help with reconciliation with their own physical and emotional selves and also with the people they love. When we cannot be on the same page, when our needs are opposing those of the people around us, it's not something we can necessarily fix or change but we can acknowledge and allow it. Ho'oponopono can help us do this whether we are saying it to ourselves or to those around us.

1. **I'm sorry**
   'I'm sorry but I need to grieve/love/act differently.'

2. **Please forgive me**
   'Please forgive my need to do, feel and see things differently.'

3. **Thank you**
   'Thank you for accepting, acknowledging and allowing our differences.'

4. **I love you**
   'I love you regardless.'

There are no solutions, no magic that can change the situation, no cure; there's no fix to dying, death and grief. Nothing can change what has happened and alter what is happening. Nothing should alter what we need and how we need to do things to honour ourselves and our relationships. All we can do is acknowledge and allow.

Think of illness and grief, in all their many guises, as a book: we all read at different speeds, we will sympathise and empathise with differing characters and situations, and our interpretations of events and storylines won't be the same. We'll envisage what the characters on the page look and sound like in a completely opposing way and we'll be frustrated and disappointed and excited and thrilled at dissimilar points throughout the novel.

Every aspect of our 'self' is unique and that's part of what makes us humans so fascinating and wonderful. We embrace our differences and enjoy the differential of being 'one-off' in everyday situations and that's what we need to try to do when life is incredibly challenging.

I am on a different page to you, and that's OK.

FIVE THINGS I WISH I'D KNOWN
WHEN MY MUM DIED

by Nicky Duffell

Nicky's mum Mary died in April 2007. She had been diagnosed with gallbladder cancer just seven months earlier.

1.

I wish we'd talked about it. We couldn't of course, we were all in denial (deep denial). But I wish that I'd said to my mum, 'I'm scared,' and I wish that she had said, 'I'm scared too.'

2.

I wish someone had told me that it's OK to grieve, In all its messiness, in its darkness. That it's OK to go there, it's OK to stay there for a while, too. It's OK to grieve, to cry, to scream. Every single messy part of it is OK.

3.

I wish I'd known that I didn't have to go on antidepressants to grieve. That grief can feel so dark that there are days when you don't know how you're going to survive, you don't know how to function and you definitely can't see clearly. But I didn't need antidepressants – I needed to feel every single part of it.

4.

I wish I'd fought harder to get my mum into proper care. My sister and I cared for her at her home, taking it in turns, we weren't qualified or emotionally equipped to do this. I wish I'd fought harder to get her the professional care she needed, and just as importantly, that we needed too.

5.

I wish I really understood that grief stays with you. I've been in denial about that for a very long time! That it lives and breathes within you. It can come in from nowhere, even 12 years later, if you let it. And you must let it. Grief can feel like it will break you, you can feel broken, but letting it live and breathe, letting it be part of you means you can live with it, you can become friends with it, rather than pushing it away and denying the energy that it needs. It's not easy, but I'm learning to do just this.

Assisted dying

[A]

There's no doubt at all that assisted dying is a contentious subject and one that we have deliberately chosen not to focus on in the book. However, very recently, the Royal College of Physicians voted to 'hold a position of neutrality' on assisted dying. It means that they will not oppose changing the law regarding it. This turn-around by such a respected medical professional body representing more than 35,000 doctors will undoubtedly have an impact, and we felt it was important to acknowledge it.

Assisted dying is, in simple terms, the act of helping someone to die. The help comes from a doctor and the person being helped to die is someone with an incurable or degenerative disease. When someone is living with a life-limiting diagnosis and their life has or will become unbearable as a direct result of their illness, in countries such as Belgium, Switzerland, Canada, the Netherlands, Luxembourg, Colombia and in some American States, they can choose when to end their lives. There are stringent processes a person needs to go through in order to prove that they are fully able to make the decision, including being considered to be sound of mind and repeatedly and clearly stating their desire to end their life to the relevant professionals. In many countries, including the UK, helping someone to die in this way is considered to be a crime.

Doctors and those working in the palliative care field are almost always opposed to the idea of assisted dying, perhaps because their entire role centres around making people as comfortable as possible during their illness and at the end. They also fully understand what good end-of-life care can provide. Palliative care professionals believe that if people understood what can be achieved with their particular branch of medicine, and the suffering that can be alleviated by it, then they would choose not to expedite their expiry date. Conversely, people who feel very strongly that assisted dying should be lawful believe it's a basic human right to end their life when they decide the time is right for them. They maintain that their life, and the course it runs, should be their own business with no one at liberty to tell them what is acceptable and what isn't. After all, what constitutes a good quality of life for one person is not the same for another.

Can we ever know what we would find tolerable and what comprises a good enough quality of life for ourselves until we are in that position? Can we judge or should we ever diminish another person's wishes to end their own suffering when it becomes too much to bear? Who are we to decide the course of someone's life (and indeed their death) for them? It's a debate that will most certainly rage long after the end of my life.

A matter of life and death

[A]

Much of the debate over end-of-life care, I believe, comes down to two questions:

1. Is a good end of life one where the medical team did everything to save a life?
2. Is the above statement still true if there is little or no chance of a happy outcome?

Culturally, we have always seen a good end of life as one we have 'fought' against. It is long overdue for us to consider otherwise. Many treatments are aggressive and futile, robbing someone of the last remaining specks of a good life.

Perhaps a good end of life is an accepted one? One where the person who is dying is in control, can be at home or the place of their choosing, can have their pain and symptoms managed. End-of-life care must be entirely individualised and person-centred; only then can we begin to offer the excellent end-of-life care that everyone deserves.

— June's Experience

June lived an incredibly full life: alone and happy. She went dancing and played snooker. She cooked everything from scratch every day. Her breathlessness became untenable and she finally went to the doctor. She had cancer and after much discussion with the medical team and her family she decided to refuse active treatment and choose a palliative care pathway. She accepted her life-limiting prognosis with the wisdom of one who knew herself well and contemplated mortality more often than many. She died in a hospice, surrounded by her family. Hers was a peaceful death. Peaceful and on her own terms.

I believe that if we discussed end-of-life issues regularly, we wouldn't find them so tricky to broach. Issues pertaining to death and dying should be taught in schools as part of the PSHE syllabus from primary and onwards. During Year 13 tutor time, when we teach young adults how to fill in job application forms, we should also be filling in Advance Directives with them.

We all have to take responsibility for communication and the decisions we make. It's extraordinarily difficult when we're unwell and vulnerable to hear these truths. If we've never considered end of life until our own life's end, it's no wonder we find it so hard. It's too much to have that conversation for the first time when we are facing death. It's so much easier to talk about it while we're living a healthy life. We need to break down the ingrained cultural barriers that prevent us from talking about death and dying.

QUANTITY OR QUALITY?

Why do we value quantity over quality of time? Why do we cling so dearly to the notion that a life well lived is the one that lasts the longest? Sometimes doing nothing is the most courageous path. Sometimes accepting there's nothing left that can be done is the bravest choice. Some may describe such a decision as 'giving up'. Pursuing treatment until the very end, on the other hand, is lauded as 'being a fighter'.

Do the words 'battle' and 'fight' compound medical teams' feelings of failure when an unavoidable and imminent death is in front of them? Changing our language may help us to change the way we think. Illness and death are a part of life. Death is not a failure: not ours, and not our doctors'.

Perhaps redesigning our expectations and language at end of life could begin with Paul Kalanithi's beautiful words:

> 'The physician's duty is not to stave off death or return patients to their old lives,
> but to take into our arms a patient and family whose lives have disintegrated and work
> until they can stand back up and face, and make sense of, their own existence.'
> **PAUL KALANITHI**, AUTHOR

If medics did this, I believe death and dying could be a richer and better experience for everyone involved.

IS THE NOTION OF A 'GOOD DEATH' AN OXYMORON?

I answer this question with another question: Is a 'good death' what we want to be aiming for? I truly believe that we ought to be striving for a good life. All the way up until the very end.

I don't really believe in the idea of a 'good death'. Describing death as 'good' makes me feel like I'm doing a disservice to life, to loss and to grief. My job as an end-of-life doula is about helping people to live a good life and that 'living' includes dying. The dying, we all hope, will be as gentle and as painless as possible but it's the living of a good life right up until your last breath, that's what it's all about.

I'm not sure a 'good' death is possible but a 'good' life definitely is. Perhaps we've come to think of a good death as a quiet death, an acknowledged death, a pain-free-as-possible death, or a death with gentle final days or moments. But I would argue that these are not *good* deaths. They could be described as death as it 'should' be, perhaps – as we would want it to be and certainly the kind of death we should strive for.

But death equates to loss – a physical and emotional loss. Its impact is felt far beyond the moment itself, and secondary loss can be felt just as acutely and indefinitely (*see* the chapter on grief for a full explanation of 'secondary loss'). Do not diminish the magnitude of someone's dying or its impact by describing it as good. Describe their life as good, as well-lived, and them as well-loved. Describe their death as gentle (if indeed it was), but not as good:

She lived a good life right up until the end. She died a gentle death.

FIVE THINGS I'VE LEARNED FROM NURSING THE DYING

By Kimberley St John

Kimberley was a palliative care specialist nurse at Guy's and St Thomas' NHS Foundation Trust in London, and was the trust's lead for transforming end-of-life care. Kim was a trailblazer and wrote this Five Things for us in April 2019. She died suddenly and unexpectedly on 12 July 2020 at the age of 32.

1.
We take our health for granted. I am so grateful to be able to run up the stairs.

2.
Music, touch, scents and tastes are often the most effective way of communicating with people who are very close to death. The little things matter.

3.
Most people don't have fancy bucket lists. For many it's being at home or having fish and chips.

4.
It's important to think about what you would or wouldn't want at the end of your life. I know that I wouldn't want intensive treatment if it wouldn't help me. I have written it down and told my family in case they have to make decisions for me.

5.
Don't delay anything that is important to you. I have known people to put off marriage, a special trip, making up with a relative. None of us know how much time we have. Use it wisely.

FIVE THINGS I'VE LEARNED SINCE THE SUDDEN DEATH OF MY WIFE, KIMBERLEY ST JOHN

By Sam Lock

'Kim and I married in October 2019. Our wedding was loud, raucous and utterly full of love. It was very befitting of the relationship that had led us to that point. To have been part of her life was an adventure – she filled her years with travel, rich experiences and countless friends. She loved genuinely and fiercely, and she loved many. She was a force of nature; her passion and effervescence inspired hope and facilitated change, even in the face of the seemingly immovable. Her brightness could fill a room, yet her intimate tenderness could make you feel like the only other person in existence. Her kindness and empathy were immeasurable. Her years, though short, were extraordinary, and I'm privileged to have been a part of them.'

1.
Love openly and leave nothing unsaid. Tell people your feelings sincerely and often. I'm comforted by the fact that Kim knew how much I loved her and I know how much she loved me.

2.
Take stock of what's around you. Appreciate what you already have. Kim saw value in things others might take for granted – even just the ability to walk up the stairs. She called it her 'morbid gratitude'.

3.
Kim's death is the tragedy – not the grief. Grief is my release; I've embraced it. Crying is a powerful tool.

4.
Being open about my grief has implicitly given others permission to be open too. It has allowed for some beautiful conversations.

5.
Death is an inevitability, but grief is not. Rather, grief is a debt that we accrue when we are fortunate enough to love. And the more we love, the more we owe to grief. The magnitude of my grief is a testament to how much I love Kim. I remind myself of this in my darkest moments.

FIVE THINGS I LEARNED WHEN MY MOTHER DIED FROM CANCER

by Ellie Reid

Ellie is an artist who lives and works in London. Having experienced the death of several family members in relatively short succession, death, grief and loss are themes that have been explored in her sculptural and paper works.

1.

Find some music you can scream, howl and rage to. I didn't want to take those feelings into the space I shared with my mum or express them in front of my young child, so when I was alone (often driving) I would listen to Florence and the Machine and LET IT ALL OUT.

2.

Know that ultimately all the decisions to be made are those of the person who is ill or dying. You may have strong ideas but you can never fully know what they are going through. Respect this.

3.

Ask the doctors, nurses or carers what the death might be like. My horror was that mum would die suddenly and I wouldn't be there or that it would be torturous in some way (fortunately it was neither). There are common signs that the medical profession can discuss with you before death happens.

4.

You can make a 'death plan' much like a 'birth plan'. You can think about what music the person might like, people who might be in the room and the stories you might want to share before that person dies. Ideally the atmosphere is calm. Steadying yogi breathing was invaluable to me to get me through being in the room as my mum died.

5.

When someone dies after a long illness, you may wonder if the memories of them before the illness will ever become more present. They will. It takes time but the memories of the illness fade and their living, vital self comes back to you.

The undeniable beauty in the impermanence of life

[A]

Understanding what 'normal dying' looks like may well lessen our fears about how we're likely to die, but this grasp of it won't ever change the fact that our dying means our end. The end of our life. It means leaving the people we love, it means missing out on all the things we hold dear. Death is a full stop. It's permanent and there's no coming back from it.

Nevertheless, there is an undeniable beauty in the impermanence of life and its inherent fragility. If we embrace our mortality, as all living beings must, we can begin to end our lives on our terms, with grace and dignity.

'Death Makes a Crown of Love'

Death makes a crown of love,
A mantle to take across the threshold
As a sign of accomplished living:
You are loved,
You have loved,
You have lived.

GREG GILBERT, FROM HIS WONDERFUL BOOK OF POETRY,
LOVE MAKES A MESS OF DYING

Funerals

[L]

'I want to live my life so well that even the undertaker is sorry to see me go.'
PAMELA FAHEY, AS INSPIRED BY MARK TWAIN, JUNE 2018

Wherever you are in the world, this section has been written to help you to have a more empowered approach to funerals. It's not a step-by-step guide to the practicalities (that will change depending on your location); instead, it has been written so you can learn about why we have funerals and discover the things the people we've worked with have found to be important when someone has died.

In this chapter, we'll share stories of the many funerals we've helped to facilitate. If you ever need to arrange a funeral, hopefully you'll be inspired to create one that works for you and honours your needs. If you're bereaved, or about to be, this might be difficult reading, but I hope you'll find it worthwhile. Take whatever you need, and leave the rest. In this section, we'll learn:

1.   Why funerals matter so much.
2.   How seeing the person who has died can be a helpful
     and healing experience.
3.   How you can arrange a really good funeral.
4.   How to plan your own funeral.
5.   Everything you ever wanted to ask a funeral director.

Why I became a funeral director

[L]

'We've had some bad news love,' my dad told me. 'Grandad's been to the hospital and there's nothing they can do for him.'

I was 26 and I'd never dealt with the death of someone close to me. I'd never even been to a funeral. My only experience of death had been when my family's pets had died. One day, our beloved border collie cross, Sally, was whisked off to the vets, never to return. Aged 10, I'd stared into her corner of the kitchen, now completely empty. Where was she? Where had she gone? What had happened to her?

Not attending a funeral due to a hangover was as close to attending a funeral as I had ever come. My friend's dad, who shared school lift duties with my mum, died from a heart attack while he was on holiday in Cyprus. His funeral was the day after my 18th birthday party. So, as my friends and I slept off hangovers on my bedroom floor, my parents dressed in the black suits they only ever wore to funerals and headed to the local church. I wanted to go, to say goodbye to the man who had picked me up from school for years, but I didn't feel as though my sadness and grief were valid.

My grandad had spent his life joking about his death, and now it was happening. Neville Briggs, or Nev as he was known, was best described as a self-made man with a wicked sense of humour, who liked a pint and enjoyed a round of golf.

One day, Grandad had taken himself to the local funeral home and planned his own funeral. He'd paid for it all in advance. He didn't want any fuss; no fancy cars for the family, no extravagant flowers spelling out 'Grandad' and no top-of-the-range coffin. He wanted something simple, and to the point. He wanted to die as he had lived.

The anticipation of his death was petrifying. I felt the impact on my family's fragile dynamic would never recover. We weren't ones for showing emotions. How would we cope? What would we do at the funeral? Would there be public displays of emotion? Would people cry? Would we have to cry? It was all a bit much.

Six months later, on a sunny morning in July, my grandad died at home in his bedroom. My grandma had been keeping vigil at his bedside, but had gone into the kitchen to make herself a cup of tea. Determined not to leave him alone, she asked my sister to sit with him. As my sister stepped into the room, she knew something was different.

'You're not to leave him alone,' my distraught grandma told my sister, as she held vigil at his bedside, holding his hand as she waited for the funeral directors to arrive.

'Why? He doesn't care, he's dead,' my sister laughed, through her tears.

A few hours later, the funeral directors loaded my grandad into the private ambulance and whisked him three minutes away to their premises – a red-brick building that was attached to a builder's yard, opposite the local fish and chip shop that did the best cod and chips in town.

As a local builder, my grandad had bought his materials from the builder's yard, which also had a business in funerals. It's common for funeral directors in the UK to have roots in carpentry or haulage. As the people who were originally asked to make coffins or transport someone who had died, expanding their business into funerals was a natural progression.

My grandad had said he didn't want a religious service so the funeral director had recommended the services of a lady called Ruth, who worked as a civil celebrant. I wondered what a civil celebrant could possibly be, imagining a woman who wore sensible shoes and ankle-length skirts and put together bland funerals on behalf of the local council.

According to my sister, Ruth had visited my grandma's house and spoken to her at length about my grandad. I was deeply suspicious. I had little confidence in anything the funeral directors had suggested. 'I don't want a stranger talking about Grandad,' I told my mum.

I knew I was the only member of my family who would be prepared to speak at the funeral, so I wrote about the grandad I knew – a man full of dark humour who reminded me, in the most charming way, of Del from *Only Fools and Horses*. He was a man of common sense and no nonsense.

The day before the funeral, my mum had written on the cards for the floral tributes with the wrong pen, smudging black ink everywhere. So she sent me on a mission to see the funeral director to ask for new cards. I stepped inside, ignoring the long queue outside the fish and chip shop.

I was terrified that I'd walk straight into the Chapel of Rest and be confronted with my grandad's cancer stricken body in a foreboding coffin. But instead, I found a reception area with patterned carpets, dark red-brick walls and mahogany furniture. A man stood up to greet me as I explained that I needed another card for the flowers.

'We might have to charge you extra for that,' he winked. I half smiled, avoiding looking any further into the office. He opened the drawer of the desk and handed over a small card with lilies and scripted writing that said, 'In Loving Memory.'

The day of the funeral arrived. I decided to wear a black silk draped dress, unsure of what else I owned that would be considered appropriate. 'Wear whatever you want,' I could hear the voice of my grandad in my head. 'Don't mourn for me.'

The hearse and a black limousine arrived at the bottom of the drive, exactly on time. My grandad had said no to funeral limousines when he pre-planned his funeral, but my parents had paid extra to get us to the crematorium in nearby Chesterfield in traditional funereal style.

Throughout the journey, my grandma sobbed, and my dad gave her tissues. I tried to hold back the tears, and wondered whether it was disrespectful to look at my phone. Was I allowed to talk? Should I make pleasant small talk? Were tears allowed? Would the funeral directors tell me off for not showing my respects in the appropriate way?

I'd never been to a crematorium before and couldn't quite work out what was going on – it seemed to be an amalgamation of a hospital, a modern church and a 1950s grammar school with a chimney sticking out of the top.

I saw the celebrant, standing outside the chapel doors. She introduced herself and said she had a copy of my tribute in case I was too emotional to deliver it. She was dressed in navy blue, not black. I wondered whether this was a uniform issued by the council, designed to be serious but not too gloomy.

The funeral director beckoned my dad and uncle to the hearse, and together with the professional pall-bearers, they carried him in to the chapel as Frank Sinatra sang 'My Way'.

Walking into the crematorium, I felt the tears beginning to stream down my cheeks so I dug my nails into my fingers. I didn't want to cry in front of all these people, especially as I was wearing black eyeliner.

Ruth did the service, giving a surprisingly well-put-together and accurate portrayal of my grandad's life and his character. I wondered whether the council had trained her in eulogy writing. We sang 'All things bright and beautiful' – the most popular funeral hymn since well, forever.

Before I knew it, it was my turn to speak. There was a lump in my throat, and my already high-pitched voice was just getting higher and higher. The tears began as I looked at my family on the front row. Ruth stepped behind me, ready to take over. That was all it took for me to pull it together. I didn't want a lady from the council reading my tribute to my grandad. So I continued.

I returned to my seat, legs still shaking and hands clammy. Ruth said something about the nature of life and death and how we mustn't cry with sadness but should smile with joy instead. I stared at the red-brick platform where the coffin was lying, surrounded by velvet curtains. It was strange thinking my grandad was there in a wooden box, an essential part of this strange spectacle, yet completely absent.

'The time has now come for us to say a final goodbye to Neville Briggs,' Ruth said. What did this mean? I wondered whether my family would be subjected to having to go up to the coffin. Would it be opened? Would I see Grandad's lifeless body for the final time? What would he be wearing? Would we stand witness as the coffin travelled into the flames?

Nothing happened. The curtains closed around the coffin and the service was over. We were directed to stand in a corridor, while the mourners filed out and shook our hands to a chorus of 'lovely service' as I choked back more tears, and frantically dug my nails into my fingers. My mum gave me tissues as I held back the tears until I spluttered them everywhere in one big undignified splurge that sounded like a loud snort. Unchecked emotion didn't seem OK at an event like this, but emotions swallowed down and spat back out were even worse.

We were directed back to the funeral limousines and taken to the local pub. We entered to see a table of beige – sausage rolls, quiche, sandwiches and cake. There seemed to be a free bar and lots of people standing around, whom I didn't know.

I was hit with a pain I didn't recognise. I'd been through distress before – heartbreak, alcoholism, suicidal depression, unrequited love – but in the form of sharp stabs of agonising pain. Grief was a pain that went deep but also felt so different – a mixture of gratitude, anger, sadness, regret and guilt. I stuffed the feelings down with plates of beige food and shook hands with people whose names I remembered from childhood. The sausage rolls ran out, the free drinks dried up and everyone went home.

I've told this story a hundred times, in a hundred different ways. I've talked about the dusty men carrying the coffin who looked like they belonged inside it, the strange crematorium, the mechanical whirring of the curtains as they closed around the coffin, and standing at the flower terrace to a chorus of 'lovely service' from people I didn't know.

At the time, I had no idea that there was any other way. I had no idea funeral directors aren't all the same. I had no idea that celebrants don't normally work for the council. I had no idea that the coffin doesn't go straight through the crematorium doors and into the flames. I had no idea that the grief I was stuffing down with sausage rolls could be dealt with in a totally different way. I assumed we had to do as we were told, stick to the rigid behaviour that was expected of us, and that would be that.

My grandad's funeral felt fitting for him. It was exactly the funeral he would have wanted and that the people who attended would have understood and recognised – a summary of his life followed by drinks at his favourite pub. He'd have embraced and enjoyed every single moment of it.

But with my grandad's funeral as my inspiration, I found myself questioning everything. What actually is a funeral? Why do we have them? What purpose do they serve? Do they serve their purpose? Do we even need them? Should we just dismiss funerals forever?

The questions just kept coming. Why do we hand over the people we love the most to funeral directors on our high streets? Why are funeral directors even on our high streets? Why do funerals cost so much? Is death just a retail opportunity? What do funeral directors actually do? If we weren't dealing with something so uncertain, so upsetting, so overwhelming, would Doom, Gloom & Son still exist? Why don't people talk about death? If people actually talked about death before it happened, would funerals be different? Would the funeral industry actually survive?

It seemed to me that funerals were incredibly important; I could feel that so deeply. Without knowing why, I knew that the way we handle death says everything about how we handle life and how we behave as a society.

It didn't take long for me to decide to leave my career. I was working for an entrepreneur in London, creating innovative campaigns that were changing how people interacted with businesses and brands. It was an intense job and very exciting. We were often still in the office at 4 a.m. eating pizzas and working on big ideas for big clients.

One day, we were sitting in the boardroom of a huge fashion brand with the executive team, discussing ideas for a campaign to sell more handbags over the Christmas period. As we looked at samples of handbags, an ambulance came slowly down the street outside with its sirens blaring.

'I can't believe this,' the CEO said. 'That noise is so inconvenient. Can someone tell it to stop? Handbags don't sell themselves you know.'

Faced with the prospect that life would eventually end, I wanted to live a life of purpose and meaning. I wasn't prepared to spend another moment working for something I didn't believe in. I couldn't ignore the important work the ambulance crew were doing, while we devised creative ways to sell expensive handbags that no one really needed.

BECOMING A FUNERAL CELEBRANT

So I left my job, with no idea how I'd be able to pay the rent. I spent that summer exploring the funeral industry, reading everything I could and wondering how I could make a positive difference.

With the permission of the superintendent, Natasha Bradshaw, I spent some time watching funerals from the gallery above the chapel at Mortlake Crematorium in London, sometimes up to 10 every day. I was a fly on the wall, catching glimpses of other people's lives, how they lived and, ultimately, how they ended.

I watched the funeral directors, who have the most precise sense of timing I've ever experienced. They introduced routine, ritual and structure into a world of the unknown. Some of them seemed to thrive on telling grieving people where to go, where to stand, what to do and how to be, others were chaotic and unsure. Most walked in front of the shiny hearses and told mourners where to go, but didn't seem to understand why they were doing what they were doing.

I saw many types of religious service, from the priests who cared, their compassion shining through, to those who treated funerals as business as usual, slamming the service book closed before the mourners had even said the final 'Amen'.

I came across funeral celebrants – some with crystal clear voices who led services that brought the person in the coffin in front of me to life, and others, dressed in uptight grey suits, who delivered the service in a voice greyer than the suit they were wearing, more befitting an accountant. I heard the same scripted template from some celebrants over and over again.

I witnessed the funeral of a man in his 40s who died unexpectedly in a car crash. His theatrical father took the service with such candour, vigour, grace and style that I couldn't help but wonder why other families didn't fire the grey-suited celebrants and take the same approach.

I watched as a mother and her three daughters sat in the chapel while 'Unchained Melody' played on repeat. Thirty minutes later, the curtains closed around the wicker coffin as the sound of their sobbing filled the chapel.

It's often said that at times like this there are no words. Yet during my summer of funerals, I heard many. From the standard poetry that's read at almost every funeral, telling everyone not to cry but to smile, to the same religious readings read out over and over again. 'God's house has many rooms,' became the soundtrack to my summer.

'So what is a funeral?' I kept asking myself. I hastily scribbled notes from the gallery of the crematorium as the funerals went on below: 'A space for grief, contained. Rituals that bring order to a chaotic series of events. Structure where there is no structure. A movement towards acknowledgement and acceptance. The ultimate zoom-out on life.'

Extraordinary lives, ordinary lives. Those who died as they lived, uneventfully, and those who lived as they died, eventfully. They all came to an end in the art deco chapel at Mortlake Crematorium. Each one a 40-minute closing of a life, however much or little lived.

What I witnessed that summer was not so much a conveyor belt of funerals, but the conveyor belt of life. I was as inspired as I was appalled. I was 28 years old and I knew this was my calling. I wanted to do something with my life; I didn't want something to do. This was it.

I decided to become a celebrant, having realised that they were neither trained nor employed by the council. I soon learned what celebrants are supposed to do: work with the family and friends of the person who has died to create a ceremony that helps them to say goodbye, in a way that works for them. Celebrants are neither religious nor non-religious; in fact, their own religious or spiritual beliefs should have nothing to do with the service they offer. A good celebrant will put together a personalised funeral ceremony that reflects the beliefs of the person who has died, and the people who survive them.

Celebrants come from a range of backgrounds, usually choosing celebrancy as a second career. Surprisingly, celebrants don't need to have any formal training, though most choose to train with one of the many celebrant organisations in the UK. The courses should teach their students how to really listen to bereaved people, and how to put together a ceremony that honours their needs. Unfortunately, most of the training courses simply teach their students how to adapt a few words on a templated script to make the ceremony seem as though it's personalised.

I hoped I'd be going to a funeral school set in a grand stately home where we'd learn everything we could ever need to know and understand about funeral ceremonies. Disappointingly, it turned out that my celebrant training would take place in a conference centre, run by a group of women who were akin to stern headteachers. We were taught how to send an email, learned a way of understanding grief that was disproved decades ago, and were told to write ceremonies from templates, which could be slightly personalised if required. My main takeaway from the course was that I'd be baking a lot of lemon drizzle cakes for funeral directors in an attempt to persuade them to book my services for their clients. The skills I actually needed – how to talk to grieving people and deliver ceremonies – seemed to be surplus to requirements.

By October 2015, I was a fully trained celebrant with a certificate of qualification showing that I was a pro at sending emails and an expert in out-of-date grief models. Armed with a stack of templated ceremonies in a folder, I set out to impress the funeral directors of London with my lemon drizzle cake-baking skills. In under two years, I somehow managed to work with almost every funeral director in London – the good, the bad, the really bad and the downright horrifying.

The current system makes funeral directors the gatekeepers to all things funeral related. The public approach the funeral director first, who then makes a recommendation as to who should officiate at the service. I found the majority of funeral directors hopelessly underqualified for the privileged role in which they found themselves. Most didn't seem to care about the ceremony, as long as it went as smoothly as possible and didn't take up too much time, preferably 20 minutes. Their interest seemed to be in the more solid and less emotional aspects of funerals – top hats, expensive coffins and shiny cars.

My real training took place outside the classroom. I was mentored by a celebrant, former opera singer, Emma Curtis. She had taken a great deal of time to learn how to become a different kind of celebrant, developing the skills required to do really profound work. She became a secular minister, using her experience as a bereavement and grief counsellor to create ceremonies that truly supported the people who appointed her.

After funerals, we'd drink coffee or eat pizza and talk about how we approached our work. Emma taught me how to put together beautiful ceremonies, to hold space for grieving people and to have firm and clear boundaries, both professionally and personally. She now teaches advanced bespoke celebrancy, ensuring celebrants have the skills they need to put together meaningful ceremonies, based on a solid understanding of grief.

It's difficult to make a career out of celebrancy; the profession is flooded with people who completed the same inadequate training as me. If done well, the work is woefully underpaid and inconsistent; if you are working from generic templates at a rate of as-many-funerals-as-you-can-cram-into-your-diary per week, it's impossible to deliver the high standard required to honour the end of someone's life properly. Hence the standardised templates with the '<insert name here>' mentality.

So many times, I found myself in a family's front room discussing the funeral ceremony, and wondering why the funeral director had booked a 20-minute service at the local crematorium for a family who clearly needed considerable time and space to say goodbye. But when I arrived as the appointed celebrant, it was too late. I found myself telling countless families that we wouldn't be able to let all 12 grandchildren tell stories from their magical childhood, and we'd have to have just three pieces of music, rather than the six they wanted. I felt I was doing them, and their grief, a huge disservice.

BECOMING A FUNERAL DIRECTOR

Out of frustration, I decided to become a funeral director in order to begin addressing some of the problems I was experiencing. I decided the best way to learn was through experience, so my training involved working alongside modern, alternative and conventional funeral directors. I went to work full-time for a funeral director in London, who taught me everything I needed to know. Eventually I decided to take some more formal training in the form of a diploma, provided by one of the major trade associations.

I collected people who had died from their homes at three in the morning. I learned how to take care of someone after they'd died, washing and dressing them if required. I learned about embalming and watched the embalmers at work. I liaised with coroners' officers after a death required investigation. I learned that hospital mortuaries are usually in the basement, badly signposted and almost impossible to find. I learned that most nursing homes insist that funeral directors collect someone who has died straight away, even in the middle of the night. I learned about the different paperwork required when someone is to be buried or cremated. I learned how to prepare a coffin and put someone inside it. I learned how to tell a widow that nature had rapidly taken its course since her husband died, that his body had changed a lot, and that I wanted her to be aware of the reality before she came to spend any time with him. She put the phone down on me, and I had to understand that her devastation was due to the news I was delivering, rather than being personal.

At the time of writing, the UK funeral industry is totally unregulated. Anyone can become a funeral director, without any qualifications, training or licence. However, following reports of variable standards, extortionate funeral costs and the exploitation of bereaved people by some funeral directors, the Competitions and Markets Authority decided to fully investigate the funeral industry in early 2019. The Scottish Government have already decided to introduce a statutory code of practice for funeral directors which will shortly come into force. Regulation and licensing could be introduced to the rest of the UK in the near future. This is both a good and bad thing, depending on who is given control of the regulation.

Throughout this book, I refer to the funeral industry, rather than the funeral profession. Some of my funeral colleagues may find this distasteful, but I consider it to be an accurate portrayal of what's happening in the UK. The industry is dominated by several big businesses, including a corporate company who is listed on the stock market and reports to shareholders. Funerals are not a feel-good service managed by the community for the good of the community; they are big business and make some people very wealthy indeed.

As a trainee funeral director, I witnessed some beautiful things, moments of sensitivity and true compassion, but I also witnessed behaviour that I'd describe as unpoetic if I were being polite, and exploitative and disrespectful if I were being blunt.

I worked from early in the morning until late at night, and was always on call. After funerals, I'd dash back to the office to begin the next task. We were often managing 25 funerals at the same time and didn't have enough staff. I went from one emotionally charged funeral straight to a meeting with a family with no time in between, usually having missed lunch. If we'd been called out the night before, I might have been awake since 4 a.m. My colleagues had no self-care or support strategies in place. It wasn't the sort of environment where talking about how you felt was encouraged. I noticed that my colleagues were not coping. Red Bull and sausage rolls were consumed in the early hours of the morning while the hearses were washed. I was always finding half-eaten Mars bars in the staff areas. The employees smoked outside in between funerals, coming back to the office smelling of smoke. The conversation was crass and the jokes were offensive. Racism, sexism and ageism were commonplace. The staff drank a lot of alcohol outside of work, and there were rumours of problematic use of other substances, too.

Eventually I burned out. I worked through headaches, illness and heartbreak. There just wasn't time to have a day off to rest. Then one day, I lost my voice completely. I still needed to answer the on-call phone because there was nobody else to do it. My voice took 10 days to return, by which point I realised that I needed to find a way of working which didn't neglect my own well-being in order to be able to offer the kind of service I wanted to clients.

THE BEGINNING OF POETIC ENDINGS

Disillusioned by most of the funeral industry, in the summer of 2017 I launched my own funeral service. I felt that everyone deserved to be acknowledged with relevance, meaning, sensitivity and style. I called it Poetic Endings. There's a beauty in poetry that's portrayed no matter what the subject matter. I promised myself that Poetic Endings would give everyone the time and space to find out what would work for them.

Every moment of arranging the funeral is important: the first call you make, the questions asked, the way the person who has died is treated, and the ceremony itself. Sitting with a family over many cups of tea at the kitchen table and asking them questions about the person who has died and inviting them to share their memories with each other, is often the most valuable part of the process. Allowing a family to sit with their dad as a simple candle burns and his favourite music quietly plays can start the process of beginning to understand that he has died. Our experiences leading up to the funeral can be more important than the funeral ceremony itself.

No two funerals are ever the same. Sometimes we'll meet a client in advance, perhaps because they're coming to the end of their life and would like to make a decision about who will take care of them and what will happen. Sometimes we'll receive a call in the middle of the night to say someone has died and asking us to collect them. Sometimes we'll be appointed several days after someone has died. Sometimes the coroner is involved and there's a long delay. Sometimes we'll take over from another funeral director, who already has the person in their care but isn't providing the service the client wants. Sometimes a person has died abroad and needs to be brought back to the UK.

Funeral directors often speak in 'trade language' or euphemisms. We are different: you'll never hear us calling the person who has died 'the deceased', saying people are 'at rest' or calling embalming 'hygienic treatment'. We don't call the people in our care 'bodies'. We use their names and treat them as individual people. We use the words 'death' and 'died', although always sensitively and gently. We avoid using funeral industry terminology and explain what happens as clearly and transparently as we can, even if what we're explaining is the process of decomposition. I've spent enough time behind the scenes to realise that the public don't really need to be sheltered from death in the way that some funeral directors favour, although sometimes the reality of what's happening may need to be explained to them in a gentle and sensitive way.

So many people have told me that they've had negative experiences of the people who have died being collected from home, a process most funeral directors call 'a removal'. They will talk about the arrival of the funeral directors as 'men in black' who smell of stale cigarettes and fail to introduce themselves. They often don't explain what's happening or ask if anyone would like to be involved in moving the person who has died. A friend talked of how the funeral directors arrived to collect her father and asked, 'Where is it?'.

Going out to collect people in the middle of the night is a tough and unenviable job, sometimes involving taking a person out of a flat on the 13th floor of a building with no working lift, but it needs to be done with compassion and care.

Just after I launched Poetic Endings, I came home late one evening to discover that my house had been burgled. The front door had been smashed, and there was broken glass everywhere. I stood in the midst of the broken glass and called 999. I waited for the police to arrive while my friend Laura jumped in a taxi to come to my house to support me.

By the time the police had checked the house and taken a statement from me, it was past midnight. There was still broken glass everywhere and the front door was broken. I knew we needed to call someone to fix the door and clean up the glass. I had a funeral meeting at 9 a.m. the next day and needed to feel safe again so I could get some sleep. I was frightened and vulnerable, shaking as though I was freezing cold, even though it was a warm midsummer evening.

Laura googled 'locksmith West London' and called the first name on the list. I told her that I didn't care how much it cost, as long as they came quickly. Half an hour later, a man in a van came and fixed the door. He charged £375 for 20 minutes spent sweeping up glass and boarding the door. He didn't say a word as I paced up and down, wondering how I would sleep that night.

When he left, I felt empty, alone and scared. I'd needed him to do much more than board up the door. I needed him to acknowledge my fears and make me feel safe and secure in my own home again, by explaining what he had done and what needed to happen next.

As I discussed my experience with friends, I realised that funeral directors have a similar role to locksmiths. Arranging a funeral is an experience people rarely think about and have usually never done before. Death often happens in the middle of the night, and in the shock and trauma of the situation, a hasty Google search and a quick phone call results in calling someone who may or may not offer a good service. The principles of what I learned that night have influenced my work as a funeral director – the need to be truly present, to communicate clearly and to *really* show up.

The funeral industry is unlike any other industry in the 21st century. It's the only business where consumers will hand over money for something they aren't really sure they want or understand. It's an industry where myths and assumptions are commonplace and left unchecked; where most consumers don't really do their research, complain, ask questions or write reviews. It's an industry dominated by big businesses who hide behind the names of the local family companies they bought years ago. It's an industry in which people still ask for your fax number and want to be paid with a cheque. It's an industry hidden behind net curtains on Britain's high street and in outdated crematoriums and cemeteries, removed from everyday life. But it is changing. The fact that Poetic Endings exists, and that you're reading this book, is a big part of that change.

A ritual without meaning is just a formality, and when overwhelmed with the shock of a bereavement, it's so easy to pay an extortionate amount of money for a funeral with little thought as to what we're doing and why we're doing it. In the UK, it's been part of our culture to keep our grief repressed, to suffer in silence by not acknowledging the depth and difficulty of our pain. The classic 'keep calm and carry on' isn't an approach that's helpful for dealing with the often catastrophic nature of loss. Mary Elizabeth Frye, one of our most popular funeral poets, tells us not to stand at a grave and weep. Henry Scott-Holland tells us that death is nothing at all and to continue with our lives as though nothing has changed. But when someone dies, absolutely everything changes. Allowing ourselves to mourn can be the biggest gift we can give to ourselves.

I wanted to create an enlightened funeral service for today and for the future. A funeral service that didn't look like anything that was on offer in London back in 2017. I wanted to take funerals away from fusty dusty shops on the high street with memorial stones, plastic flowers and faux Victoriana. There'd be no photographs of the queen or gloomy men in top hats on the walls. I'd create a genuinely helpful professional service that helped people not to just say goodbye, but to work out how exactly to do that, in a creative, gentle and sensitive way. My first step was to unplug the fax machine.

Not all funeral directors are the same

[L]

Before I became a funeral celebrant, I thought there were two types of funeral directors: Victorian funeral directors, who wore top hats, carried canes and worked in a dark and mysterious fashion; and green funeral directors, who arranged something called a humanist funeral with a cardboard coffin in a woodland full of bluebells, which somehow bloomed all year.

It didn't take me long to discover that funeral directors aren't *either* Victorian *or* green, as the mainstream media would have us believe. There are many different kinds of funeral directors, all with very different approaches.

There are funeral directors who would consider themselves to be 'traditional', use words like 'dignity' and 'respect' to describe their work and display photos of their fleet of cars in gold frames in a dusty window display; traditional funeral directors who have embraced a more modern approach; modern funeral directors with a traditional approach; modern funeral directors who are defining a new way to do funerals; corporate funeral directors riding on a reputation they don't deserve; corporate funeral directors disguised as local family firms; local family firms who are more like corporate funeral directors; actual local family firms; progressive funeral directors who are speaking out and challenging the status quo (like Poetic Endings); alternative funeral directors who might wear green fleeces and use vans instead of hearses; alternative funeral directors who use essential oils, incense and crystals and will laugh and cry with you; undertakers; home funeral guides who will help you to arrange a DIY funeral in your own home; community-led organisations serving particular communities, cultures or faith; and last but definitely not least, the direct cremation companies, who specialise in efficient disposal of the dead without any form of ritual or ceremony.

Some of the most heartfelt funeral services are provided by rural funeral directors who serve their communities with traditional values, in a way that leaves me almost envious. A client once told me that her mother's funeral in the Yorkshire Dales involved the local funeral director, a well-known figure in the community who was also a joiner. He came round to her mother's house to discuss the coffin and burial. There was no talk of fancy coffins or limousines. He made the coffin while friends and neighbours came together to put on a big spread – sausage rolls, cheese sandwiches, plenty of cake and vats of tea. Everyone in the small village came to the burial, walking to the cemetery, before returning to the local pub to eat the food and share their memories. This was as recent as 2013.

In comparison, my life in London feels lonely and isolated. I don't know many of my neighbours, my community feels transitory and most of my friends and family live in other parts of the city. If I died soon, this Yorkshire ideal wouldn't be the reality of my funeral.

Most funeral directors in the UK sell their services in packages. They've created set options based on the kind of coffin and the number of funeral limousines required. They've named their coffins after significant local towns or long-dead politicians, and managed to get a reputation for upselling products with carefully timed comments such as: 'A lot of people feel this is the last thing they can do for their mum. Perhaps you'd like to consider this beautiful solid oak coffin?'

While I wish this weren't true, it's a reputation deserved by at least some of the funeral industry. During my time as a celebrant and a trainee funeral director, I came across funeral directors who had different price lists depending on the perceived wealth of their clients. I came across funeral directors who had extortionate mark-ups on coffins. 'If it's oak or bespoke, charge whatever you want,' a funeral director once advised me. I came across a funeral director who had an illicit partnership with nursing home staff to ensure it was always in their financial interests to send bereaved people his way (to the tune of £200). One funeral director confessed to arranging funerals for babies and children for free because it was good marketing: 'If you do the baby, you'll definitely get the grandparents.'

I've been told about several companies who have different prices for each branch, even though the clients are given the same funeral with the same cars and the same staff. The difference for travelling to a branch three miles down the road can be hundreds, even thousands, of pounds.

There has been great resistance from funeral directors to put their prices on their websites, mostly because their inconsistencies would be revealed. They also know most clients won't shop around. Once they've got a client in their office, shared some kind words and given them a cup of tea, they know that they're unlikely to go elsewhere.

Wherever there's vulnerability, there will be people willing to exploit that vulnerability for their own financial gain. Asking about the cost of a funeral has been categorised as distasteful, as though there's shame in enquiring about how much one of the most expensive purchases most people will ever make will be.

I was once taken aside by a funeral director after I'd spoken out about the lack of transparency in funerals on radio. 'You're saying some dangerous things,' I was warned as I was walking through a cemetery on my way to a funeral.

'Like what? That funeral directors should put their prices online?'

'Yes. You need to watch what you're suggesting or we'll be coming for you.'

I believe that putting prices online is the funeral industry's first step to proving it can serve the needs of today's society by behaving transparently – showing that it has absolutely nothing to hide.

Fortunately, it's not all doom, gloom, plastic flowers, dusty net curtains, thinly veiled threats and exploitation. If you're looking for a different kind of funeral service with a more enlightened and flexible approach, there are funeral directors who will help you to feel empowered with your choices, and not charge the earth for doing so.

These funeral directors will work with you in a flexible way. They will listen to you. They will spend time with you and help you to work out what's important to you. They won't tell you what to do. They won't sell you a funeral package named after a dead politician. They won't guilt trip you into buying a more expensive coffin. You'll know what's going to happen, what to expect, and how much it's going to cost. They all have websites explaining their approach and services. They even have their prices online!

The funeral directors who are leading the way in setting up creative, helpful, ethical and well-meaning funeral businesses are almost exclusively women (with a few notable exceptions). This shouldn't be surprising – women's involvement in taking care of our dead really isn't anything new.

THE EVER-CHANGING NATURE OF FUNERALS

In the 19th century, dying was a very different experience to what it is today. People died at home and stayed there until the funeral. The local 'laying-out woman' (who also helped with births) would visit the home to carry out the last offices, ensuring the person who had died was dressed in a clean nightgown or perhaps their Sunday best.

Local carpenters or joiners were asked to make a coffin when someone in their community died. They would visit the house to measure the person and would then make a coffin, sealing it to prevent any unpleasant leakages. The person who had died would then be placed in their coffin in the front parlour at home. These men became known as undertakers because they were literally tasked with *undertaking* the jobs that no one else wanted to do. Flowers were placed around the room to help disguise any unpleasant odours so friends and neighbours could come to visit. The funeral would take place three or four days later.

Death was messy and uncontrollable, but that didn't stop the women in the community from taking care of their dead. It was seen as something that belonged at home and in the community, as much as birth or illness. It was just another part of life.

In America, embalming had grown in popularity after President Lincoln's body had been embalmed and transported from Washington DC to Ohio for burial. The American Civil War also helped to increase its profile; the bodies of young soldiers were embalmed on the battlefield so they could be returned to their families back home, often hundreds of miles away. By 1900, American training in embalming techniques was being offered to undertakers in the UK, who spotted a business opportunity and became the funeral directors we know today. They trained as embalmers and opened their own businesses, replacing the front parlours in people's homes with 'funeral parlours' and providing 'Chapels of Rest' where the dead could 'rest'. They commercialised death, providing mass-market funerals for anyone who was prepared to pay the price, turning funerals into a retail opportunity for the British high street.

In 1948, the National Health Service was established in the UK and, with that, attitudes towards health care began to change. People died in hospitals rather than at home. Death was seen as something that was unhygienic, unpleasant and frightening and care of the dead was willingly handed over to the now well-established funeral directors, who charged for the service.

Some funeral directors have made it their mission to protect us from the perceived horrors of our dead, as though we couldn't possibly cope with the reality. As if what we don't know, and can't see, couldn't possibly hurt us. All of those net curtains and dusty plastic flowers in their shops confirm the view that death should be hidden away, shielded from public view. Out of sight, and preferably out of mind.

Change is inevitable, nothing ever stays the same. As our society and culture changes, so do our traditions and the systems we have in place. The funeral system we have now isn't even that old. As society continues to change, so will our funeral system. It needs to serve the people who use it, in a way that is relevant to them.

Today it's more feminine traits – compassion, empathy, flexibility, gentleness and creativity – that are leading the way in changing funerals for the better. Although it's unlikely that we're going to re-establish laying-out woman in our local communities, we do need to create a way of taking care of our dead that works for our society and embodies these feminine traits. As society is moving away from more patriarchal attitudes, so is death.

I've noticed that many of our clients don't want to be shielded from the realities of death. They ask questions and want to be told the truth in response. They want to get involved with washing and dressing the person who has died, even if they don't want to have the person at home. We don't necessarily need to return to how things were in the early 19th century, but we can take the elements that resonate with us and interpret them in a way that works for today's society.

Even the funeral directors of the 1960s, who were trained to offer a distraught bereaved person a cigarette, could understand that women were a valuable addition to their business, although women were permitted to be 'lady assistants' rather than fully fledged funeral directors.

It was considered deeply reassuring to have a 'lady assistant' standing at the door to the Chapel of Rest, tilting her head to the side in a sympathetic manner and saying, 'He's at peace now,' as the family said their goodbyes.

This came directly from a training manual for funeral directors written in the 1960s: 'Her natural aptitude for the arrangement of flowers (this should be backed by special training), her skill in the setting of hair, and her fastidiousness in the dressing of the deceased. All this is second nature to a woman and is appreciated by other women.'

Women's role in society has changed. We're no longer relegated to the role of 'lady assistants' in our home lives, careers, politics, society, communities or culture. It's not that the value of those feminine traits wasn't recognised before, it's just that women are now leading the way in setting up new kinds of funeral businesses that embody them. Because we can. And because we know that it matters.

Not all funeral directors are stuck in the principles of the training manuals of the 1960s, but many are. I know of several funeral directors who refuse to allow women to work as funeral directors, insisting that they stay in the office arranging funerals with clients, rather than being allowed to go out and conduct funerals. I'm waiting for the day when someone takes one of these funeral directors to court for discrimination.

It's important to point out that just because you've appointed your local high street funeral director doesn't mean you're definitely going to be guilt tripped into buying an overpriced coffin. It doesn't mean you didn't do the right thing for your loved one. It's just important to make a decision knowing that there are choices, and you don't have to choose something if it doesn't feel right. You need a funeral director who is going to support you in a way that works for you.

How to choose a funeral director

[L]

As we'll learn in the next chapter, grief affects our brain. A time of tragedy isn't the best time to be shopping around and asking difficult questions. If you're not prepared and find yourself needing a funeral director, go with your gut instinct. Take your time and don't worry if you get it wrong. You can change funeral directors later on if you need to.

The Good Funeral Guide's online directory is a good place to look for a funeral director in the UK. You can read about how they work, what they value, and read reviews written by previous clients before you make your decision.

Fran Hall, the CEO, scrutinises funeral directors for qualities such as emotional intelligence, transparency, creativity, flexibility and integrity. Her inspections are thorough, and not all funeral directors make the grade. She might want to know what they're most proud of, why they do what they do, what kind of language they use to talk about their work, how they answer the phone and how they deal with the stress and trauma of being a funeral director.

I believe that trade associations exist to protect funeral directors and the general industry. The Good Funeral Guide is an independent, not-for-profit resource that exists to protect bereaved people. It's there to help you. Make good use of it.

DECIDING WHAT MATTERS TO YOU

You don't need to ask all the questions below, but they may give you something to think about when considering the right kind of funeral director for you:

1. Where is the funeral director based? Does this matter to you? You don't have to go to your local funeral director if they're not a good match. You can travel further afield.
2. Is it important to you to have a connection to the funeral director? Is there someone you've used before and with whom you've had a good experience? Can a trusted friend recommend someone?
3. Where will the person who has died be cared for? Does this matter to you?
4. How will they be cared for? Will they be embalmed?
5. Do you want to be involved in their care? Will you want to wash and dress them?
6. Can you spend time with the person who has died? Where will this be? Will you need to make an appointment? Can this happen in the evening and at weekends?
7. Can the funeral director take your cultural or religious considerations into account?
8. Do you want to have a traditional funeral or would you like something more contemporary and creative? Does it seem like the funeral director has experience in facilitating the kind of funeral you want? If you care about shiny cars, choose a funeral director who cares about shiny cars. If you want to do something creative, choose a funeral director who can facilitate your creativity.
9. Who owns the funeral directors? Is it a genuine family business or a corporate chain in disguise? Some corporate chains are well disguised, so if it matters to you, make sure you ask who owns the business.

10. Will the person who arranges the funeral with you be there on the day? Some companies, especially the larger ones, will have funeral arrangers who work in the office and will be your point of contact. It will likely be a different person, who you've never met, who will conduct the funeral on the day.

THE IMPORTANT QUESTIONS

You might want to ask yourself these questions once you've met the potential funeral director:

1. Can you talk to the funeral director openly and honestly?
2. Do they listen to what you're saying? Do you feel as though they understand what you want?
3. Do you like them?
4. Are they transparent about their services and costs?
5. And the crucial question: Do you trust them to take care of the person who has died?

GETTING INVOLVED

Good funeral directors will allow you to participate as much or as little as you feel comfortable with, providing restrictions aren't in place.

You might want to wash and dress the person who has died. You might want to paint their nails and do their hair or make-up yourself. You may wish to create your own orders of service, have members of the family carry the coffin or put together flowers from your own garden for the service. You might even want to take the service yourself.

If the funeral director says no to any of your requests, consider changing funeral directors. You're allowed to do that, even if most of the funeral is already arranged. A good funeral director will listen to you, support you and facilitate whatever you want to do. You're in charge. Funeral directors are there to provide guidance, but not to tell you how things should be done.

Remember – a good funeral is whatever you want and need it to be. A good funeral director will recognise this and work with you, for you.

DIY funerals

A DIY funeral isn't for everyone. But for some people, it really works.

Using a funeral director is not a legal requirement in the UK, even if professionals tell you otherwise. You may want to handle the funeral arrangements yourself, or decide the parts you'd like to do and appoint a professional for the rest.

You can take care of the person who has died at home and make all the arrangements for the funeral. You'll need to consider how you will collect the person who has died from the hospital, hospice or coroner's mortuary, take care of them at home, arrange the burial or cremation, manage the paperwork, and transport them to the funeral. There's a lot to do, and the reality of it can be over-whelming, so it's worth having a back-up plan.

There are home funeral guides who will be able to support you in doing as much or as little as you like. You can also use the services of a flexible funeral director, who will let you rent space in their mortuary and provide specialist body-care, if required.

— Ray's Funeral

Raymond Natkiel died in Charing Cross Hospital. His stepdaughter, Liza, had arranged for me to meet him at the hospital to talk about what he wanted for his funeral. Unfortunately, he died sooner than the palliative team had expected, so I met Liza at his supported living flat in West London instead so we could begin making arrangements for his funeral.

I marvelled at his artwork and his impressive collection of books, mostly rare editions. His entire flat was full of paintbrushes, half-completed projects and eccentricities. The window of the lounge looked out on to the street below so he'd wave at all the neighbours. Everyone in the area knew and loved him. He was a bohemian and a revolutionary who belonged in both 1950s Paris and 21st-century London. He wanted his funeral to honour the way he'd lived his life, and everything he loved.

When I meet clients, I often ask about their previous experiences of funerals so I can understand what's important to them. Liza talked to me about her mother's funeral in the North Pennines of Cumbria. She explained how she'd taken care of her in her house in the middle of nowhere with the help of an understanding funeral director from Carlisle. Liza had loved being able to look after her at home, in her own space, surrounded by her artwork.

Liza didn't realise Ray could come home from the hospital, but after some discussion about the realities of what it entailed, we decided it was a possibility. I spoke to the hospital bereavement team about our plan and then went to see Ray in the mortuary. His body was in good condition so I felt we could bring him directly home without needing to take him into our care for preparation first.

Liza helped to bring Ray back to his flat. We put his beloved French flag over the stretcher and used the lift to transport him to the second floor, and then wheeled him along the corridor to his home. It took a bit of manoeuvring to get the stretcher through the front door, but we managed it.

Ray was inside a body bag, provided by the hospital. With the help of Liza's friend Joanna and Ray's good friend Angelique, we moved him from the stretcher and on to the chaise longue. I asked Liza if she'd like to unzip the body bag herself. She wanted to do as much as she could, so I stepped back and allowed her to be in control. Sometimes my role is simply to invite people to do whatever it is they want and need to do.

That afternoon Liza, Angelique and Joanna bathed Ray using hot water and essential oils. I put eyecaps (similar to contact lenses but made of plastic) in his eyes to keep them closed, but his friends and family did the rest. They dressed him in corduroy trousers, his favourite T-shirt, a waistcoat, a red scarf and pointy white brogues – his self-proclaimed 'pimp shoes' – with green socks.

Liza had chosen a flatpack coffin, a prototype from a company in Holland. It arrived in the post so the pieces needed to be slotted together. We spent a few hours despairing over our DIY skills as we assembled it.

Once it was ready, we transferred Ray into his coffin and then lifted him on to trestles in the front room. Liza added a few final touches – his favourite books, artwork by Angelique's children, a cigarette in one hand and a glass of red wine in the other.

That night, Ray's neighbours and friends came to say their goodbyes to him. They'd spent many a long evening talking about philosophy, politics and art over red wine, and Ray's final night in his flat would be no exception. They stayed until late, drawing on his coffin, drinking wine, eating cheese and sharing memories of their beloved friend, as he laid among them in his coffin.

The next morning, Ray was cremated in a simple ceremony at Mortlake Crematorium. In the chapel, we listened to Bob Dylan, The Rolling Stones, Edith Piaf and Louis Armstrong. Everyone danced and sang as they went up to Ray's coffin. When the time came, everyone gathered round to say their final goodbyes.

Ray's funeral wasn't totally a DIY funeral, but it was a funeral that empowered the people who cared about him the most. My role was to simply be there to invite them to do whatever they felt they needed to do, and to support them by providing guidance and expertise.

YES, YOU CAN BE BURIED IN YOUR GARDEN

— Mary's Funeral

Mary had lived in a cottage in Lancashire for 85 years of her life, but when her health declined, she moved to London to live with her daughter Kirsty. Although Mary was happy to spend her final days in London, she wanted to be buried in the garden of her cottage in Lancashire when the time came.

Mary died at home on a Sunday morning. Kirsty wanted to honour her wishes but wasn't sure whether they were legal. She spoke to the Natural Death Centre, who assured her that it was legal to bury someone on private land. They sent over instructions on how to dig a grave and a sample burial register.

Mary stayed in our cold facilities in London until the time came for her to go to Lancashire. The local farmers she'd known her entire life had already prepared her grave and were enjoying a cup of tea with Mary's grandchildren when we arrived. We helped them to move her coffin into the front room of her cottage, where she would spend a final night surrounded by her family and friends.

The next morning, Mary's family buried her in her own garden, next to the flowers she'd planted and tended her whole life.

It's perfectly legal to be buried on private land in England and Wales. If you'd like to do this or if you'd like to handle the funeral arrangements yourself, it can be a profound, meaningful and healing experience. It can also be confusing, challenging and difficult. I suggest you talk to the Natural Death Centre, who will be able to provide support and guidance and advocate on your behalf, should you come up against any resistance. You can find them here: www.naturaldeath.org.uk

Seeing the person who has died can be a profound and meaningful experience

[L]

'Confront a corpse at least once. The absolute absence of life is the most disturbing and challenging confrontation you will ever have.'
DAVID BOWIE

Most people have never seen a dead person, and have no idea what happens to someone after they have died. We find that people are often worried about what the person will look like, and concerned that they could be left with a harmful memory. However, we've witnessed how helpful, healing and meaningful it can be to see someone after they've died.

— Mimi's Funeral

Although Mimi was 89, about to turn 90, it seemed like she would live forever. She sang in the local choir, she baked cakes to raise much-needed funds for the community garden on her street, and she regularly took trips to visit beautiful gardens around the UK.

A week after one such trip, Mimi was taking a stem ginger loaf cake, her favourite, out of the oven when she had a stroke. She was taken into a busy hospital by ambulance and over the course of the next week, she was moved from ward to ward. Nurses and doctors gave her family contrasting information. A doctor told them to prepare themselves for the worst; 10 minutes later a physiotherapist told them about the exercises she could do at home to get her back to her previous level of fitness.

Mimi died at 4 a.m. in a renal ward, surrounded by her three children and eight grandchildren. The bed in the ward had been the only one available in the entire hospital. Her family felt as though they'd watched her choking to death in huge amounts of pain, and came away traumatised by what it was like to die in hospital. They described her final week as a chaotic, distressing and awful time. To her family, it was inconceivable that she'd not only died, but that she'd died in a hospital ward in such a traumatic way.

I talked to Mimi's family about what was important to them and how they felt they needed to say goodbye. What became clear was just how traumatising everyone in the family had found that last week of her life.

'I want to forget what happened at the hospital,' her daughter Julia wrote. 'After everything she did to make the end of Dad's life so peaceful, I feel like we've failed her. I wanted Mum to have that too.'

When we collected Mimi from the hospital, she was in a hospital gown and the paraphernalia of her final days in hospital was still present. We washed her hair, then gently bathed her with warm water and lavender oil. We closed her eyes and her mouth and dressed her in her favourite nightgown and slippers. We gently placed her inside her willow coffin before covering her with a blanket she'd crocheted herself.

I told Mimi's family that although her skin was quite fragile, she looked peaceful in her willow coffin, wearing her favourite nightgown, and promised that if her family did want to spend some time with her, it wouldn't be like the experience they'd had at the hospital.

'I think I might want to see her,' Julia said. The others agreed.

Her family wanted to spend time with her in a way that was meaningful to them. They wanted to replace the images of her traumatic death with something gentler and kinder, the end they'd wanted for her.

Despite the fact that Mimi's body had begun to change by the time the family saw her, they still recognised her as their mum and grandma, although they felt like the essence of her was gone.

It's not always so simple, though: the reality of our work depends on how someone died, how long it's been since their death, how quickly they were found, and what's happened to them since.

We gave Mimi's family the opportunity to be with her in a beautiful room overlooking the river. The family had filled the room with daffodils, photographs of them all and plenty of lightly scented tealights. A big pot of Earl Grey tea was left to brew next to a stem ginger loaf cake.

'Oh Mum,' Mimi's daughter Julia said, as she entered the room and slowly made her way over to the coffin. 'You look so beautiful.'

It didn't take long for those who were nervous about seeing her to join the rest of the family. They spent an afternoon gathered around Mimi in her coffin, refilling the pot of tea and eating the cake until there were only crumbs left. There were tears, but there was also lots of laughter. They told stories and placed the cards and letters they'd written for her 90th birthday in her hands and kissed her forehead. Their final act as a family was to come together to put the lid on to her coffin.

'I am so overwhelmed at the reality of Mum being gone,' Julia later wrote. 'But now I think of her looking so peaceful in her nightclothes, surrounded by the people who loved her, rather than those horrible final days at the hospital. It's now a beautiful image, rather than a traumatic one.'

What really happens after someone has died?

[L]

After death, most people are kept inside a refrigerated unit in a mortuary, not in a 'Chapel of Rest' as some funeral directors will lead you to believe. The mortuary might be at a hospital, a hospice, a coroner's facilities or at the funeral director's premises. The idea is to keep the person cold, to slow down the rate of decomposition – a vital natural process, when the dead tissues break down and are converted into simpler organic forms, which begins just a few minutes after a person has died.

I was once explaining how we take care of people in a cold environment, when the daughter of the lady who had died interrupted me.

'So in the same way that a banana kept in the fridge will change over time, so will a person?'

She was exactly right. Refrigeration doesn't stop decomposition, it just slows it down. Just because someone has been kept cold doesn't mean their body won't change.

After death, skin will sallow and may become waxy or fragile. There might be discolouration. Fluid and blood may begin to accumulate in the lower parts of the body as circulation stops and gravity takes effect. The eyes will sink into their sockets, and it may be difficult to keep them closed. Limbs may become stiff and the body may release fluids. The mouth may be open, and it may be necessary to use invasive techniques to keep it closed.

Some funeral directors will have mortuary facilities on their premises, others won't. Some of the bigger companies have 'mortuary hubs', often a unit on an industrial estate which they may call a 'care centre'. If you say that you'd like to spend time with the person who has died, they will be taken from the hub to the branch of the funeral directors where the funeral arrangements have been made. You can ask your chosen funeral director where the person who has died will be cared for. Expect them to give you a clear and honest response.

Some funeral directors don't have refrigerated facilities. Instead, they will embalm everyone in their care, and keep them in coffins at room temperature, although this approach is frowned upon now that modern mortuary facilities are readily available.

WHAT IS EMBALMING?

Embalming is the act of temporarily preserving a body by slowing down decomposition. It involves replacing the body's blood and fluids with preservative

---

chemicals, including formaldehyde. It also involves piercing the major organs of the body using a sharp implement called a trocar, then draining the contents using an aspirator. Some funeral directors will call embalming 'hygienic treatment' in an attempt to disguise what it really is. Some will insist that it's necessary to embalm someone if you want to see them. Most of the time, that's simply not true.

Over the last century, the appeal of embalming has been in allowing funeral directors to present a perfect 'memory picture', whereby people look like they're just sleeping or resting, rather than dead. It's meant that many people have seen the person who has died covered in heavy make-up. At the time, it was considered to be helpful for the grieving family from a psychological point of view. That perspective is now changing.

HOW WE LOOK AFTER THE PEOPLE IN OUR CARE AT POETIC ENDINGS

Our emphasis is on helping family and friends to acknowledge that the person who has died is really dead, without it being a distressing or traumatic experience. We don't want people to look like they're still alive, but we don't want them to look like a waxwork doll as they sometimes do when they've been embalmed and then heavily made up. We want them to look clean and well cared for. Whatever they did to feel like themselves in life, we can do that in death, whether that's styling their hair in a particular way, painting their nails, or giving them a shave.

We're not totally against embalming, but we have found few situations where the result has justified the nature of the procedure. Our philosophy is to take a considered view on everything we do as funeral directors, based on our commitment to take exceptionally good care of the person who has died, while considering what their family and friends want and need in order to say goodbye to them.

'Would you like me to talk you through how your dad looks right now?' we might ask, if a client is considering seeing their person. If they say yes, we might feel we need to say: 'There are changes taking place, which we can't stop. Your dad's face may look darker than it did last time you saw him and the skin on his hands is very fragile. There's a scar across his chest from the post-mortem, but you won't be able to see this as it's hidden underneath his roll neck jumper. Apart from the change of colour, he looks peaceful.'

We firmly believe that it's important to have the opportunity to say goodbye, in a way that's beautiful and peaceful, without causing undue distress or damage, but without denying that someone has died.

FIVE THINGS I'VE LEARNED ABOUT CARING FOR PEOPLE WHO HAVE DIED FROM WORKING IN A MODERN MORTUARY

by Annika Caswell

Annika is a specialist bodycare artist working as part of the team at Poetic Endings in London. She has a long history of craftsmanship within the bespoke tailoring and couture industry but transferred her skills to funerals after the profound experience of seeing her father sensitively prepared in his coffin.

1.
Seeing a person who has not been embalmed is not unhygienic, dangerous or illegal. In our experience, non-chemical and less intrusive alternatives can present the person who has died in a kinder and more natural way, often more closely resembling how they were in life.

2.
No matter what the circumstances of the person's death are, there is always a way to spend time with the person who has died. Even if it is just to be in the same room with them with their coffin closed, or just to have their hand revealed.

3.
In our experience, nature takes its course differently for every person and presents, in turn, unique challenges to the mortuary team. Everyone has unique needs in terms of how much they want to know or not know about the preparations that may take place.

4.
The majority of the products used in taking care of the person who has died are the same as those used for the living. If the person had a favourite shampoo, nail polish or aftershave you can absolutely ask for those to be used in their care.

5.
The human body is a profound vessel, and even though we may never understand what happens to 'us' when we die, the physical being we leave behind deserves and commands care and respect to the end.

FIVE THINGS I WISH EVERYONE KNEW ABOUT POST-MORTEM EXAMINATIONS

by Dr Suzy Lishman CBE

Sometimes, after a person has died, a post-mortem examination may be necessary. We asked consultant pathologist Suzy to write a Five Things so we could better understand what happens and why. Suzy has carried out over 1000 post-mortem examinations, and gives regular public talks about the procedure and its benefits.

1.

Around one in five people who die in England and Wales will have a post-mortem examination (also known as an autopsy). The examination is usually carried out when the cause of death is unknown, the person who has died hadn't seen a doctor recently or if death was not due to natural causes.

2.

Post-mortems are carried out with care and respect. We never forget that the person who has died is an individual, and somebody's loved one. The procedure resembles a surgical operation, with precise incisions being made to expose the internal organs. Occasionally a small amount of tissue is removed for further testing. All other tissue is returned to the body.

3.

Post-mortems involve a team of skilled specialists, including anatomical pathology technologists (APTs) and pathologists, who are specially trained doctors who also examine tissue from the living. They work together to provide a respectful, professional and timely service.

4.

The majority of post-mortems in the UK are performed at the request of a coroner. These do not require the consent of the next of kin, but you will be kept informed of the process by the coroner's officer. The coroner will sometimes hold an inquest into a death, to allow them to consider evidence from several sources.

5.

Post-mortem examinations often provide valuable information that can't be discovered in any other way. Despite many people having scans and other tests during life, post-mortems frequently reveal conditions that weren't suspected or are more extensive than expected. They provide important education for doctors and help bereaved families understand what happened to their loved one.

WHEN IT'S JUST NOT POSSIBLE TO SEE
THE PERSON WHO HAS DIED

— Akachi's Funeral

Akachi was found 10 days after he died alone in his studio flat. As his death was unexpected, his case was referred to the coroner, who carried out a post-mortem. By the time Akachi came into our care, his body had decomposed to a point where he was no longer recognisable.

His niece Zoya knew that her uncle's community would expect to have an open coffin in their church. It felt important to honour what the community expected, but also to acknowledge the reality of how Akachi's body had deteriorated. Having an open coffin just wasn't possible.

Zoya still wanted everyone to be able to come up to her uncle's coffin to say goodbye, so she designed a special coffin, which had photos of her uncle and the things he loved around the sides. The lid was painted with blackboard paint. At the point in the church ceremony when everyone would usually file past the open coffin to pay their respects, everyone was instead invited to write a message on to the coffin lid as music played.

'The coffin helped so much,' Zoya said. 'Everyone knew how he had died so was scared to go up to the coffin. But being able to see the photos of him around the sides, and write messages to him, enabled us to be close to him and say our goodbyes without it being a horrible experience.'

As you can see from Zoya's experience, there's often a lot that can be done to help people to say goodbye. It involves talking honestly but gently to the people involved, and also establishing what's important to them. Then a solution can be found.

For instance, we've draped cotton sheets over a lady to enable her husband to hold her hand for the final time, without being exposed to the reality of her body after she was knocked from her bike. We've helped three sons to safely say goodbye to their father, who died from complications related to hepatitis C. We've helped a family to sit with the body of their father, who died by suicide, covering his body bag in their own blankets so they could say what they needed to say to the remains of his physical form. We've arranged for a teenage girl to be fully reconstructed by an embalming and restoration specialist, when her parents wanted to kiss her goodbye after she was murdered. During the first COVID-19 outbreak, we arranged for a family to see their grandfather via Zoom so they could say goodbye to him without the risk of being exposed to his body.

Why would I want to see someone after they've died?

[A + L]

Some people view the body of someone who has died as something fundamentally inhuman. In philosopher Julia Kristeva's theory of 'Abjection' she describes the horror we feel when we move from being a living, breathing, moving capable 'subject' to a lifeless 'object'. We transform from being an animated human to being a corpse or a body. We go from being 'someone' to 'something'. She believes that one of the reasons we find it so difficult to see someone who has died is because, either consciously or unconsciously, it reminds us of our own fragility and mortality. According to Julia: 'Corpses show me what I permanently thrust aside in order to live'.

Our work is based on the belief that we remain who we are right up until the point of cremation or burial and even beyond. We remain the subject in the hearts and minds of the people we were fundamental to throughout our lives. Our lack of physical presence, or our physical being, does not objectify us. Our lack of movement or our inability to process thought in death does not render us a mere object to be 'viewed'.

By spending time with someone once their heart has stopped beating we are able to begin to process their absence, and we're able to begin grieving for their physical disappearance from our lives. When we wholeheartedly believe someone has died we are able to begin the process of learning to live without them.

When an animal dies, we're advised to show the dead animal to the other animals in the household, allowing them to see, smell and understand that their animal friend has died. If they are not made aware of this, they may spend the rest of their lives looking for them. If we use this theory with humans, it makes sense that having time with someone who has died can be an important part of grieving.

The people we've talked about in this section all wanted the opportunity to spend some time with the person who had died. They needed to know, for themselves, that the person they loved was really gone. The physical reality of the body in front of them meant it was unavoidable and unquestionable. For them, being in the presence of the body of the person they'd loved made their death very real.

In some cultures, people will wail or may shout the name of the person who has died over and over again, to ascertain that they're really not coming back to life.

If a person has died suddenly or unexpectedly, there's no time to prepare or to say goodbye. Some people may not have a choice about whether or not they see the body of the person who has died – they may have been there at the time of death, such as in an accident. Or they may have been the one to find the person, perhaps at the scene of a crime or a suicide. Having the opportunity to say goodbye to them at a later time, in a calmer setting, can be really helpful.

Sometimes, though, it's not. When John's wife died in surgery, he decided he didn't want to see her again. 'She's not really there,' he said. 'Her body is just her physical remains. She's gone.'

Jane felt differently about seeing her lifelong partner Heidi after she'd died. 'Seeing her was such a precious gift. I needed time to get my head around her death. Even though something felt different, she was still my Heidi. Looking back, it really helped to be in the room with her and just have that final time together.'

Deciding to see someone who has died is a big decision. It can be a powerful and moving experience. Death isn't a time to be logical. Do whatever feels right. Do whatever works for you.

'VIEWING'

Most funeral directors in the UK will call the experience of seeing the person who has died a 'viewing'. It's usually held in a room inside the funeral director's premises, called a Chapel of Rest or a family room.

You might want to ask to see the room first, so you can familiarise yourself with it. Most traditional funeral directors have a room in their premises that may have been blessed by a priest. They often contain religious artefacts and plastic flowers, which you may want removed. More progressive funeral directors have understood the importance of spending time with the person who has died, and have created more healing and nurturing environments in which this can take place.

At Poetic Endings, we've been trying to redefine the word 'viewing' but haven't yet settled on a word that describes the experience. 'Viewing' indicates that it's a situation in which you remain detached, just stand back and look. If it's possible, it's helpful to be involved. You might want to lay some flower petals or sprigs of rosemary on the person who has died, spray them with their favourite perfume or be the one who closes the coffin for the final time. It's important to remember that they're yours, not ours. As funeral professionals, we're just there to offer guidance and support.

No one should ever be forced to see the person who has died, but if there's any doubt, we do encourage it. We talk it through and let people know that it doesn't need to be a frightening or alien experience. We don't promise anything. We make it clear that we'll do what we can, but that we'll be gentle and honest about the reality of how someone is, so they can decide for themselves whether it's something they'd find helpful.

THINGS TO CONSIDER WHEN SEEING SOMEONE AFTER THEY'VE DIED

1. **How would you like the person who has died to be cared for?**
   - Are there any cultural or religious sensitivities to take into consideration?
   - Do you need to take precautions for any infectious diseases, such as COVID-19 or hepatitis C?
   - Would you like them to be embalmed?
   - Does your chosen funeral director insist on embalming if you'd like to see the person who has died? Remember that embalming is not a legal requirement in the UK and it's not necessary for people to be embalmed in order for you to spend time with them.
   - If it's possible, would you like to be involved in washing and dressing them?
   - Would you like them to be wearing their own make-up or have their hair in a particular style?

2. **What would you like them to wear?**
   People who have died don't need to be dressed in a suit or the polyester gowns favoured by some funeral directors. They could be dressed in something more casual, such as comfortable pyjamas or a favourite summer dress. If they didn't wear formal clothes in life, why would they wear them now? They could also be dressed in a simple cotton gown, or a shroud. Do what feels right for you and for them.

3. **Where will you have time with them?**
   - Will you see them in the hospital, hospice or in the coroner's facilities?
   - Will it be at the funeral directors' premises?
   - Or perhaps at the funeral itself with an open coffin?
   - Would you like them to come home?

   You can see someone in the hospital, but they will probably still be in a hospital gown and it will be in a more clinical setting. If it's possible, seeing them at a later time after they've been prepared and they're wearing their own clothes could be a different and more healing experience.

4. **Ask what to expect**
   - What do they look like now?
   - Have they had a post-mortem?
   - What will the room be like?

- Who will be there? If you're feeling uncertain, ask your funeral director, or a friend, to go into the space first and describe what they see to you.

5. **How would you like to use the time you have with them?**
   - Would you like to write a letter to place in their coffin?
   - Do you want to hold their hand?
   - Would you like to talk to them?
   - Is there something you'd like to place with them?
   - You could play music, light a candle or just be in reflective silence.
   - You might want to bring a friend for support, or you might want to be alone. If you're at a funeral home, you may wish to ask the funeral director to be in the room with you, or you may wish to be alone. This is your time.

6. **You can touch them, but they may feel cold**
   We don't need to be scared of someone who has died. They might look a bit different and may have begun to change but they're still your person. You can touch them, kiss them goodbye or hold their hand. Depending on how they've been cared for, they will probably feel cold if you touch them. Some people can find this shocking, but it's perfectly normal. If it isn't possible to touch them, for whatever reason, your funeral director will be able to advise.

7. **Even if the funeral director says no...**
   Just because someone isn't in good condition doesn't mean you can't spend meaningful time with them. A good funeral director will be able to help you to find a way to be with the person who has died in a way that works for you.

8. **What will you do afterwards?**
   Spending time with the person who has died is likely to be an intense and emotional experience. Make sure you give yourself time and space to process it and ask for support if you need it. Be gentle with yourself.

9. **Do what's right for you**
   Everyone has differing needs. Some people might find it helpful to see the person who has died, others won't. We all grieve in different ways. Just because someone else doesn't want to see them, doesn't mean you shouldn't want to. It's not about 'doing it right', it's about working out what's right for you. That's different for everyone.

Allowing children to do what is right for them

[A]

— John's Funeral

When John, Laura's husband, died at the age of 37, her three children, Kim (11), Joseph (seven) and Jenna (three), were vocal about what they wanted. They asked their mum to let them be with their dad for the last time so they could say goodbye.

It was a difficult choice to make and although it wasn't met with approval from her family and friends, Laura wanted to honour her children's wishes. Having time with their dead father went against convention and challenged our culture's ideas about death, but it helped her children to understand the reality of what had happened.

We helped them to be with him in a peaceful family room, where they were given plenty of time and space to do whatever they needed to do. It was important for them to say goodbye to him on their own terms and in their own way.

They wrote letters and made cards, tucking them next to him in his coffin. They sang songs to him and played the music he loved. They baked the chocolate brownies he used to make for them as an after-school treat. They wrapped one up in a napkin and put it in his coffin. They drew pictures and decided to keep them to remember their special day with him. They picked flowers from their garden and sprinkled them over him.

We talked about what was going to happen next – where their daddy would be going, how he'd get there and who would be looking after him. They understood he'd be in a cold room in the mortuary until the day of his funeral and how a special car called a hearse would bring him to the crematorium.

On the day of the funeral, they saw his hearse approaching at the top of the crematorium's drive. They ran over to say hello, choosing to walk alongside as it arrived at the chapel.

With the celebrant's help, they'd helped put together every part of the service. They'd chosen the music and the readings and had asked if they could sit right next to his coffin during the service. No one hurried them or told them how to be or what to feel. When they were ready to say goodbye, they kissed his coffin and left the chapel in their own time.

Laura gave her children a priceless gift. She listened to them. She gave them agency. She let them be in control. She let them express their grief in their own way. She let them say the goodbye they wanted and needed to say.

Laura wrote about why it had been so important to her: 'I had wanted to see my husband's body with our children, so they could see with their own eyes that their daddy was no longer alive.'

With guidance, support and an openness to allow her children to respond in the ways they needed, Laura gave her children the best opportunity to live a really good life despite the sadness of the situation. By acknowledging their needs and giving weight to them, she lightened the load of their grief by helping them to be present with the reality of it.

CHILDREN SHOULD BE SEEN AND HEARD

We actively encourage children to both talk and write about how they feel about death, dying, funerals and grief. Giving them the space to express how they feel is important. It can be thought-provoking, profound and beautiful. Allowing their voices to be heard is something we can all facilitate.

I miss you Dad. Wish I had talked and spent more time with you before you left.

#UNSAID

You drank too much.

#UNSAID

I wish that I spent more
time with my grandad

#UNSAID

To gran

I hope you reach 100
and go to the queen

good wishes from Fiona

xxxxxxx

#UNSAID

Gran, I wish I could have
come out to you before I died.
I still miss you.

#UNSAID

Why funerals really matter

[L]

'I'm so sorry,' people often say to us. 'I'm not very good at funerals.' 'You're not supposed to be,' we tell them. 'It's a funeral.'

Funerals aren't supposed to be something we're good at. Most of us have never arranged a funeral before. Some of us have never even been to a funeral. Some of us have been to a funeral where we've questioned whether it was a good reflection of the person who died. But a funeral doesn't have to be like the ones you've been to in the past or the ones you've seen on TV. You can create a funeral that works for you, is appropriate for the circumstances of the death and fits the way you're grieving.

When someone dies, our life changes. The enormity of the change can be huge, in many ways beyond the physical loss of the person. Funerals can serve as an acknowledgement of that enormous change and can help us to adjust to our new reality.

The person who has died may be a spouse, a partner, a relative, a friend, or the person we said hello to every day at the bus stop. Whoever it is, a funeral can serve as an acknowledgement that the physical presence of that person is now gone. A funeral is a way of making the death real.

It's not about perfection, it's about doing something that honours the person who has died while also allowing the living to do what they need to do. A good funeral can be a profound and transformational experience that can help the living to accept and acknowledge that someone has died.

It's not just the funeral itself that matters – it's the process of deciding what's important and meaningful, completing the paperwork, ordering the sandwiches and the sausage rolls, collecting photographs, watching old videos, coming together as family and friends to share memories and stories. The process of arranging a funeral gives us something to do at a time when we can feel like our lives are in chaos.

When my granny died in February 2018, we didn't have the opportunity to acknowledge her death. Before she died, she'd seen an advertisement for something called a direct cremation, where a person is cremated with no ceremony and no one in attendance. Having attended so many formulaic funerals for her friends, she decided funerals were a waste of time and money and insisted that she didn't want one. Like so many people of her generation, she didn't want any fuss.

This meant that we didn't come together as a family when she died. It meant life went on as normal, as though she were still sitting in her armchair in Devon, waiting for *Countdown* as she did her weekly shopping on her iPad. Whenever I thought of Granny, I couldn't imagine that empty chair in Devon. There had been no opportunity to come together as a family to acknowledge that she had died.

There was talk of organising a memorial with her ashes – but then life got in the way. A cousin was moving house, another had a new job in America, I was busy working. Without the urgency of a dead body to dispose of, the ceremony was put on the backburner, and it never happened.

We never had the opportunity to acknowledge the reality of my granny's death and this made grieving the loss of the matriarch of our family really difficult.

A funeral offers the opportunity to come together as family, friends or community, no matter how big or small, to offer support to each other. It gives everyone in that community a space in which to share their thoughts, feelings and memories about the person who has died. It's an opportunity to cry together, to laugh together or just to be together, with the sadness, pain, grief and tragedy of the situation.

It's also an opportunity to come together to learn new things about the person who has died. After a funeral, we often hear people saying 'I never knew Mum was so popular at work!' or 'Uncle John helped so many people at his church yet he never talked about it.'

A good funeral is created with the belief that funerals are about the dead but for the benefit of the living. A funeral can be whatever you want and need it to be. In the UK, there are no rules or laws about where it's held, who takes it or what it should include. The most important part of a funeral is to make sure that it does what it needs to do.

THINGS THAT ARE OK AT A FUNERAL

It's OK to wear black.
It's OK to wear colour.
It's OK to carry the coffin.
It's OK to touch the coffin.
It's OK to include children.
It's OK to feel everything.
It's OK to feel nothing.
It's OK to applaud.
It's OK to laugh.
It's OK to smile.
It's OK to cry.

How to have a good funeral

[L]

'That was the best and worst funeral I've ever been to,' is something we often hear people saying when they leave a funeral. That means it's been a good funeral.

They'll say it was the *best* because it was an accurate reflection of the person who had died – it really honoured them – and the *worst* because it made them feel something – it provided space for them to feel what needed to be felt.

Wherever you are in the world, and regardless of whether you're planning a more traditional or modern funeral service, you might want to take inspiration and encouragement from the points below. I've written them to help you to have what I understand to be a *good* funeral. Depending on where you are and what you believe, some of it might be suitable for you, some of it won't. Take what you need and leave the rest.

REFLECT ON THE PERSON WHO HAS DIED – WHAT MIGHT BE FITTING FOR THEM? WHAT WILL SERVE THOSE LEFT BEHIND?

Whenever I meet a client for the first time, I often talk to them about the person who has died over several cups of tea. We'll discuss their life, loves, work, passions, values, hobbies, family, relationships, beliefs, aspirations, dreams and desires as well as the circumstances of their death and the effect it's having on those who are grieving.

If you're faced with planning a funeral, you might want to begin by considering the questions below:

- Did the person who has died leave any wishes?
- What are the circumstances of their death? How will this be reflected in the funeral ceremony? Will it be traditional? Solemn? Informal? Formal? More creative?
- Who is the funeral for? Who will be attending? What do they need from the funeral? Are there any restrictions in place?
- What are the beliefs of the person who has died? What are the beliefs of the people attending? Is this important?
- What did they love? What did they value? What was their life like? What words come to mind when you think about them?

There are no rules where funerals are concerned. You can start from a blank page and work from there. There's no standard way to live, die or say goodbye.

TRADITIONAL BURIAL, NATURAL BURIAL, SEA BURIAL OR CREMATION?

Unless the person who has died has left explicit instructions, you might not know whether they'd like to be buried or cremated.

— Susan's Funeral

Philip was visibly distressed when I met with him to talk about his wife Susan's funeral. She had died suddenly and they'd never had a conversation about what either of them wanted for their funerals.

I reassured Philip that lots of people don't talk about it and that's OK. This meant he could decide what would work for him and their large family, which included several stepchildren and lots of grandchildren, spread out across the UK.

We talked about burial in a traditional cemetery in their local area, which meant that Philip could erect a headstone and then have somewhere to visit. We discussed cremation, and talked about how this would mean he could have Susan's ashes and could decide what happened to them. We talked about natural burial – the idea that Susan would be returned to the earth in the most environmentally friendly way possible, either in a woodland, field or meadow. He liked the idea, but was concerned that many natural burial grounds won't allow any kind of marker for the grave. Some do, perhaps a tree, a bush or a wooden marker, but his local natural burial ground's ethos was all about becoming part of the landscape.

Susan could also have been buried at sea, one of around only 12 such burials that takes place in the UK every year.

Philip decided to cremate Susan so he could bring her ashes home with him. He was aware that he would be moving into a nursing home at some point in the near future, and didn't like the idea that he'd be too unwell to visit her grave. Having her cremated meant that he could keep a part of her with him, wherever he was.

FIVE THINGS I WISH EVERYONE KNEW ABOUT THE CREMATION PROCESS

by Natasha Bradshaw

Natasha is the superintendent of Mortlake Crematorium in London.

1.
The cremation does not take place when the curtains close. It takes place in a different room called the crematory up to 72 hours after the service.

2.
Each person is cremated separately. However, cremations of two people can take place together if the cremation applicant or next of kin makes a request. This might happen when partners or a parent and child die.

3.
Ashes of pets can be cremated with the person or mixed together afterwards.

4.
Any metals such as artificial hips, knees, and pacemakers are recycled and the money goes to bereavement charities in the UK.

5.
In cases where a coroner is not involved, doctors will complete paperwork to ensure all is correct. This can be reassuring to anyone who worries they won't be dead when they're cremated.

YOU DON'T ACTUALLY HAVE TO HAVE A FUNERAL CEREMONY

David Bowie *allegedly* did it (although we're not convinced). Karl Lagerfeld did it. Even my granny did it. It's called direct cremation: when the person who has died is cremated without a ceremony or anyone in attendance. There are various forms of direct cremation.

There are the big companies who operate nationwide and will collect the person who has died from wherever they are and then cremate them at their convenience with no one in attendance. The ashes will be returned to their family at a later date. These are the true direct cremation operators, who are turning the disposal of our dead into an industrial process.

You can also ask your local funeral director to arrange a direct cremation. Most will do this and may allow you to attend, others won't. They might also allow you to come to see the person who has died before the cremation takes place. I call this a simple cremation rather than a direct cremation because it's more flexible. There might not be a formal ceremony, but you might still be allowed to go to the crematorium to witness what's happening.

A direct cremation is undoubtedly a lot cheaper than a traditional funeral. There's no hearse, no funeral director and no fuss. Which is why a lot of people like it.

It's growing in popularity in the UK but it's controversial – the effects of not acknowledging the death on long-term grief are currently unknown.

Direct cremation is popular with a generation of people who might say, 'Oh don't waste your money on a funeral for me.' Whenever someone is pre-planning their funeral and requests a direct cremation service, I ask them to think it through very carefully and to find out from the people who will be affected by their death what they might want and need. There's often tension between what the person who is going to die wants, and what their family and friends need.

Sometimes direct cremation can be helpful. It all depends on whether you think there's value in the body of the person who has died being present when everyone gathers to say goodbye. When strict restrictions were in place due to COVID-19, many people had to organise a direct cremation for the person who had died, even when they really wanted to attend the funeral service.

— Frank's Funeral

Frank's family were ill with COVID-19 and couldn't safely attend his funeral. They asked the funeral director to play Frank's favourite music as his coffin was committed. They played the same music and lit a candle at home as the committal was taking place. They later arranged a memorial service when it was safe for his closest family and friends to come together.

YOU CAN CHOOSE THE KIND OF CEREMONY, RELIGIOUS OR OTHERWISE

If you decide to have a funeral service, you'll need to make some decisions about the kind of ceremony you'd like.

If you've chosen a religious or faith-based service, you will have to follow the structure, rituals and traditions of that particular faith. Depending on your religion, you might still be able to incorporate some of the ideas from this section into the funeral.

If you're coming from a secular perspective, it's wise to think carefully about introducing rituals that are going to be helpful, meaningful and relevant, because you won't be able to defer to the customs of a particular faith. This gives you a blank canvas to create a funeral that works for you.

Religious/faith-based services

If you want to have a religious funeral, you will be in the hands of a religious leader such as an imam, a vicar or a rabbi. A religious ceremony has a fixed structure to follow and is likely to concentrate on worshipping God and preparing for the afterlife. Some denominations, such as the Church of England, will allow a degree of personalisation, others, such as Catholic funeral services, will be more rigid.

Some of the loveliest funerals we've facilitated have been when the local church has been at the heart of the community surrounding the person who has died. Friends and family have come together to decorate the church with flowers from their gardens, the choir have all been friends with the person who has died and everyone has walked behind the hearse from the family home to the church. It has felt like a community truly coming together to support each other in their loss.

Celebrant-led ceremonies

Funeral celebrants will facilitate the funeral that you'd like to have based on your beliefs, not theirs. There's a whole spectrum of celebrants with different styles and offerings. Some celebrants are brilliant, others aren't so good. Some will include religious elements such as prayers and hymns, others won't. Some will work from a template, others will write a ceremony that's totally personal to you and the person who has died.

A good celebrant will visit you at home and spend time talking about the person who has died before putting together the funeral. They'll then work with you to make sure the ceremony flows in a way that works for you.

A Google search will reveal celebrants in your area. Call them and have a chat about what you want. If you're working with a good funeral director, they should be able to recommend a suitable celebrant. If you don't like the person they suggest, you can choose someone else. Because standards are so variable, it's a good idea to talk to several funeral celebrants before you appoint the person who feels right for you.

Multi-faith ceremonies

Belief systems can be complicated. Everyone may have differing needs, but they don't need to clash. I once worked with an imam to put together a funeral ceremony for a young woman who had died unexpectedly. Her family were religious so prayers were important to them; her friends from university were mostly secular and needed to talk about the life she had lived and what she had meant to them. By being flexible and considerate of the beliefs of others and being prepared to work together, her funeral met everyone's needs.

Friend-/family-led ceremonies

You (or a relative or friend) can lead the funeral service yourself. You can put together the ceremony or appoint a flexible celebrant to assist you with certain elements, such as the structure. It can be a lot of work and pressure on the day, especially if you're emotional, so it's good to have a back-up plan.

WE CAN CELEBRATE A LIFE WITHOUT FORGETTING TO MOURN A DEATH

Grief is a mix of numbness, sadness, regret, anger and gratitude with no set timeline or structure. Making sure we allow space at the funeral for all these emotions is important.

Although we have choreographed the arrival of a coffin to enter the chapel at the exact moment the beat dropped to a dance track from Ibiza, it's not about turning funerals into parties, nor is it about only celebrating life and just acknowledging the positives.

It might be that a pink coffin, fireworks and champagne are relevant and meaningful to the person who has died as well as suitable for the circumstances of their death. But it might be that a funeral that allows people to express the extent of their sadness while still acknowledging what a wonderful life the person lived is more appropriate. It really does depend on the circumstances.

A celebration of life fit really well for Lily, who died at the age of 104 surrounded by her huge family after a long and joyful life. But a celebration of life that dismissed the deep sadness and despair everyone was feeling wasn't so fitting for Ben, who died by suicide on his 25th birthday, having lived with depression for many years.

The most helpful funerals we've seen have been brave and bold in being exactly what is required of the situation, however painful that is. They've allowed the people attending to do exactly what they've needed to do. We can still celebrate a life, without forgetting to mourn a death. As my friend and colleague, humanist celebrant Natalie Charles says: 'If you can't cry at a funeral, where can you cry?'

THE DEAD

They've got a nerve, the dead,
with their insufferable absences
while we are left to dig
deep for the funeral director's
order of service,
coffin, music, flowers –
at the wake
distant cousins devour
pleasantries and leave early for trains.

They are never alone, the dead,
their unholy alliance with
the loved relative,
the stolen friend,
the young, the beautiful, the doomed,
injustice like
a blind scythe whistling in the high field
while we, resigned,
fill in paperwork for
doctor, registrar,
poet.

They've got places to go, the dead,
behind veils they steal,
mysterious, incorporeal,
a conspiracy of silence,
raised and translated
to grandeur,
to questions no answer.

Pressing your head against cold stone,
you cannot move
at the thought
of clearing her room.

STEVE HALLIWELL

YOU DON'T HAVE TO GO TO THE CHURCH OR CREMATORIUM

There are no rules concerning where funerals can take place. You're not restricted to the crematorium, cemetery or a religious centre.

Crematoria
Some crematoria are beautiful spaces, others operate more like a conveyor belt. You don't have to go to your local crematorium if it doesn't suit your needs. You can make an appointment to have a look round in advance and decide if the crematorium is right for you.

Crematoria usually have service times from 20 minutes up to an hour. If you know that there's going to be a lot of content during the ceremony, it's advisable to book extra time.

Cemeteries
Traditional cemeteries will often have a chapel where the funeral can take place. These chapels are often beautiful and historic spaces that are hardly used, so you could consider having the service there, even if the burial will take place somewhere else.

Churches and other religious centres
If you subscribe to the beliefs of a particular religion, and you're willing to go along with their customs and rituals, you can have the funeral in a religious centre such as a synagogue, mosque or temple.

Natural burial grounds
These are usually set in beautiful and peaceful locations you can return to over time. Some have ceremonial buildings on site where the funeral ceremony can be held without the time pressures of the crematorium. You could even hold the whole service outside at the graveside.

Other venues
There are no laws about where a funeral can be held, although restrictions may be in place during a COVID-19 outbreak. Community centres, cafes, pubs, theatres and historic houses may work well for you, but check that they will allow the coffin to be there if that's what you want. You can even hold the funeral at home or in your garden.

Alternatively, you can go to a venue first for the main part of the ceremony, and then go to the crematorium or burial site. You can also have the cremation or burial first, and then go somewhere else afterwards.

MAKE IT PERSONAL

Cars

Hearses come in every colour of the rainbow, including an actual rainbow. You can choose to transport the coffin with horses, carts, flatbed trucks, bicycles, motorbikes, converted camper vans, tanks, fire engines, Morris Minors and more. There's also a hearsette, which is a normal vehicle that has a hidden coffin deck in the back. You can even use your own vehicle, provided that the coffin can fit into the back safely and securely.

Some people like to have a funeral cortège with limousines following the hearse on a specific route. We've taken people through their favourite parks, driven past their first home, their children's schools, their nursing home and their friends' homes. We've witnessed people who haven't been able to attend the funeral due to COVID-19 restrictions, old age or ill health, stepping outside to wave as we slowly drove by.

— Iris' Funeral

Iris had lived in South West London for her entire life, so for her funeral we met at the entrance to her local park and then wound through the streets in a cream vintage Daimler hearse, passing the places she loved: the pub where she'd met her husband, the schools her children had attended and the places where she'd hung out with her friends. Her family and friends followed in their own cars, with bunches of pink roses attached to both wing mirrors to show that this was a funeral cortège.

You can also use your own cars, or taxis, and meet the hearse directly at the crematorium or cemetery – it will save lots of money on the funeral bill.

Coffins

Long gone are the days of funeral directors only offering expensive mahogany coffins and enquiring about your preference for 'coffin furniture'. Just to give you an idea of the many options available, here are some coffins from the brochures currently on my desk:

Wood-effect coffins, veneered coffins. Solid wooden coffins made from oak, golden oak, walnut and mahogany. Biodegradable pine coffins for burial. Solid wood coffins carved with scenes from the Bible. Painted coffins in any colour of your choosing. Zinc-lined coffins and caskets for repatriation. Coffins made from recycled pallets. American caskets, wooden or metal. Coffins painted in blackboard paint for writing on. Natural and environmentally friendly coffins including but not limited to seagrass, banana leaf, pandanus (wild pineapple), Yorkshire wool, bamboo, sweetcorn leaves, English or European willow, coloured willow. There's the option to weave a willow coffin yourself. Coffins covered in glitter. Cardboard coffins (note – cardboard isn't as cheap as most people think, due to the extensive labour required to make them strong enough to hold a person). Flatpack coffins. Build-your-own coffins. Shrouds. Cotton shrouds. Bamboo shrouds. Cradles. Felt cocoons. You can even get involved with decorating the coffin yourself if you wish.

This list isn't exhaustive!

We've seen interactive coffins featuring crosswords and puzzles, a coffin that was covered in handprints and paw prints, and even a coffin that had a small post-box at the end, so family and friends could write messages to the person who had died and post them to him.

— Chrissy's Funeral

When Chrissy Robinson died, his friends wanted to come together to celebrate his life in a way that was characteristically *Chrissy*. He had a boat in Emsworth, which he loved to sail. Inspired by his pastime, his friends commissioned a boat-shaped wicker coffin. He arrived at the crematorium in serious style – in his wicker boat in a leopard-print hearse full of beautifully vibrant wildflowers.

YOU'RE NOT RESTRICTED TO THREE PIECES OF MUSIC

We've been compiling a list of misconceptions people have about playing music at funerals. The most common is the idea you're only allowed three pieces of music at the crematorium. A client once told us that you have to have hymns. Another client claimed that you're only allowed to listen to each piece of music for 20 seconds before it's faded out. Another client thought that the organist would have to play the songs she'd chosen on the organ. She was struggling to imagine what Beyoncé would sound like when played on the crematorium's organ.

Whether it's Elgar or Eminem, you can play the music you want to play. Don't let anyone tell you otherwise. You can also have as many pieces of music as you want provided that it fits into the time available. You might want to have a piece of music as everyone goes into the funeral, and another piece as the coffin is brought in. You could also have music for reflection, for the committal (more on this later) as well as when everyone is leaving. There are no rules.

It's worth considering that whatever music you choose will forever be linked with the funeral. For instance, when Jason chose a popular track for his wife's funeral, he didn't realise that it would be played in every shop, bar and cafe he went into that summer. He found it unbearable to listen to.

You don't actually have to have any music at all. Silence can be powerful, but it can also be painful. Music tends to lead our emotions. Even a short silence can feel like it's lasting a lifetime.

— Bob's Funeral

Bob's four children couldn't remember a time when he wasn't listening to his local radio station. We made sure the time of his funeral coincided with his favourite radio programme so it began as his coffin was brought into the chapel.

— Peter's Funeral

Peter's funeral was at a natural burial ground. His friend, a guitarist, played 'Whole Lotta Love' by Led Zeppelin as a procession of his friends and family walked through the woodland to his grave

— Charlotte's Funeral

Charlotte's family serenaded her arrival with her favourite song and a candlelit procession. They each held a lantern and sang 'She'll Be Coming 'Round the Mountain' as her coffin was carried into the service hall.

WORDS MATTER

Although there are no rules, this is a simple structure for a funeral service. You may wish to change it depending on how much content you have and what you'd like to include. It may also depend on how you're saying goodbye and where the service is going to be.

Entrance music
Words of welcome (including remembering those who can't be there)
The eulogy/tributes/poems/readings
Committal (the formal farewell)
Closing words
Closing music

Writing a eulogy or tribute
Writing a eulogy or giving a tribute at the funeral can feel like a huge and daunting responsibility.

Sometimes a eulogy is a chronicle of a person's life from when they were born until they died. I've heard eulogies that have listed every detail of someone's life, including the names of all their infant school teachers. Others are more creative, insightful or poetic.

You don't necessarily need to speak for everyone present, or to document the person's whole life in painstaking detail. You might want to talk about:

- Your memories of them.
- Your favourite stories.
- What they loved.
- What they represented.
- Their values.
- The impact of their work.
- The things you've learned from them.
- How they made you feel.
- Any good advice they gave.
- What you will miss about them.
- The legacy they will leave.

Some of the most touching tributes we've heard have worked because they were just so honest and heartfelt. They didn't glorify the person and most of them weren't perfectly written, they were simply genuine and sincere in the way they honoured the person who had died.

You might want to read your words out loud several times both on your own and in front of people. It's a good idea to get used to the emotion behind the words you're going to say before you read them at the funeral.

Don't put pressure on yourself to deliver the tribute perfectly. It's OK to be overwhelmed and upset. Just take a moment and then continue if you can. You might want to have someone allocated to take over if you decide you really can't continue.

— Lindsay's Funeral

When Lindsay died, her mother wrote a tribute based around the letters of her name. Each letter of her name represented a different memory of her daughter. She asked her grandchildren – Lindsay's children and her nieces and nephews – to stand at the front as she read. As each letter was read out, each child held up a print of a giant illustrated letter. By the end of the tribute, LINDSAY was spelled out.

Sometimes tributes are refreshingly honest. Often in the most difficult of circumstances, speaking the truth is the most direct way of dealing with the elephant in the room.

When 13-year-old Joel's father died from the consequences of his drug addiction, Joel spoke with a rare openness and honesty about his life:

'My dad died because he had problems with drugs. I always knew that he loved me, my mum and my sisters. But because of his problems with drugs, he was unable to be there for us. He was very poorly at the end and I'm glad he doesn't have to go through pain any more. I will miss the dad I never got to properly know.'

CHOOSING POETRY

Poets can be our spokespeople when we're otherwise lost for words. In the words of my friend, writer Rose Heiney: 'I realised there's a poem for every situation, every feeling that you've ever encountered. EVER. There's pain in life, and there's the antidote for pain, which Is poetry.'

Putting together the order of service

The order of service is the programme that's given out at the beginning of the funeral. It may list the order of events, as well as anything that needs to be mentioned, such as details of the wake, any announcements or any charitable donations as well as any words of thanks.

The order of service is important: it guides the mourners through the funeral service and is something they may wish to take away with them as a keepsake. It also provides an emotional focus while planning the funeral. It's usually a collective effort, serving as an opportunity for everyone to come together to decide what's meaningful and relevant to them. Agreeing what goes in it can also be incredibly stressful, so if there's any time that tensions between family members are going to be tested, it's when the order of service deadline is approaching!

We often put together orders of service with collages of photographs. This is another important part of the process: it's an opportunity to look through photos together, share memories and remember things that may have been forgotten.

There's often someone who is happy to take responsibility for the order of service. Perhaps a family member or friend will be willing to design something beautifully, too. The more hands on you can be, the better. It's all part of the process.

Some orders of service are really unique. David's order of service contained a letter from him about his life and his death, written before he died. Our friend Jon Underwood's order of service included a joke he'd posted on Facebook a few weeks earlier.

An order of service doesn't need to be a traditional booklet. You can get creative.

— Florence's Funeral

Florence was a prolific baker. She had piles of handwritten recipe cards in her kitchen. For her funeral, her family had her most-loved recipes printed out on to postcards that were given out during the service. One postcard detailed the funeral itself, the others were handwritten recipe cards for her lemon drizzle cake and Yorkshire puddings, accompanied by photographs of Florence in her kitchen wearing her favourite apron.

Apart from the format and the design, you can also get creative with the wording. You might want to find a way of thanking the people who have attended the funeral, shown up for you in your grief or for the support shown towards the end of someone's life.

— Charlie's Funeral

The words on the back of Charlie's order of service were heartfelt: 'Charlie's family would like to extend their love and gratitude to you all for being a part of his short but extraordinary life. Thank you.'

— Ben's Funeral

Ben's order of service had very few words at all. The order simply listed who would be speaking and in what order:

'Remembering Ben
A Friend
A Brother
An Uncle
A Father
A Son
A Husband'

The rest of the order of service was taken up with beautiful photos of the beautiful relationships that made up his life.

GETTING EVERYONE TO PARTICIPATE REALLY HELPS

Funerals don't have to be static, stiff affairs during which we worry about what we're supposed to do and where we're supposed to stand.

Participating in the funeral can really help us to feel involved at a time of overwhelming sadness. It's an opportunity to do something for the person who has died, to express our love for them and be part of something much bigger than ourselves.

— Jenny's Funeral

Six of Jenny's friends from her choir carried her coffin into the chapel. They were all women and didn't know that, as women, they were allowed to carry their friend. They had previously believed that only professional male pall-bearers, provided by the funeral director, could do so.

— Dawn's Funeral

Gina didn't feel that she could do very much at her partner's funeral other than be there. Her role was to light a special candle (which she'd chosen) at the beginning of the funeral to mark the opening of the space. At the end of the funeral, she closed the space by blowing it out.

— Hetty's Funeral

At Hetty's funeral, everyone came together to sing a song. Her family chose 'Thank you for the Music' by Abba.

— Jyoti's Funeral

For Jyoti's funeral, her friends donated their old teapots. On the day of the funeral, the aisles of the church were lined with teapots, now full of wildflowers. Guests were invited to pick a teapot and take it home with them after the service.

— Milly's Funeral

Message writing can be a powerful way of getting everyone involved while giving them the opportunity to express their thoughts and feelings about the person who has died. During Milly's service, everyone was handed a heart-shaped tag and asked to write a message to her. Her family and closest friends had already written letters to her then wrapped them in wildflowers. As music played, they were invited to come up to her banana leaf coffin to tie on their messages and place their letters. The words of love and gratitude went with Milly to her final resting place.

— Laurence's Funeral

Mark arranged for his friend Laurence's coffin to be painted in his favourite shade of vivid green. The celebrant then invited everyone to place a white rose on the coffin as his favourite song played.

CHILDREN CAN BE INVOLVED TOO

We're often asked whether it's OK to include children in the funeral. Parents and guardians are often concerned that it will just be too distressing and traumatic for them to experience.

It's very much an individual decision but our experiences have led us to believe that funerals can be a positive, healthy and helpful experience for children (and adults!). It's possible to create a safe space in which they can feel welcome and part of the proceedings.

Children are creative, resilient and curious and we frequently encourage them to participate in the funeral itself, as well as the planning. They often have ideas of their own about how they'd like to be involved.

— Fred's Funeral

At Fred's funeral, his grandchildren (aged five, eight and 10) played an active role. They stood at the entrance to the chapel and gave out orders of service. At the end of the service, they handed out packets of forget-me-nots for everyone to take home and plant in their gardens.

— Charlotte's Funeral

Jessica (aged four) and Katie (aged six) loved to sing to their Auntie Charlotte. At her funeral, they stood up together and sang their favourite goodbye song to her:

'See you later, alligator,
In a while, crocodile,
Give a hug, ladybug,
Blow a kiss, jellyfish.'

— Chunhua and Lijuan's Dad's Funeral

Chunhua (aged three) and Lijuan (aged five) came to their dad's funeral. They were always blowing bubbles with their dad, even when he was in his hospital bed. So at the funeral, everyone was given a small bottle of bubble mixture and blew bubbles as his favourite song played.

— Lottie's Dad's Funeral

Lottie (aged seven) felt shy around people she didn't know. She didn't want to do anything at the funeral itself, but she wanted to be involved in putting it together. She helped her mum to choose the coffin for her dad, deciding on a cardboard one that could be decorated. Lottie drew lots of pictures of her memories of her dad on pieces of paper and stuck them on to the coffin with butterflies, glitter and stickers. At the funeral, she was delighted when the vicar mentioned her contribution.

— Noah's Sister's Funeral

Noah (aged four) wanted his favourite bedtime story to be read to his stillborn baby sister, after it had been explained to him that she had died at the hospital and wouldn't be coming home to join their family.

Although we may want to protect children from the truth, talking in euphemisms about the funeral can do more harm than good. 'Granny is going on a journey' or 'Uncle Ben's going for a long sleep' can cause confusion and distress.

Children will make up what they don't know so it's best to be straightforward and direct: 'Uncle Benjamin has died. That means he isn't going to be around any more but it doesn't mean he loves you any less. We're going to be going to a special event for Benjamin, called a funeral, where we're going to hear lots of amazing things about him as we say goodbye.'

THE COMMITTAL

At some point during the funeral, the time will come for the formal goodbye. This is called the committal and it's when the person who has died is taken away for the final time. It's the moment of separation – when the person who has died is separated from the living and 'joins' the dead. This is when you may hear the traditional committal words – 'ashes to ashes, dust to dust' – taken from the Book of Common Prayer.

Cremation and burial both have different forms of committal.

Cremation

Each crematorium is set up very differently. The coffin may be placed on a platform called a catafalque. When the moment comes, a set of doors may open behind the coffin and it will glide away. Sometimes the coffin will go down instead. At most crematoria, catafalques are surrounded by mechanised curtains. Once a button is pressed, the curtains will close around the coffin. This may mean that you don't see the coffin gliding away or going down.

It's up to you whether you'd like the curtains to be closed or if you'd prefer them to stay open. You might want to press the button yourself.

You can also ignore the catafalque completely and ask for the coffin to be placed on trestles, which can be placed closer to the mourners.

WITNESSING THE START OF THE CREMATION

It's a popular misconception that the coffin will go through the doors and straight into the flames. The reality is that it will go into a room behind the catafalque, and then be taken to the crematory for the cremation to take place. If requested in advance, you're allowed to watch the charging of the coffin. This is when the coffin goes into the cremator. Some people want to watch for religious reasons. Others want to watch it because it's the genuine moment of goodbye. It can be very beautiful – as the coffin is pushed into the cremator, hundreds of orange sparks light up the air, and then the doors quickly close.

Burial

Burying our dead is possibly the most earthly expression of our grief. The reality of the grave confronting the mourners and the sheer physicality of the coffin being lowered into the ground as the person returns to the earth makes the death crushingly and heartbreakingly real. Rabbi Maurice Lamm talks about 'the heart-rending thud of earth on the casket' as being enormously beneficial from a psychological perspective. There's no avoiding it, no denying it. This is the substance of life itself, as earthy, raw and real as it can get.

The point of committal is more obvious when someone is buried. They are lowered down into the earth, accompanied by words, music or just silence.

— Nancy's Funeral

Nancy's family and friends sang a well-known lullaby as her coffin was lowered into the earth. They threw handfuls of rose petals mixed with sprigs of rosemary into her grave.

— David's Funeral

David's family asked everyone to collect a golden autumnal leaf as they walked through the cemetery, following his coffin to his grave. After he'd been lowered into the earth, everyone filed past, throwing their chosen leaf into the grave.

— Adam's Funeral

Adam's family stood around his grave in silence as snow began to fall, gradually covering his coffin.

YOU DON'T HAVE TO LEAVE THE FLOWERS AT THE CREMATORIUM

At the crematorium, flowers are usually placed on the flower terrace, where they may stay for several days. Traditionally, this is where everyone will gather after the service to make small talk and look at the flowers. At a burial, the flowers are usually placed on the grave after it's been filled in.

If you don't want to leave the flowers at the crematorium or on the grave, you can take them away with you.

— Betty's Funeral

At Betty's funeral, we dismantled the beautiful wildflower coffin spray and gave small bunches out to the mourners. They went to the wake with purple and yellow flowers in their hair and buttonholes.

— Rosalind's Funeral

At Rosalind's funeral, her family took a selection of flowers home with them and then had them pressed and placed into a special album along with photographs of the funeral.

You don't have to have flowers. Some people prefer to ask for donations to a charity. Others prefer to get creative.

— Rod's Funeral

Rod loved growing vegetables in his allotment so his family made a special wreath of the autumnal vegetables he'd grown before he died.

— Seamus' Funeral

Seamus loved the country of his birth, Ireland. His coffin was draped in an Irish flag. His daughter placed his favourite hat, scarf and pipe on top of the coffin.

— Mickey's Funeral

Mickey didn't like flowers, but he liked cake, so his partner made a multi-layered cake to put on top of his coffin. After the funeral, the cake was taken to the wake and cut into generous slices for everyone to enjoy.

— Celia's Funeral

Celia loved arts and crafts. Her family made garlands of flowers out of tissue paper and had them draped around her coffin. They also decorated the pews in the church with matching tissue paper flowers in every colour of the rainbow.

ARRANGING THE WAKE

It's thought that wakes were originally an opportunity to ensure the person who had died was really dead. Mourners would keep watch or 'vigil' over them before their funeral. In the UK today, a wake is more like a party or a gathering after the funeral has taken place.

Organising the wake is like organising the order of service. In the chaos following someone's death, it's an opportunity for everyone to come together as a family (or friends) to argue over sandwich fillings and sausage rolls! It can provide an important focus.

If you're the main person organising the funeral, it's worth not taking on too much responsibility on the day itself. Delegate! It's best not to be the sole person responsible for doing all the catering, for example. Either ask guests to help out or employ professionals.

After the funeral service is over, generally everyone wants some good hearty food, cups of hot tea and coffee and some cake. Some people like a stiff drink.

Wakes don't need to take place at home or in a pub. We've seen families go to historic houses for afternoon tea or for a walk in the park followed by a picnic.

Wakes also don't need to be called wakes. They can be after-parties, celebrations or simply gatherings. They might be short and sweet or they might go on late into the night and beyond.

You might want to fill the venue with photographs or have albums on display. You might even want to create an altar, where people can leave their memories in a book.

— Julia's Wake

When his wife Julia died, Paul created a memory board and displayed it in the function room of their favourite pub. Everyone was invited to bring their favourite photograph of her to add to the collection.

— Craig's Wake

At Craig's wake, his family had brought along his huge collection of books. Everyone was invited to take a book home with them.

— Laura's Wake

Laura loved food and many of her relationships centred around her passion. After her funeral, everyone was invited to bring a dish they associated with her to her parents' house for the wake. They created an altar where everyone placed their dish and shared the story of why they'd chosen it. After the sharing, everyone was invited to tuck in to the feast.

THERE ARE LOTS OF THINGS YOU CAN DO WITH THE ASHES

My grandad's ashes were buried in his beloved garden. My grandma planted flowers and installed a bench there, so she could sit and have a cup of tea next to him every day. Florence, my niece, was five at the time. 'Grandad died and is now growing into a flower,' she told me.

There's no rush to decide what to do with the ashes, but the options are endless. Just a few ideas: ashes can be made into jewellery, be released into space, become a firework, become incorporated into a tattoo by being mixed with the ink, be scattered in the sea, be stored in a barrow in the countryside, or simply sit on someone's fireplace in an urn.

Although there are thousands of different styles of urns, you don't necessarily have to buy one. You might want to use an old biscuit tin or jam jars – whatever's meaningful to you. You could also commission an artist to create something special in which to store or incorporate the ashes.

— Jayne's Experience

When Jayne's mum died, she decided to release her ashes into the Thames. We hired a boat and sailed down the river until we found a quiet area. Jayne then leaned over the edge of the boat and scattered her mum's ashes into the water. The ashes looked like a universe exploding into the water, as they dispersed into a million tiny fragments.

Funerals & COVID-19

[L]

'Our duty was to the people who had placed the dead in our care, and to those yet to do so. We had all freely chosen this path, and now we would fulfil our duty, just as those in the NHS and other essential services would do.'
DAVID HOLMES, FUNERAL DIRECTOR

Most of the world had never even heard of PPE until March 2020. Then overnight, personal protective equipment (PPE) became one of the most highly sought-after commodities of recent times.

As coronavirus spread through China in January 2020, I earnestly stocked the mortuary cupboard with plentiful amounts of PPE – FFP3 respirator masks, eye protectors, gowns and gloves. My colleagues in the funeral industry looked on in confusion and bemusement.

By April 2020, we were looking after three times the number of people we would normally have in our care. 90% of them had died either with or from COVID-19. Our plentiful supplies of PPE from earlier in the year were running out. New supplies were impossible to find. Everything I could find was being sold at an outrageous premium.

As coronavirus-related deaths were peaking in London, uncertainty and confusion reigned. Funeral directors tried to serve the people in their care whilst also keeping everyone safe. Questions were left unanswered. How infectious was the virus after death? Would our entire workforce fall ill? Could we safely collect and take care of people who had died with COVID-19?

We began taking calls from nursing homes where the virus had already spread uncontrollably and PPE was in short supply. We watched as huge temporary mortuaries were constructed all over London. We tried to source coffins as suppliers became overwhelmed. We waited for the government to act to restrict, or even ban, funerals. We collaborated with other funeral directors to share equipment and provide moral support. Every week, we reported the number of people in our care to the London Resilience Forum, who were tasked with ensuring the funeral system didn't collapse.

When lockdown was finally introduced, funerals became remote and restricted, and had to be reimagined. We had to go against all of our beliefs as progressive funeral directors. We stopped encouraging people to participate in all elements of the funeral and found ourselves saying, 'I'm so sorry, it's just not safe to do that right now.' At the peak of the first wave of the pandemic in April 2020, funerals became less about allowing grieving people to do what they needed to do, and more about the efficient and safe disposal of the dead during an international crisis.

Every hour, we dealt with another shocked and traumatised family. 'But how do I know it's really my father?' Hossein asked my colleague Joanna every day. He'd last seen his father, Abir, when an ambulance rushed him to hospital with COVID-19-related breathing difficulties. Two weeks later, we gathered at the cemetery for Abir's funeral. Abir was zipped into two body bags within a sealed coffin. The service lasted just 10 minutes before the gravediggers, wearing full PPE, sprayed the grave with disinfectant and began filling it with soil. Wearing our masks, we stood far away from the family, and watched as they fell to the floor and wept.

With so many restrictions in place, there had never been a better time to dismiss funerals altogether. But funerals weren't dismissed. People *really* wanted to be there to say goodbye, even if the funeral was restricted and often remote. They found creative ways to stay safe whilst honouring the life of the person who had died. Sometimes that meant simply blowing a kiss from a distance or playing a pre-recorded voice note over the crematorium's sound system. For many, it meant watching the funeral remotely on a computer screen at home and trying to find a way to connect with the other virtual attendees. People lit candles, raised glasses and shared photos, using the wonder of technology. Everyone wanted, and needed, to find a way to connect, to acknowledge their pain and to mourn together.

Communities came together in a way I haven't seen in my lifetime. People stood outside their homes in droves to honour the person in the hearse as it made its way to the crematorium. Streets of strangers donated flowers because florists were closed. People showed up for their friends, for their family and for total strangers.

As I write this, the pandemic is far from over. Restricted and remote funerals have now become the norm. The number of people allowed at a funeral may have increased from 10 to around 30, but with infection rates rising, we're waiting for stricter restrictions to be re-introduced.

We're prepared this time. The team has become skilled at arranging funerals without meeting bereaved people face-to-face. We understand a little more about the virus and how infectious it is after death. Our PPE cupboard is re-stocked and ready to go. We're used to wearing masks whilst having sensitive conversations. Hosting funerals on Zoom no longer seems like an alien concept.

It's difficult to arrange a funeral in normal circumstances, never mind during a pandemic. Even with restrictions in place, I've been constantly inspired by people's resilience, resourcefulness and creativity. In the midst of enormous grief, impossible circumstances and a highly infectious virus, funerals *really* matter.

— Ekon's funeral

Very few people were able to attend Ekon's burial due to the strict restrictions that were in place. His friends came together to create a live radio show that honoured his love for music and career as a DJ. On the evening of his burial, everyone was able to tune into the show, and listen to music and tributes in his honour, from the safety of their own homes.

— Beth's funeral

Beth's family lived abroad and could not travel to London to attend her funeral. Her daughter, Ruby, asked her closest childhood friend to attend on her behalf. They connected over Zoom so Ruby could be more intimately involved with the funeral than the crematorium's fixed camera would allow.

— In Salvo's honour

When Salvo died abroad during lockdown, my friends were unable to attend his funeral. They felt they needed to acknowledge the shock and tragedy of his death so they contacted the Catholic church he attended in London. The priest suggested dedicating a mass to Salvo. We attended the mass on a Saturday morning then gathered in a local park to reminisce, observing social distancing but still coming together in our collective grief.

FIVE THINGS I'VE LEARNED ABOUT FUNERALS THROUGH THE COVID-19 CRISIS

by Hannah Jackson-McCamley

Hannah works as a celebrant in London. She has worked throughout the pandemic, helping people to find meaning within a restricted funeral ceremony.

1.

When someone we love dies, our world can feel like it's been turned upside down. To experience a death when the world actually is upside down is even more fraught, confusing and scary. Yet amidst all the madness during the initial COVID-19 outbreak, I witnessed more kindness, resilience and compassion than ever before.

2.

Funerals were restricted with fewer people allowed to attend, sometimes no flowers available, not even a picture on the catafalque. It was awful to have to say 'no' to the smallest request. Yet people showed unbelievable gratitude for the simplest things – a recorded tribute by someone not there, holding a picture brought from home, wearing a piece of their loved one's clothing or even knowing that a candle was being lit that night in their memory.

3.

COVID-19 made many people realise the most important aspects of a funeral: not excessive flowers or expensive hearses, but the acknowledgement of grief, a space to pay tribute to the person who has lived and to ensure that the person who has died is not simply a statistic. That space doesn't have to be in a chapel or crematorium – solidarity can be shown online, on the phone or even in simple private gestures.

4.

I was struck by how many people touched by the tragic consequences of COVID-19 thought of others before themselves by setting up fundraising pages and doing donation drives. It's as if the forced distancing liberated a sense of humanity, kindness and unity like never before.

5.

Although it was and continues to be a highly fraught time, everyone tried their best. Empathy, compassion and flexibility are key to all involved in funerals and, despite the pressures, it's more important now than ever for grief to be acknowledged, understood and respected.

Planning your own funeral

[L]

Funeral directors will be happy to help you plan your funeral. Many will restrict this to a discussion about how many limousines you want, the three pieces of music you'd like to be played during the service and the pre-payment plan you'd like to sign up for.

There are so many advertisements on daytime television for pre-paid funeral plans, showing glamorous older couples wearing white linen, smiling as they plan their funerals together. They always have a tan from the many cruises they've enjoyed, and exude financial responsibility, security and freedom.

But pre-paid funeral plans aren't really for the benefit of the people who buy them or their families. I believe pre-payment funeral plans are mostly for the benefit of funeral directors and their suppliers. It means *their businesses* are protected for the future.

This targeted and persuasive marketing and advertising has created a situation in which many people think that pre-paying for their funeral is a good idea. Wherever there are vulnerable people, there are people prepared to make money. The situation has got so bad that in June 2019, the UK government announced plans to regulate the pre-paid funeral sector, to bring to an end the high pressure and misleading tactics in the sale of these plans.

IS IT HELPFUL TO PLAN YOUR FUNERAL IN ADVANCE?

— Fred's Funeral

Fred had planned his funeral back in the early 1980s, after a close friend of his had died from cancer. He'd hidden his funeral plan in a tin box under the floorboards in his bedroom with other important documents. When he died at the age of 92, his children came together to create his funeral. They made it meaningful to them, sharing stories and choosing the music he'd played to them during their childhood.

At the 11th hour, Fred's funeral plan was found under the floorboards. He'd written a detailed itinerary of the ceremony, the music and the words. His family were torn between honouring it or ignoring it in favour of the funeral they'd so lovingly put together. They chose to honour it, and the resulting funeral just didn't work for them. It didn't flow together and the music was unfamiliar – no one knew what it meant or why Fred had chosen it. They left the funeral feeling confused and dissatisfied, like they hadn't been able to say a proper goodbye to the father they loved and admired.

Leaving no instructions at all can be disconcerting for the people arranging your funeral, who may wonder if you wanted to be buried or cremated, but leaving detailed and prescriptive instructions can cause extra stress and prevent people from working out how they want to say goodbye to you.

The best kind of funeral plan is a loose framework that allows the people arranging and attending the funeral to do whatever they need to do.

A funeral plan isn't static. It changes over time. As your life changes, so will your funeral. If I die in three weeks' time because I'm involved in a tragic accident on the way home from work, my funeral will be very different to the one I'll have if I die at the age of 100, surrounded by my family.

I decided to plan my funeral when I first became a funeral celebrant, and have since revised it because I realised that the main people who would be affected by my death would be my parents and my sister in Derbyshire, and my friends in London. The funeral I had initially planned would fit the needs of my friends in London, but it would be alienating and unhelpful for my parents and immediate family. However, the more funerals I was involved with, the more I understood what was important. At a time of pain and uncertainty, I felt my funeral needed to be familiar and reassuring for my parents, while giving them an opportunity to participate as much or as little as they were comfortable doing.

My current funeral plan is nothing like the original. It involves a natural burial, at a woodland burial ground of my parents' choosing in a place that's meaningful to them. I've asked to be buried in a banana leaf coffin wearing the simple white nightgown I found for 5 Euros in a flea market in Italy. I've created a playlist on Spotify (featuring Max Richter and Massive Attack), and I'd like my family and friends to throw wildflowers into my grave. But my funeral plan makes it clear that I'm not tied to anything – they can do whatever they want and need to do after I've died. If what I've planned doesn't work for them, it's OK. They can change it.

If I get married and have children, my funeral plan may change again. It will depend on what's relevant and meaningful to the people who will be most affected by my death.

WHEN PLANNING YOUR FUNERAL IS A HELPFUL THING TO DO

— Ellie and Chen

Ellie and Chen got married in 2018. They'd bought their first house together and were planning to start a family. They'd written their wills and decided to talk about their wishes for their funerals so they were clear about what the other wanted. Ellie wanted to be buried, Chen wanted to be cremated, but they decided they wanted to end up in the same place. After many discussions, they planned for Chen's ashes to be interred in Ellie's grave. They agreed the surviving partner would be able to decide the rest of the arrangements.

— Maryam

Maryam had rejected the religion of her upbringing. She decided to plan her funeral when she found out she had terminal cancer at the age of 52. She wanted to put firm instructions in place for her sister to easily follow when she died, so the rest of the family didn't revert to the customs of their religion. She included them in the planning process, so they knew what to expect and didn't feel alienated by the funeral she wanted for herself. When she died, they knew what she wanted and were able to honour her beliefs while acknowledging their own.

— Janet

Janet wanted to put plans in place because she didn't want a funeral at all. Her grown-up children disagreed with her wishes and felt they would want to have a funeral for her. We talked about why Janet didn't want a funeral. Her parents had died when she was a teenager and she'd found both funerals distressing. She had avoided funerals ever since, always coming up with an excuse for why she couldn't attend. She wanted to spare her own children the discomfort of the same experience. After we'd unravelled the reasons why she didn't want a funeral for herself, she decided to take some time to reconsider her decision.

Thinking about your own funeral doesn't need to be a gloomy experience. It is also not a precursor to dying. However, there can be a surprising side effect to thinking about your own funeral: by working out who you are in life by looking at your death, you may be inspired to make changes before it's too late.

— Benjamin's Experience

Benjamin was a photographer who was working as a courier to pay his bills. When he heard that I was helping people to plan their funerals, he decided to plan the one he wanted to have in the future, using the process as a milestone to check where he was in his life, and whether he was going in the right direction. After doing so, he decided to leave his courier job to become a full-time photographer

— Margaret's Experience

Margaret was an 85-year-old retired doctor who decided to put plans in place for her funeral. Halfway through the process, she thought about all the open conversations she'd had with her family and friends about life and death. She decided her funeral was for the benefit of the people who would survive her. Her funeral plan was simple: 'In the event of my death, I give you permission to do whatever you want and need to do'.

CREATING YOUR EMOTIONAL LEGACY

Our funerals are our emotional legacy. They matter. They help the people who survive us to begin to work out how to live their lives without us. It's important to give them the time and space to figure out how they want and need to say goodbye.

When I first started working with funerals, I realised that we needed a way of planning funerals that went beyond just looking at the basics of the funeral and how we would pay for it. We need to look deeper by considering why we are having a funeral, who the funeral is for, and what they might need from it.

You might believe that you'll be present at your own funeral, you might not. If you're religious, you might believe that a funeral is about the glory of God and the afterlife.

The following questions will help you to get a clearer understanding of how you're feeling in relation to your life, your death and your funeral. This will assist in the process of creating a funeral that's a reflection of who you are as well as being helpful and meaningful to the people who survive you.

The questions have no right or wrong answers. If you don't feel the question is relevant, it doesn't resonate with you or you just don't want to answer it, move to the next one. I suggest taking some time to reflect on these questions over a few weeks or months. Whatever works best for you.

You

1. Who are you? What do people call you? Do you have any nicknames?
2. How old are you? How old do you feel?
3. How would you describe what you do?
4. What would you have liked to do with your life?
5. What brings you joy? What makes you sad?
6. What was your first thought when you woke up this morning?
7. When did you last say thank you and really mean it?
8. What would you call your autobiography? What would the back cover say?
9. Why do you want to plan your own funeral?
10. Have you ever been to a good funeral? What was it like?
11. Have you ever been to a bad funeral? What was it like?
12. Are you ready to die? Are you afraid of dying? Are you afraid of death?
13. You're going to die tomorrow. What will you do today?
14. Do you believe in life after death?
15. Do you believe in God?
16. How would you like to be remembered?
17. What's the nicest thing someone has ever said about you?
18. When did you last cry? When did you last sing?

The people who will survive you

1. Who do you think will miss you?
2. Who will be most affected by your death? What would you like to say to them?
3. How have they previously dealt with other deaths and losses?
4. Do they have any religious or cultural beliefs you'd like to consider?
5. What do you think they will need from you after your death?
6. Do you think they'd like to be involved in caring for you after you've died?

Your funeral

1. Would you like to be looked after by a funeral director? If so, do you have a preference?
2. Do you have a preference for your coffin/shroud?
3. Do you want to be cremated or buried? Where?
4. Where would you like the funeral service to be held?
5. Do you want your funeral to incorporate any elements of your religion or culture?
6. Would you like to choose a reading(s) or poem(s), or write a letter to be read on your behalf?
7. Would you like to request that someone specific does something? Such as reading a tribute, letter or poem or singing a song?
8. Do you have any requests for music?
9. How do you feel about flowers?
10. If you're going to be cremated, what would you like your relatives to do with your ashes?
11. Is there anything you really want at your funeral?
12. Is there anything you really don't want?

IMPORTANT THINGS TO REMEMBER

1. Funeral plans aren't legally binding. Once you've spent some time thinking about your funeral, you might want to take the opportunity to talk to the people who will be responsible for arranging it. You might want to keep a copy somewhere safe, and ensure that the people responsible know where to find it. But it's best if that's not even necessary – if you've had an open and honest conversation about what you might want, and what they might want, a written plan isn't so important.
2. If you want to pay for your funeral in advance, it's worth looking into ethical funeral plans or simply putting the money into an account that can be used to pay for your funeral after your death. In the UK, the funeral can be paid for directly from the bank account belonging to the person who has died by submitting the invoice to the bank with a copy of the death certificate.
3. If you don't feel able to think about your funeral, or have an open discussion with your family and friends, you might find it helpful to leave a copy of this Five Things by Fran Hall in a safe place.

THE FIVE THINGS I WISH EVERYONE KNEW ABOUT FUNERALS

by Fran Hall

Fran is CEO of the Good Funeral Guide and oversees the GFG accreditation scheme, the gold standard for recommending funeral directors in the UK.

1.

You don't have to rush. Take your time. Dead people don't have to be whisked away. Dead people aren't usually a health hazard They're just the same as they were before they died. Stay with them. Feel the absence of the essence of the person. Let yourself adjust.

2.

Organising a funeral is surreal. You'll probably only do it once or twice in your life. If you're using a funeral director to help you, find one who shares your values. Do your research. Or get someone you trust to do the research for you.

3.

Funerals are important. They are the public acknowledgement of the ending of a life. The rituals of a funeral play a part in the processing of loss. But there is no right way. Create the funeral that works for you. Find the right people to help you to do this. And don't be afraid to say no to things (or people) that don't feel right. Trust your instincts.

4.

Funeral directors are useful if you want to delegate, but they are not in charge – you are. You are paying them to do things you can't or won't do. And only employ people you like. Ask questions. Ask to see where the person who has died will be kept. Ask who will be involved with caring for them. They are yours, and you have a right to know.

5.

Help carry the coffin. It doesn't have to go on your shoulders, you can carry it by the handles if you make sure the coffin you choose has load-bearing handles. Even small children can help carry their relative. That physical connection to the weight of the person's body helps your body to recognise the reality of their death. You are allowed to lower the coffin into a grave, to fill in a grave or to witness a coffin go into a cremator. If you feel you can, then do it. Be involved in the final act. It will help.

Ask a funeral director anything

[L]

We asked the people of Twitter and Facebook what they'd most like to know about anything and everything related to funerals. We've answered the most popular questions here.

Do I have to have a funeral director?
No. In the UK, there's no law saying that you must use a funeral director. You can take care of the funeral arrangements yourself, or work with a flexible funeral director who will do as much or as little as you need them to.

Do I have to have a funeral?
No, you don't have to have a funeral service. Direct cremation and burial is when someone is cremated or buried with no service or ritual and no one in attendance.

Do I have to wear black at a funeral?
There are no rules about what people wear to funerals. You might want the attendees to be as stylish as the person who died, or request strictly no black, or even only wear black. You just need to make it clear so people know what to do.

Is it OK to announce the funeral online?
Yes. Whatever works for you. You might want to think about the age of the person who has died and how their family and friends would prefer to communicate. Sharing details of the funeral on social media can avoid the need to make lots of telephone calls. You may want to be mindful that this could be the first time that people are hearing the news of the death, so make the announcement with care and consideration.

Do funerals have to be expensive?
There's so much talk in the press about the rising costs of funerals, mostly encouraged by the companies trying to sell pre-paid funeral plans to vulnerable consumers.

The reality is that a funeral can cost a little, or a lot, depending on what you want, and the kind of funeral director you use. If you want horses, shiny cars and lots of floral tributes, and you go to a corporate company, it's going to cost a lot. If you'd prefer something simpler, do your research and find a flexible funeral director who will provide the service you want.

You can reduce the overall cost by encouraging your family and friends to be pall-bearers, using fresh flowers from the garden, or driving yourself to the crematorium. If you're prepared to get creative, resourceful and embrace the reality of dealing with the body of someone who has died, you could also have a DIY funeral at minimal cost.

Why are post-mortems sometimes necessary?

A post-mortem, also known as an autopsy in America, is the examination of the body of a person who has died to determine the exact cause of death. The coroner is required by law to carry out a post-mortem when a death is suspicious, sudden or unnatural.

Does the coffin go straight into the flames at the crematorium?

No. At the point of committal (when the curtains close or the doors open and the coffin glides away), the coffin will go into a room behind or below the chapel before it's taken to the crematory. The coffin is then charged into the cremator.

What are ashes?

Ashes are what remains after a body has been cremated, mostly comprising the bones that survive the cremation process. The extreme heat inside the cremators means that little to no traces of the coffin or shroud will survive. Larger bones, such as the hip bones, will still be fairly intact. Metals (such as hip replacements) are then removed before the ashes are put through a machine called a cremulator. This reduces them to the fine dusty and gritty grey substance we call ashes.

In the UK, there are strict procedures in place to ensure that the ashes that are returned to you are always the remains of the person who has died.

Is it OK to take photographs at a funeral?

Some people find it really helpful to have photographs, or even a film, of what happened on the day of the funeral. It's such an overwhelming time and people find they often can't remember exactly what happened, and who was there. In some cultures, it's standard for everyone to have their phones and cameras out, recording every detail of the day.

Can I really bury someone in my back garden?

In the UK, burying someone on private land (such as in a garden or in a field) is relatively straightforward, and surprisingly free of red tape. First of all, you'll need to either own the freehold to the property or have the landowner's permission. You must then make sure that there are no covenants on the land prohibiting burial and that the grave is 10m (33ft) away from standing water, 50m (165ft) away from a drinking water source and a minimum of 1.3m (4ft 3in) deep.

You'll also need to make sure that the burial is added to the deeds of the property or land. It's important to note that, should you wish to sell in the future, private burials may dramatically affect the property's value!

When can we have the funeral? Do we have to wait a month?

This depends on whether the coroner is investigating the death, as well as the availability of the church, crematorium or cemetery, and the funeral director. In the UK, funerals usually happen anywhere from a day to a month after someone has died, but there are no rules. It also depends on how quickly the paperwork can be completed, and whether religious customs are being followed.

If your funeral director tells you there will be a long wait, it's worth checking directly with the crematorium or cemetery. Bigger companies can only facilitate a certain number of funerals at any one time due to the availability of their cars and their team, so this causes a delay. If you have a special date in mind, call several funeral directors and see who is available.

Do we have to have our grandad embalmed?

Embalming is legally required if someone is going to be repatriated to a country outside of the UK. If they're staying in the UK, embalming is not a legal requirement.

Embalming is mostly an unnecessary and invasive procedure but can be helpful in certain situations, such as if there's a long delay before the funeral. Many funeral directors will call embalming 'hygienic treatment' and imply that it's necessary. It's not. It's important to know that the person who has died does not need to be embalmed in order for you to see them.

What if I want something but my family doesn't?

It's worth knowing that funeral wishes aren't legally binding in the UK. So even if you leave explicit instructions, the people arranging the funeral don't have to follow them. You may wish to think about who the funeral is for and what they might need from it before you put any plans into place.

We want to have an alternative funeral for my dad but we're worried about the reaction from his siblings, who are much more traditional. What should we do?

People have different experiences and expectations of funerals, and it can be alienating to attend a funeral that's doesn't conform to tradition or expectations, especially when overwhelmed by grief. It can be as simple as announcing, 'In the spirit of coming together to celebrate the many different parts of Mark's life, we're going to do things a little differently today.' By guiding the attendees through what's happening and why, everyone can leave the funeral feeling as though their needs have been met.

Do we have to use a coffin?

In the UK, there is no law requiring that a coffin must be used. If the person who has died is going to be cremated, most crematoria will require a coffin, although a few of the more open-minded ones will allow a shroud instead. It's worth knowing that the law states that it's 'an offence to expose a dead body near a public highway as this would outrage public decency'. This just means that the body of the person who has died needs to be covered in public.

What happens if the person who has died carries an organ donor card?

In the UK, thousands of people are waiting for an organ transplant. Three people die every day due to a shortage of organ donors. Donating your organs is a generous act that can save lives. Organs that can be donated after death include the heart, lungs, kidneys, liver, pancreas and small bowel. Tissue such as skin, bone, heart valves and corneas can also be donated.

The decision about whether some or all organs or tissue are suitable for transplant is made by medical specialists, taking into account the potential donor's medical, travel and social history.

The donation operation is performed as soon as possible after death by a specialist team. The donor is treated with the greatest care and respect during the removal of organs and/or tissue. Only those organs and tissue specified by the donor or their family will be removed.

The body of the donor is then treated in the same way as any other death in a hospital where donation has not taken place. Family and friends can still see the person who has died and an open coffin is usually still possible.

In 2020, organ donation law in England is changing to an 'opt out' system. This means that all adults in England will be considered to have agreed to be an organ donor when they die unless they have recorded a decision not to donate or are in one of the excluded groups. You can read more on the NHS organ donation website: www.organdonation.nhs.uk

Can I donate my body to science?

Yes, you can decide to donate your body to science, and many medical schools will welcome the offer of a donation. If you are interested in doing so, you will need to contact a medical school to find our more information, as well as to fill in a consent form. Under the Human Tissue Act 2004, written and witnessed consent for anatomical examination must be given prior to death. Consent cannot be given by anyone else after your death. You should also inform your family, close friends and GP if you wish to donate your body.

You should ensure that you have an alternative funeral plan in place should your body donation not be accepted. If it's not possible to donate your entire body, it may be possible to donate your brain. More information is available on the Human Tissue Authority's website: www.hta.gov.uk

A truly poetic ending

[L]

I wrote this chapter in honour of Emanuele Follett, who taught us so much about the power of a good funeral.

Emanuele died on 12 June 2018 at the age of 49, just as the sun was setting over London.

His funeral took place in a wildflower meadow in Surrey on the hottest day of the summer. In spite of the heat, more than 150 people gathered around the grave of their partner, son, brother, uncle, nephew, cousin, bandmate, colleague and friend.

As his coffin was lowered to his final resting place by his oldest and dearest friends, his father read the words he'd chosen, ending with 'good night'. A long line of family and friends spiralled around his grave, taking it in turns to throw handfuls of petals down into the earth. Ella, Emanuele's dog, sat dutifully by his graveside, watching the proceedings.

There was a pile of earth next to the grave, with two shovels ready for the gravediggers to use to fill it in. Rolling up his sleeves and wiping the sweat from his forehead, Emanuele's friend took a shovel and began moving the earth into the grave. Another friend took a shovel, and did the same. It didn't take long before everyone was joining in. A mix of soil, tears and petals in every colour of the rainbow settled on top of his coffin as the sound of a saxophone playing filled the meadow.

Emanuele adored his nieces and nephews, and they adored him right back. His eight-year-old niece Coco had chosen to wear a bright pink tutu dress to the funeral. Having watched everyone else, she picked up a shovel and joined in. Her final job was to sprinkle the remaining petals into her uncle's grave. She leaned over the grave and made sure every single petal made it into the earth.

There were no dry eyes – a combination of hayfever from the meadow, sweat from the heat and tears from the raw emotion of what we had experienced.

That day we went home feeling like we had been involved in something profound. Something that spoke to the most human part of us. We were so moved that Emanuele's family and friends had wanted to bury their son, partner, brother and friend. That they'd rolled up their sleeves and stayed until the very end. That everyone who knew him, no matter how old or young, had been involved. That we were simply there to invite them to do what their hearts were telling them to do. That they acted on what they felt, without holding back. With no one telling them what they could and couldn't do.

What the brilliant, bold and brave family and friends of the brilliant, bold and brave man did that day in Surrey was to sit with the overwhelming emotion of what had happened, and allow it to be, to consume and engulf them while they did what they needed to do – lay him to rest.

Grief

[A + L]

When someone dies, it can be like finding ourselves in a play, having never read the script, or sitting an exam we've never studied for. We have to try to make sense of something that often makes absolutely no sense.

Grief is unique yet universal. It eventually affects everyone yet no one experiences it in the same way.

If we know love, one day, we'll know loss. It's inevitable that, at some point, we'll all experience grief.

This chapter is for when life, as we know it, ends. We'll learn:

1. What grief feels like.
2. What you really need to know about grief.
3. How others have found a way to live with their grief.
4. How to support a grieving friend.
5. What it's like to lose a partner.

'Alexa, What is There to Know about Love?'

Alexa, what is there to know about love?
What is there to know about love?
A glove is a garment that covers the hand
for protection from the cold or dirt and –
Alexa, how does a human heart work?
How does a human heart work?
Blood is first received in the right atrium via
two veins, the vena cava superior and inferior –

Alexa, where do we go to when we die?
Where do we go to when we die?
Activating Google Maps. Completed activation.
Would you like to start from your current location?

Alexa, what does it mean to be alone?
What does it mean to be alone?
It is the silence left by words unsaid,
the cold expanse of half a bed.
It is the endless stretching of the hours,
the needless tending of plastic flowers.
It is an echo unanswered in a cave,
the fateful ping of the microwave.
It is the fraying of a worn shirt cuff,
and the howl – Stop, Alexa. That's enough.

BRIAN BILSTON

GRIEF HURTS IN EVERY POSSIBLE WAY

Sometimes, it's physical. Breathing hurts. Moving hurts. Just being alive hurts. You have a constant headache. Your heart feels heavy. Your chest feels tight. Every part of your body aches. You're exhausted yet sleeping is impossible. Your brain doesn't work properly. You can't focus or remember anything. You forget what day it is. You have no idea whether it's sunset or sunrise. Should you be eating breakfast or making dinner? You have no idea. You're not hungry. Who cares? They're dead.

It can be emotional. From uncontrollable crying to feeling OK and then suddenly, the tears are streaming down your cheeks again. From numbness to fear to numbness to overwhelming pain to numbness all over again. It's lonely. It's isolating. How can anyone else possibly understand? The guilt. Could I have done more? What if I'd just...? Then the rage, the unadulterated RAGE that this has happened yet life still goes on. That the sun still rises and sets and the buses are still running. How could the world possibly continue turning? Followed by rage at the person who has died. How could they do this? How dare they die and leave you like this. But oh, the gratitude. They lived and they brought so much to your life. How you loved them and how grateful you are for everything.

One moment you're fine, congratulating yourself on how well you're doing, and then all it takes is a letter landing on the doormat with their name on the envelope for the tears to begin all over again. Then there are the days you forget they're dead. Calling out their name to ask if they'd like a cup of coffee. Or hearing the phone ring and expecting it to be them. Before remembering the horrifying truth. *They're gone.* First the devastation and then the apathy. What's the point? Why bother? Why take the bins out or change the bed sheets? Why even get out of bed? Even making a drink is too much. Taking a shower can feel like climbing Mount Everest. Getting through the next hour can seem impossible, even the next minute, never mind the whole day. Waking up and remembering they're dead feels like doomsday all over again. Going to sleep alone, reaching out and finding no one at the other side of the bed. It's overwhelming and it's unbearable.

There might be times it's spiritual. Why did this happen? Why did this happen to you? What's the point in anything? What does life mean now? How can anything possibly mean anything ever again? Where is God when you really need him? If there's a God, how could they do this? Life seems overwhelmingly fragile, and can end so easily. How does anyone manage to survive?

Welcome to the club that no one wants to join.

The requirements for membership are simple, but the repercussions of joining are huge. Wherever you are in the world, your membership goes with you. Membership can never be cancelled or revoked. Once you've joined, you're a member for life.

What is grief?

[A + L]

*'Grief is like glitter. No matter how much you try to tidy it up, you're never gonna get rid of it all.
You're always gonna find bits of it somewhere.'*
GEORGE SHELLEY, WHOSE SISTER DIED AT THE AGE OF
21 AFTER BEING INVOLVED IN A ROAD ACCIDENT

Grief is the natural set of emotions we feel in reaction to a situation we would not choose to be in. Something may have happened, or is happening, and there's nothing we can do to change it. Somehow we must find a way to live with the unchosen reality of our new life.

Grief is multi-faceted. It's understood and experienced differently by everyone who encounters it. Grief is most commonly described as an emotional response to death but in reality, we can grieve for anything that has had a fundamental impact on our lives that has been taken away, we worry will be taken away or no longer exists in the same way it once did. It could be a divorce, the end of a relationship or a friendship, children leaving home, pets dying, redundancy or life not being what we imagined. The list is endless.

We don't believe there's a single person in the world who hasn't experienced grief in some way. Grieving is universal and it's a natural and normal part of life.

In this chapter, we'll talk mostly about the grief we experience following a death, although some of the principles apply to all kinds of loss. When someone dies, our lives change irrevocably. Grief isn't a problem we can fix or solve. It isn't a competition. Pain is pain. There's no one way you should be feeling, and no one-size-fits-all prescription for dealing with it.

'Bereavement is what happens to you; grief is how you feel; mourning is what you do.'
DR RICHARD WILSON, CONSULTANT PAEDIATRICIAN, WHO
WORKED CLOSELY WITH PARENTS WHO LOST A CHILD THROUGH
SIDS (SUDDEN INFANT DEATH SYNDROME)

It's not so much the grief itself that can cause us so much damage – grief is natural – it's the things we do to actively avoid feeling it. We have to express our grief by finding ways to mourn. If we don't, our grief could stay stuck. Pain demands to be felt. If we don't find a way to feel it, it might find a way to leak into our lives. We might drink too much, overeat, undereat or become addicted to drugs. We might feel depressed, resentful, angry, unable to cope and alone.

'There are periods when I've been furious that he is not here any more. For a long time I couldn't watch TV dramas or films because so many actors have worked with my dad. Seeing them alive while my dad is dead made me burn with white-hot rage. I've realised that I have no choice but to let it out; I've screamed into pillows, thrashed it out while doing strenuous cardio and even taken a plastic baseball bat to a cushion from the sofa. It's essential that the anger comes out, because if it stays in it will turn into poison and make me bitter and sad. Pain that is not transformed will be transmitted; I have to work through those feelings so I don't take them out on those around me. I used to be afraid of my rage but now I let it do its thing, then I let it go.'

ROSA HOSKINS, WHOSE FATHER, ACTOR BOB HOSKINS,
DIED IN 2014 AT THE AGE OF 71

As a society, we need to express our grief by finding a modern way of mourning. We need helpful and supportive funeral ceremonies that let us express the extent of our pain. We need poetry that encourages us to feel whatever it is we're feeling. We need to find ways to support each other in our grief. We need to know that it's OK to cry when we need to cry. We need to know that it's OK not to be OK. We need to know that it's OK to ask for help. We need to know it's OK to do whatever it is we need to do until we don't need to do it any more.

'Recension Day'

Unburn the boat, rebuild the bridge,
Reconsecrate the sacrilege,
Unspill the milk, decry the tears,
Turn back the clock, relive the years,
Replace the smoke inside the fire,
Unite fulfilment with desire,
Undo the done, gainsay the said,
Revitalise the buried dead,
Revoke the penalty and the clause,
Reconstitute unwritten laws,
Repair the heart, untie the tongue,
Change faithless old to hopeful young,
Inure the body to disease
And help me to forget you please.

DUNCAN FORBES

FIVE THINGS I'VE LEARNED ABOUT GRIEF

by Charlotte Philby

Charlotte's father died in 2009, when she was 24, having been ill for most of her life. She spent most of her childhood terrified he would die at any moment.

1.

Grief isn't a linear path. It's twisted and rough, with curves and drops that appear out of nowhere. It is so dark at times that it can make you feel like you've lost your way; and then, just when you think you're lost forever, you find yourself in a clearing and in that moment everything is a little bit brighter and you can see again.

2.

Nothing is as terrifying as losing someone you love, but amidst that terror, that sharp stinging reminder that life is fleeting and fragile, grief makes us hold tighter to the ones who are left behind. In losing old friends, I have made new ones; in accepting the absence of the ones who made me who I am, I have found new parts of myself.

3.

In grief I've learned that those who leave us never really go, but that everyone leaves eventually. Grief carves our names in the bark of trees, for all to see, and, while our back is turned, strikes out every one.

4.

Death has taught me that grief is the purest emotion. It is agony and ecstasy; it is the greatest unknown and the only certainty.

5.

Grief lights a candle against the image of the ones we love, and waits, patiently, for death to blow it out. Grief teaches us to warm our hands while the flame still casts its gentle light.

Your life after their death – the things we want you to know about grief

[A + L]

We both work with grieving people every day and have experienced grief of our own. Over the years, this is what we've learned about the reality of grief.

1. **There is no such thing as the 'five stages of grief'!**
   Contrary to popular belief, grief doesn't come in neatly defined stages. Elisabeth Kübler-Ross first proposed the infamous 'five stages of grief' in her book *On Death and Dying* in 1969. The stages – denial, anger, bargaining, depression and acceptance – were developed to describe the process patients go through as they come to terms with a terminal illness. It's since been misused by the media to describe what we may go through when someone dies.

   The truth is that grief isn't a box-ticking exercise that means we can complete one stage and move on to the next. The idea of 'getting over it' is deeply unhelpful. As is the idea that 'time will heal'. Grief has no schedule, timeline or structure. You don't have to get over it, you just have to go through it. It's about learning to live with it rather than waiting for it to get better. We'll learn more about this later.

   Everyone deals with his or her grief in a different way. Some people will be very expressive and visibly upset; others will be stoic and may come across as cold and unconcerned.

   The writer Anne Lamott describes grief as like having a broken leg that never quite heals. When it gets cold, it still hurts, but you can learn to dance with the limp.

2. **The period after the funeral is a really vulnerable time**
   The build-up to a funeral is busy and often intense. There are things to arrange, paperwork to complete and difficult decisions to make.

   Following the funeral, the intensity of activity stops overnight. Calls from concerned family and friends are less frequent; condolence cards stop arriving on the doorstep and the flowers from the funeral begin to wilt.

   It's then that we have to deal with the reality of our new life, our new normal. This is when the real work of grief and mourning begins, and is often the most vulnerable time for someone who is bereaved.

3. **It's *your* grief, no one else's**
Life is complicated. We may have emotional connections with people who aren't our immediate family. A significant loss can be but doesn't have to be a partner, parent, child, sibling or grandparent. It could also be a friend, a neighbour, a celebrity or someone you've never even met, such as an online friend.

You'll notice that we haven't once referred to 'your loved one' in this chapter. That's because we don't always have healthy and loving relationships with the people around us. Sometimes our relationships are difficult and painful. When someone dies, it can bring up all sorts of different and complicated feelings. We can grieve the relationship we wanted to have, rather than the one we actually had.

When society doesn't recognise or acknowledge the grief we feel, it's described as 'disenfranchised grief'. This could be the death of a celebrity, ex-partner, colleague, pet, online friend, the termination or miscarriage of a pregnancy or even something that happened in the distant past or to a previous generation.

Grief is deeply personal. Whatever the nature of your relationship, your grief is still valid. If it hurts, it hurts, regardless of what anyone else thinks or says.

4. **It's important to be gentle with yourself**
Grief changes everything about our lives. It changes relationships with the people around us and the world itself. We may not know who we are any more.

It's essential for us to give ourselves space and time to get in touch with what we need. We might crave safety and security. We might want to put a gentle routine into place to make sure we eat well, exercise regularly and make plans for ourselves. All of these can help to build a good foundation for dealing with the reality of our loss, by dipping in and out of grief, dousing our pain.

Self-care might feel too ambitious. Self-maintenance is doing whatever it takes to get by. Some days, that might just be getting out of bed and opening the blinds.

5. **Death is the end of a life, it's not the end of a relationship**

'Your absence has gone through me
Like thread through a needle.
Everything I do is stitched with its color.'
W.S. MERWIN, AMERICAN POET

You can still love the person who has died in their absence. The feelings you have for them have not died, your relationship with them has just changed. You can continue your connection to them by establishing rituals that mean something to you. This might include visiting their favourite places, cooking their favourite dinner or wearing their clothes. It might include honouring them on their birthday or remembering them at Christmas with their favourite music, stories and food.

This is often called 'continuing bonds'. It allows us to stitch their love and influence into our present and our future. It was developed in 1996 by Klass, Silverman and Nickman as a response to the most popular models of grief at the time, which suggested that a grieving person should detach themselves from the person who has died in order to build an entire new life without them.

Maintaining the ties we have to the people who have died is both normal and healthy. Death does not diminish our human attachments and acknowledging the lifelong impact someone has had on our lives is essential to finding a way to live with our grief. Time doesn't necessarily heal but it can give us a different and new normal, one that we can fill with life and living to allay the intense pain of our grief. We may even be able to find joy and happiness again.

— Kaila's Experience

Kaila and her sisters meet every year on their mum's birthday. They gather in their family home and make spaghetti bolognese with garlic bread, their mum's favourite. They bring photographs and share stories about their mum, as they talk about how much they miss her and what she meant to them.

— Billy's Experience

Billy and his wife Joyce discovered a joint love of sailing after their retirement. Joyce was diagnosed with breast cancer a few months later and died in her local hospice. After her cremation, Billy chose to scatter his wife's ashes in the sea where they'd both learned to sail. He continued his membership of their sailing club, and embraced everything it had to offer, making a valuable new community of friends and acquaintances who supported him in his new life as a widower. He went out on his boat every day, always thinking that Joyce had been released into the waves below, cherishing the thought that she was always with him in some way.

6. **When someone dies, it's not just about the loss of the person**
   When someone dies, we experience a whole range of secondary losses, too. It might be the inability to pay the mortgage; missing having someone to talk to after work every night; the loss of income, shared hopes, dreams and ambitions, self-confidence and the future. The way we do the shopping changes. The food we have in the fridge changes. Suddenly the grass needs mowing and the bins need emptying because the person who once did those things is no longer there. We can also miss our former selves, the people we were before:

   'Sometimes I still miss who I was before he died. It's been so long now ... he has been gone very nearly the same amount of time that we were married. I miss the person who didn't know such loss ... who could go about her day without having known such pain.'
   GINNY MCKINNEY, WHOSE HUSBAND DIED SUDDENLY
   AND UNEXPECTEDLY AT THE AGE OF 62

7. **Sometimes you just don't know what you've lost**
   Death brings with it a finality that we cannot question. But sometimes, loss involves an ambiguity that means we grieve, without any of the usual markers.
   It might be that someone has been 'taken' from us by the ravages of illness such as dementia or Alzheimer's. Someone may go missing and never be found. A relationship may end with no explanation or conversation. It might be that we never stop looking for them. How can we begin to properly mourn if we have no confirmation that they're really gone?
   The strain of living with such uncertainty has a large psychological toll. It can affect us physically, too.

8. **It's OK to let people know exactly what you need (if you can)**
   It's hard to ask people for what we really need, even if we've received so many offers of, 'Let me know if there's anything I can do'. It helps to be explicit and direct in reaching out to ask for what you need the most. 'I wondered if you'd come round to help me clear out Pete's wardrobe,' or 'Could we meet for coffee to talk about how I'm feeling?' or 'Can we see a film together?'
   Most people will be grateful for the clear direction about what would be helpful and will be pleased to offer their support.

When Jamie's partner died, he found he was inundated with supportive messages from friends and offers of, 'Just shout if you need anything.' But no one was stepping forward to actually offer him what he needed – company on the long nights he was now spending alone. After weeks of frustration, he reached out and asked for what he needed. His friends then put together a plan so one of them was always with him at night, until he felt OK enough to be alone.

9. **Express your grief**
   We need to recognise our feelings, give them a name and then find a way to express them.

   It doesn't matter how we express our grief, as long as we find a way that resonates with us. It might be writing a blog or diary, creating artwork and memory boxes, playing music, gardening, dancing, singing or writing poetry or stories.

   It can be so healing to let ourselves express our pain without anyone else trying to change it, diminish it or fix it. Some of the most beautiful work in the world has come out of the depths of grief.

'The Colour of Grief'

I do not think that there is a colour for grief.
No black or grey,
No icy blue or putrid green or acid yellow
Could express the feeling.
It is like having ashes in your mouth
And gravel in the skin of your palms.
It is like weeping with every pore of your body.
It is like freezing all the way
From the centre of your heart
To the furthest edges of the universe.
Grief has no measure, no shape and no horizon.
Perhaps only an artist
Who could create a colour that is beyond all colour
Could depict the colour of grief.

JONATHAN STEFFEN

10. **It's OK to ask for help**

Grief can be overwhelming and unbearable. When faced with something as massive as death, underlying issues may suddenly surface. What may seem like an insignificant loss to other people can bring up something much bigger.

When someone dies, it's a normal and natural response to grieve. Finding a way to live with grief is something most people will be able to do even if they feel that nothing will ever be OK again.

When someone dies suddenly and unexpectedly, the trauma or the violence of the death, coupled with the unexpected nature of it, can trigger something called 'traumatic grief'. It leaves the people who are grieving not just in mourning for the death, but traumatised by the shock of it.

'Complicated grief' refers to the kind of grief that continues to be all-consuming and does not allow for any semblance of normal life to resume. Being consumed by grief is not a choice. People can't 'pull themselves together' or 'snap out of it'. Complicated grief is an unconscious response to death.

Whatever's going on for you, there's no shame in seeking professional help. A grief counsellor or therapist will talk through what's going on in a safe space and help you to find a way through it.

You might also want to consider joining a grief support group. There's often great solace to be found in spending time with people who have been in a similar situation to you.

11. **Do whatever you need to do**

Grief can be messy and unpredictable. One minute you might feel fine; the next minute you're crying in the queue at the Post Office.

Allow yourself to feel whatever it is you need to feel, and to do whatever it is you need to do. This could include:

- Wanting to leave the house; not wanting to leave the house.
- Feeling the need to be with people; feeling the need to be alone.
- Wanting to talk about the person who has died; not wanting to talk about the person who has died; wanting to talk about other things.
- Making lots of plans; cancelling plans; leaving social occasions early.
- Having a normal day, just going to work and getting on with life; waking up and feeling like it's doomsday all over again.
- Feeling OK; feeling guilty for feeling OK.

FIVE THINGS I'VE LEARNED FROM WRITING ABOUT THE DEATH OF MY SON, TEDDY

by Elle Wright

After the death of her son, Teddy, at three days old, Elle started writing to navigate her new life and as a way to feel purpose again.

1.

Things really do get easier. I know it's a cliché, and definitely one I wouldn't have believed if you had said it to me after our son died almost three years ago. When I look back over my earlier writing about Teddy compared to my writing now, even I can sense the weight of that grief lifting. Whether it's because we become more expert at wearing grief, or because it actually lessens over time, I'm not entirely sure. The words on the page don't feel so raw when I write them now, and it doesn't sting so much when I see those two words together: 'Teddy died'. Of course, that sadness is there every day, but time has definitely softened the crippling emptiness I felt in those early days.

2.

Happiness will creep back in. Don't get me wrong, this takes time and willingness to let it do so. There were days when I was convinced I would never feel truly happy again. That I was destined to spend the rest of my days without ever really feeling that familiar rush of true happiness as I laughed out loud with friends and family. That every smile would be forced and faked through gritted teeth and under a blanket of overwhelming sadness. That just isn't true. The more I wrote about Teddy and shared my experience of his birth and death, the more I noticed happier days creeping in. More jokes made their way into my writing, and well, I even dared to feel true happiness again (on more than one occasion I might add!). A huge part of my writing has become giving that hope of happiness returning to others, the ones who are where I was three years ago, who feel like it might never happen again.

3.

A problem shared really is a problem halved. I didn't begin writing my blog until nine months after Teddy died; I simply couldn't get the thoughts and feelings straight in my mind before then, let alone in an orderly fashion on a page. I shook with nerves before I pressed 'publish' on my first post about losing him. I wondered whether anyone would read it, or whether anyone else felt the same. The truth is, I shouldn't have worried about anything. As the weeks, months and now over two years have rolled on since I first began writing, I have been able to connect with so many parents whose narrative of parenthood is similar to ours. I will never tire of people sharing their stories, their children and their incredible human spirit with me; it is both an honour and a privilege to be able to share this with so many other people.

4.

The ripples of grief spread so much further than we could imagine. My first thoughts when Teddy died were for myself and my husband. How would we carry on? How could this happen to us? The more I have written about our grief and that of those close to us, the more I have come to appreciate just how far-reaching those ripples of grief are to those around us. I think especially when that loss is of a baby or a child, it shocks us all to our core and defies what many of us see as the natural order. So many of the kind people who take the time to write to me or comment on my blogs aren't bereaved parents themselves, but grandparents, siblings, friends, work colleagues or even people who have just that day been chatting to someone for the first time and learned that they have lost a child. That shock and grief, it affects us all differently, and we all need time and space to be able to talk about it.

5.

It's good to talk. I was so scared to talk about Teddy at first; so worried that I might upset someone else, or ruin their day when they innocently asked me, 'So, do you have any children?' Carrying that fear and guilt around with you can become really exhausting. When I began writing, not only did I find it really cathartic, but I discovered that the ripples slowly went out further than I could have imagined. People began contacting me and saying that they had felt more empowered to say their baby's name out loud, too, or to get involved with local fundraising or support projects for others. I soon realised that in ripping off that plaster myself and not being afraid to talk about Teddy, I was in turn doing that for others, too; and that was a very powerful thing indeed.

Growing around grief

[A]

This is the thing you really need to know – THERE ARE NO STAGES OF GRIEF! We'll keep repeating this throughout the book because it's really important.

Out of all the theories and models of grief that have been proposed, we've found Dr Lois Tonkin's 'Growing Around Grief' to be the most helpful and understanding. It's the model we use in our work, and our own grief.

Accepting bereavement in our life is difficult, but there is no escaping that grief is a part of life, in all the forms it takes. In those first few weeks and months after someone dies, grief can be overwhelming and all-encompassing. It can feel like a weight that will never be lifted. Grief is not just a companion during the day but it can also infiltrate our dreams and impact on our sleep.

Grief is stressful. The stress often floods the body with hormones, specifically cortisol, which cause that heavy feeling in our hearts. We may wonder if it's possible to ever be happy again, or to experience joy, laugh and feel carefree.

Grief can imprint on everything. Things might taste, feel and even look different. Research suggests that grief can have a significant impact on our brain and can even result in memory loss and our ability to process information. It can cause anxiety and trigger depression but it's important to differentiate the two. Grief can be a catalyst for depression but it's not depression; feeling sad is a normal part of grieving.

Lois believed that grief isn't something to get over, it's something we have to learn to live with. Our feelings of loss don't get any smaller and will be there forever, but as our lives evolve and grow, our grief becomes more manageable. Some days we will feel it as acutely as the day it happened; some days we will feel more at peace with our reality.

We're often told that 'time is a great healer', but grief isn't a wound to heal. The person-shaped hole in our heart may remain the size and shape of them, but with new experiences, friendships and different responsibilities, our new life can begin to grow around our grief, tempering our pain.

There will always be triggers, when grief comes hurtling to the forefront with full force. Perhaps it's when walking into the supermarket and the song you shared is played. Perhaps it's an anniversary or a birthday or the festive season. Everyone is different. And it's OK. Life will help dull our grief again in spite of the triggers. Remembering can actually be hugely cathartic.

Lois's model of grief has eclipsed so many of the outdated stages of grief models. It resonates with us because it's just so human. It's changed the way we witness, experience and understand grief: we can and do learn to live with grief. It is a companion to reconcile rather than a foe to be vanquished.

A BALL IN A BOX

Lauren Herschel tweeted a grief analogy she learned from her doctor in Canada, after she saw a lady who reminded her of her grandmother in a supermarket. The image and the accompanying words quickly went viral with people really resonating with the description of grief. Since then, it's been retweeted around 7000 times.

This is how it works:

There's a box. Inside the box there's a pain button and a ball. When someone fundamental to our lives dies, the ball takes up pretty much the entire box. You cannot move the box without the ball hitting the pain button. All the time. You can't control it. It is unrelenting.

Over time, the ball inside the box reduces in size. There's a bit more room inside the box and the ball doesn't hit the pain button quite so frequently. When it does hit that button, it still hurts just as much. It feels more manageable though and you're able to function better day to day. The downside is that the ball hits the pain button without warning, sometimes when you're not expecting it at all.

The ball will always be in the box. The pain button will always be there. There will probably be fewer hits on the button and a shorter recovery period, but the ball will never stop hitting the pain button. The ball, the box and the button will last a lifetime.

FIVE THINGS I'VE LEARNED SINCE THE DEATH OF MY WIFE RACHAEL

by Steve Bland

BBC radio presenter Rachael Bland's death from triple negative breast cancer at the age of 40 made headline news. As the creator of the acclaimed podcast, You, Me and the Big C, she did so much to change the conversation around cancer and death along with her co-hosts Lauren Mahon and Deborah James. Since Rachael's death in September 2018, her husband Steve has joined the You, Me and the Big C team to continue those important conversations. Here, he writes about his experiences of grief as a widower and dad.

1.
However you're feeling, it's OK
The reality of how you feel after someone close to you dies is so far removed from how you imagine it might feel. I didn't imagine for a second that anything would make me smile or laugh in the days after Rachael died, and when it did, I felt guilty. But I soon realised that however you feel, just go with it. If you want to laugh, laugh. If you feel like a good cry, go with that.

2.
It's best to let people in
I really didn't feel like speaking to anyone after Rachael died. Even close friends were getting the cold shoulder. But then some of my closest friends took it out of my hands. They just turned up at my house and pretty much forced me to let them in. It was the best thing they could have done. They didn't always say the 'right' thing but they were there for me. On that note, cut people a bit of slack if they do say the wrong thing!

3.
Be honest with kids
All of a sudden, I'm a single dad of a wonderful three-year-old boy who has a lot of questions. He doesn't understand the finality of what has happened, but he knows that his mummy isn't around any more. So what do you do? Well, I think the only way forward is to be as honest as possible. Trying to sugar coat anything is only going to lead to problems down the line.

4.
Don't rush to find your new normal
I was so desperate to be OK, and to prove to everyone that I was going to be OK, that I think I might have been guilty of trying to get to whatever normal was going to be too quickly. Take your time. No one is going to rush you, so do everything at your own pace. If you don't fancy going out, or feel like every once in a while that you need a day under the duvet, go with it.

5.
Don't be afraid to have difficult conversations
Before Rachael died, we had a lot of difficult conversations, but by talking about things like what my financial situation might be like or how I should dress Freddie without her guiding hand, she was able to get so much comfort. And not only that; by dealing with stuff like her will, or her funeral plans, it took away the pressure of working through these tricky decisions on my own. I know these are horrible things to talk about, but the earlier and the more willingly we have these conversations, the easier it all is.

THE FANDANGOE KID

The Fandangoe Kid came into our lives when Anna noticed her profoundly moving and bold work on Instagram. We're constantly in awe of how she has navigated her grief and trauma, finding ways to not just survive, but to flourish. We talked to her about her experiences of grief, and how she's found a way to live with it.

— The Fandangoe Kid's Experience

'Grief and loss have transformed my life. 2011 was the year my mother, sister and sister's partner of 20 years (who was like a sister to me) died in an accident in New York on the East River. In 2012, my oldest friend died by suicide and another close friend was killed in an accident with her husband and two children. In 2016, my dad died from cancer.

Much of my late 20s and early 30s were spent not knowing who to grieve first and attempting to untangle each complex story of love and loss. I don't feel I have had the mental space to grieve for everyone but I've accepted that I'll carry grief for the rest of my life. It's always there but it doesn't dominate my heart as it did before.

I talk about my grief to help others. As a young grieving woman, I struggled to find people who could receive and absorb my pain in a way that allowed me to open up and be understood. Many people were unable to find the words to help me.

Grief is a complex landscape full of ebbs and flows. It begins as a powerful heart and gut pain that is unmanageable, wild and out of control. All you can do is lie in a ball and protect yourself. It transforms over the years into a dull ache deep in the depths that you have to work with and manage. I think I'm a better person because of my grief. If I could rewrite my life I would still write it out, but it's made me connect to some seriously incredible souls and reach a point of emotional depth that I may never have got to otherwise.

I work with the subject of grief so much because I feel truly lucky (and sometimes amazed) to have survived the trauma. It's been essential to express my grief through my art. I really wanted to use my work to create a platform that helps challenge the ridiculous taboo around death.

In the early years I found myself banned from every institution imaginable because I couldn't contain my extreme disappointment and anger with the world. Looking back, it's like seeing a different person. I was so uncontainably furious. If I had kept going like that I would most certainly be dead by now.

I've had to modify, take time to allow it in, to let it take me down, to really feel EVERYTHING and sit with the pain. I've had to find rituals to help process that pain. I found that meditation and running really help me to create distance from the omnipresent grief. They give me the headspace to sift through the particular pain of any given day, to accept what is and to understand that it will not feel like this tomorrow. Tomorrow may be worse even but it will be different.

Dancing is a very important ritual for me. I have danced every single morning since my family died. It is something my sister and I did every day and it reminds me that there is beauty to be found amidst agonising pain, no matter what degree of trauma.

Sudden death is traumatic and the landscape as a survivor of trauma looks entirely different to when you watch someone you love die. Trauma is having the whole order of life removed and having to rebuild everything from scratch. It takes a while for the trauma to not be on the tip of your tongue at any given moment and to not totally engulf you. It's a process of rebuilding EVERY SINGLE THING in your life. Nothing is ever the same again. When my dad was dying, things were very different; I had had years to engage with the impending loss, but regardless, you never are prepared for what it actually feels like when it does come.

I was so proud of myself when I managed to begin to take care of my basic needs after my sister, her partner and my mother died. Finding some routine and self-care amidst extreme pain was an act of survival. I celebrate each small achievement in terms of trauma recovery: I remember toasting the first time I went out for a dance (three years later) and the first time I went on a date (years later).

My dad's death hit me hard. It signified the loss of everything that I come from. I agonised over legacy and was sometimes crippled by the feeling of being 'the last woman standing' in my family. That's an immense pressure and I feared I couldn't live in a world without my immediate family. I learned a lot about celebrating the beauty in the everyday, about the small wins and how to cultivate a genuine lust for life.

I have worked so hard on my grief, grabbing it firmly with both hands. I was nearly involved in the accident that killed my family, so I feel I've been given a chance to live that they would have loved to have had. When everything feels hopeless, I try to remember that there was a chain of events that kept me alive and I determinedly work hard to live as well as I can.

There is something very liberating about having already experienced some of the worst things that can ever happen to you – a fearlessness that so many people don't have.

I wished people had either said something useful or not said anything at all. So many people said unknowingly painful things: 'I've been speaking to my friends about you and we wonder how you'll survive because you've lost everything and you must just want to die.' 'You'll not have your mum at any of the important events in your life, how will you cope?' All kinds of unhelpful bullshit.

So many of those words have informed my work over the years in terms of slowly building a mental toolkit for things that may be useful to say. I think many people are just lost for words and we certainly live in a culture that struggles with being able to openly grapple with death. I don't think British people typically cope well with 'ugly emotions' – but they are an essential part of the process and they need to be treated with respect and given a place in our often-uptight world.

It is absolutely possible to live a good life after the death of people fundamental to our existence. I have lost the people I loved unconditionally but I've also been kept alive by the most incredible love of people who have now become my family.

You CAN survive grief and you CAN be happy too. It may seem unimaginable but there is nothing remarkable about me and I have managed to survive it. Not in my wildest dreams did I ever imagine I would ever be truly happy again. To me, where I am now is just a dream, I never thought it was possible and I feel really lucky most of the time.'

Grief SOS

In our work, we often get asked questions about how to cope with grief. Everyone's grief is different but we find approximations of the questions below come up time and again. The questions might resonate with your experience. We hope that the answers might help.

My husband died four years ago. I've met someone else and I'd like to start a new relationship but I feel like I'm cheating on my husband. I'm worried about how my in-laws will react and I'm nervous that my kids will think I'm trying to replace their dad.
The most important thing is that you say you feel ready to start a new relationship. We can never control anyone else's reactions and I'm sure some people will have strong opinions about the right and wrong time to embark on new love It's important to remember, however, that everyone will almost certainly want you to be happy.

Having a happy mum will be good for your children even if they find it hard at first. I'd suggest taking it very slowly. I'd talk to your kids honestly and openly about your worries and about your hopes for the future. Reassure them that no one will ever try to replace their dad and that their happiness is a priority. Explain that you've thought long and hard and that you'll always love and miss their dad but that you feel ready to take the next step with someone else. Make sure they know they can come to you with any questions and be mindful of how what you are doing impacts on them. Introduce your new partner slowly and carefully.

Your in-laws may well find it hard but they'll also understand that you need love and companionship and I hope they'll do all they can to support your new relationship. Let them know that you very much want them to continue to be a part of your family and that their support is invaluable to you.

You're not cheating on your husband, you're allowing yourself the opportunity to love again and to be loved. Remember, it will be different and it will be strange for everyone at first. There will potentially be some fallout but that's entirely natural and to be expected. The idea of change is difficult for some people, but follow your heart.

Lastly, remember that they are not the only ones who may find the change difficult; you may too. Try not to expect too much of yourself. It might be you that's finding the changes hardest to accept. If you're happy and in the right place with the right person, your family will be happy for you. Keep talking. Don't hide your feelings or your new partner. New love is a gift, enjoy it.

My beloved wife of 37 years died six months ago from COVID-19. I am absolutely furious with her for leaving me. We had the rest of our lives planned out and now she's left me alone with only a future without her ahead of me. I'm so angry with her and I don't know how to stop feeling like that.

It's OK to be angry and it's perfectly normal. Your life has been turned upside down and you're trying to find reasons and apportion blame to make some sense of it all. Sometimes there is no reason.

I'm sure you will stop being angry with your wife. It might take some time but allowing yourself to feel how you feel, whatever that is, will help the process. It's still very early days and you must be gentle with yourself. Not only has your wife died, but the future you were looking forward to has gone. If that makes you feel angry, allow yourself to be angry. Try not to fight your own emotions. To experience grief can be like learning to ride a wave. Its ebbs and flows, its ups and downs – they can be expected, of course, but they are never predictable.

Don't expect your grief to follow a particular path. Don't expect your experience to mirror the stages of grief you read about. The truth is, there is no pattern or logic – and certainly no set time when you 'should' be feeling a certain way. There are no 'shoulds' at all in grief. Allow yourself to just be. Look after yourself. Reach out. Ask for help. Find a good therapist. Talk. Cry. Reminisce. Do the things *you need* to do. Someone you loved and treasured has died and this is never going to be an easy road to travel. Be gentle with yourself.

Grief is ripping my family apart. My dad is dying and we are all trying to deal with it in our own different ways. I need us to support each other but at the moment all we seem to be doing is tearing each other apart.

Anticipatory grief often takes the form of our unconscious rehearsing for the death and a future without the person we love. People often cannot grasp how someone could be grieving for someone who is still alive. It can be lonely and isolating if you are feeling this and no one seems to understand it. Everyone grieves differently. Dr Lois Tonkin famously said that 'grief is like a fingerprint: it's different for everyone'.

You're grieving for the same man but you're all doing it differently. You'll each find your own coping mechanisms and you'll all need to take a different approach. Understanding that it's OK to do things differently and to feel things differently will help you find a way through. Respect the differences in the way you're all managing your own grief. Communication is essential. Talking to each other honestly and openly and really listening to what each other is saying. It may help you to find someone who can facilitate the conversation – a therapist or someone who is impartial. If you don't feel able to broach the subject with your siblings directly, writing them a letter could be the way forward. Remember to hold on to what you do have in common: your love for each other and your love for your dad.

FIVE THINGS I'VE LEARNED SINCE MY DAUGHTER, TALIA, DIED

by Sadie Tosun

Sadie's daughter, Talia, died from Acute Lymphoblastic Leukaemia – an aggressive blood cancer – in March 2020. She was 25 years old.

1.

Being able to swap anecdotes, photos and thoughts with your loved one's friends can be a massive source of comfort. Laughing about their quirky ways and the things that they did, with the people that love them best, is a tonic that is priceless.

2.

Do not be afraid to talk about how you REALLY feel. Burying your emotions will hit you ten-fold when you least expect it, often manifesting itself in physical symptoms that can make you feel far worse. So talk, talk, talk, cry, scream and shout.

3.

It's absolutely crazy to stop talking about your loved one like they no longer exist. A person that has been a massive part of your world doesn't just disappear because they have died. Saying their name is far more natural than not doing so. Unfortunately, society has been conditioned to become avoidant about death. Until we are part of the grief club, we do not know how to deal with all matters death-related. Break those barriers – shout their name, keep their essence alive – it's the best we can do to honour their being, and in turn teach others that it's OK.

4.

Prioritise self-care, in whatever form it takes. Love the people that are important to you. Snuggle on the sofa under a cosy blanket. Watch meaningless box sets. Put on their favourite music and sing and dance. Read quotes. Tune into podcasts. Go for long walks and most definitely immerse yourself in nature. Listen to the sound of the sea in your ears, hear the birds singing and look at the ever-changing signs of nature. Do WHATEVER it takes to get through your day.

5.

Absolutely never feel ashamed for doing whatever you need to do to navigate this life that you find yourself in. Friends and family have the best intentions, but remember that sometimes you just want to be alone. That is totally fine – you're healing, and that, my friends, is one of the hardest things you can ever do.

FIVE THINGS I'VE LEARNED ABOUT DEATH SINCE MY DAD WAS KILLED WHEN I WAS PREGNANT

by Aimie Geraghty

Aimie's dad Simon was killed in May 2017 whilst on holiday in Kefalonia, Greece.

1.

Everyone, literally everyone, will tell you that you need to look after yourself. That's fine, but all you want to do is scream and cry and scream and cry. Grief plays with your emotions. It makes you feel like your brain has a million thoughts spinning round, you're juggling your emotions and you feel like you are carrying other people's, too. Grief has a very good way of making you think you're drowning.

2.

I was seven months pregnant when my dad was taken away and I heard 'Your baby was sent to you for a reason' a lot. Something I didn't believe when I first found out I was pregnant. But now I firmly believe he was. Grieving makes you reassess how things in life happen, it makes you start believing in coincidence, it makes you believe in strange things you didn't know you could ever truly believe in.

3.

Grieving, unintentionally, makes people feel sorry for you, especially when the loss was sudden. You will feel so very, very angry at the start. The anger will slowly ease but then it will strike again at any moment. Nothing can prepare you for it.

4.

Grief makes memories come alive; a smell, a film or a song. So very often it plays tricks on us and a sudden glance out of the corner of your eye can make you think you see your loved one. The rational part of your brain knows it's not them but you just want to believe.

5.

Grieving makes you want to talk. You want to continually talk about the person who has gone and you start thinking that people around you think you're weird because all you want to do is talk about this person. It's not weird or odd; it's keeping that person alive. Keep talking, keep sharing the memories. My son will never meet his Pops but he knows who he is from pictures, knows he lives in the sky and knows he had a white van.

How to support a grieving friend

[A + L]

When Tom died by suicide, his parents spoke at his funeral about what they wanted and needed from the community around them: 'If you see us, please say hello and share your favourite memory of our beloved son. We want his name to continue being mentioned, we want to remember him, we want you to remember him. That way, he will live on.'

They were prescriptive about what they wanted because they felt so let down by their friends and family. They had noticed that people were actively avoiding them and it was adding to their pain.

There's no denying that it is difficult to be in the presence of someone who is in a great deal of pain. It's uncomfortable. There might be awkward silences. There will probably be tears. We might be scared of doing and saying the wrong things. We may well do and say the wrong things. As a society, we're just not taught how to be with people who are in pain.

In her mid-20s, when depression led Louise to not wanting to live any more, she was used to people telling her how she shouldn't be so silly. They would tell her she had everything to live for and should be feeling something, anything, other than the reality of what she was actually feeling.

One morning, a friend took her for a walk in the park and just let her talk about how and why she didn't want to live any more. She didn't interrupt.

After Louise had stopped talking, her friend just nodded and said: 'I totally get why you wouldn't want to be here any more.'

Her words were a breath of fresh air. For the first time, Louise felt listened to, acknowledged and understood. She felt heard and immediately felt better.

Diminishing other people's feelings or telling them how they 'should' be feeling doesn't help, no matter how well intentioned. The same principle applies to grief.

WHAT TO DO (AND WHAT NOT TO DO)

1. **Show your love**
   People need to feel loved when someone dies. They need to know that people care for them and about them. A kind, warm and thoughtful message in a card or a note with some flowers can help someone to feel less alone.

— Don's Experience

Showing your love doesn't require a grand gesture. Don talked about how moved he was when local shopkeepers asked about his wife after she died following a short illness. They'd lived in the same area for 45 years, shopping and eating in the local restaurants. He felt a real sense of belonging and was touched by the care and consideration of the community, even if they'd only known his wife to wave and say hello to.

— Charlotte's Experience

When Charlotte Augst's husband, David Mepham, died, she thanked those who had shown up and spoke of what had mattered most at his funeral:

'What has become so very clear to me over the course of this journey is this: the only way we can possibly respond to this heartbreaking, mind-bending vulnerability of us humans, is with love. So, I want to thank all of you who have loved us, and continued loving David, during this endlessly impossible time. You have made lasagne, you have written cards, you have sent chocolate, you have watered plants, you have assembled furniture, you have logged me into bank accounts, you have designed booklets, you have ferried our children and made plans for them, you have provided massages and poured glasses of wine. And maybe most importantly you have sat with David, in his agony, his fear and his despair. And for that I will forever be grateful.'

2. **Be really clear about what you can offer**

   Make a firm and clear offering of what you can do to help rather than saying, 'Let me know if there's anything I can do'.

   The value of practical help is often overlooked. Perhaps you can walk the dogs, feed the cats, cook a meal or take the children to school. You might want to suggest a cup of coffee or a trip to the cafe at the garden centre.

   If you offer to take them to the theatre or the cinema, check what the play or film is about first. The person you are supporting may need a trigger warning. For example, a friend took her grieving friend to see *A Star is Born* featuring Lady Gaga. She wasn't familiar with the story and didn't realise it was about addiction, depression and suicide.

3. **Don't compare your grief with theirs**

   'I know how you feel.'

   Oh no, you don't! Your grief is not the same as anyone else's so don't claim to know how they feel. You haven't walked in their shoes.

   We all deal with grief differently. Even if the loss feels similar, it's not. Someone's grief following the death of their mum may be very different to your grief after your mum died. You both had very different relationships with your mums and you're very different people. Your grief will be different.

4. **IT'S NOT ABOUT YOU!**

   People will really appreciate hearing a story about their person who has died; they'll love to be told how much they meant to you and the impact they had on your life but what they really don't want to have to do is support and comfort you. THEIR person has died, not yours.

   During a grief support session Anna spoke to a father whose son had died unexpectedly after a very short illness. He spoke of feeling unable to leave the house, unable to pick up the phone, unable to even send an email or text because whoever he saw, whoever he spoke to, whoever's arms he sought solace in 'highjacked' his feelings with their own and he almost always ended up comforting *them*, telling *them* it would all be OK, showing *them* the empathy and compassion he so desperately needed himself.

   'I've spent the last week managing other people's reactions to the news. It's exhausting.
   They're more upset than I am and I'm his wife!'
   SUSAN, WHOSE HUSBAND DIED IN 2019

5. **Leave all judgement at the door**

Some people might continue with their daily lives – they'll go to work, attend meetings and behave as though nothing has happened. It doesn't mean they're any less devastated, it just means they're finding a different way through their pain.

Others might go to bed and not want to get out again. Others will keep busy, making plans to fill every moment of the day and night until they feel ready to face what's happened.

'Why don't you go home?' or 'Take some time off work' isn't always helpful advice. Some people may prefer to have a place to go, a structure, a routine, a purpose and a timetable. It may give some order to a time of overwhelming chaos.

— Anne's Experience

Anne talked about how helpful daily messages from her manager were, when her father died. The messages simply said, 'Just checking in.'

'She didn't put a question mark so there was no need to reply if I didn't want to. She made no assumptions about what I wanted to talk about. Sometimes I'd respond with an outpouring of my deepest darkest grief or I'd tell her about the breakfast I was eating. Sometimes I'd simply send her a "Thank you". But it was always warming to know she was there, checking on me.'

6. **Don't dismiss or diminish their feelings**

Your friend may feel as though what's happened is the end of their world. Don't tell them it's not. You're not there to minimise, diminish or invalidate their pain. Mirror whatever it is they're feeling.

If they say it's unfair, say, 'Yes, it really is so unfair.'

Now is not the time to tell them how amazing they are and how bright their future might be. Stay in the present moment and deal with whatever comes up for them.

Whatever you do, don't tell them not to be sad or upset. If they want to cry, let them.

7. **Ask open-ended questions**

Try asking 'What are you feeling right now?' rather than 'Are you feeling sad?'. Ask questions that invite more than a yes or no answer. Let people explore how they feel. Be interested in their responses.

8. **Say their name, talk about them**
   Don't be scared to talk about the person who has died. Share a favourite memory or something about them you really loved or valued.

   People often avoid talking about the person who has died because they worry that mentioning them will be upsetting. Most people want to talk about them. If they don't want to, they'll let you know.

9. **Don't project**
   Don't tell them how they must be feeling or make assumptions about how they're coping.

   Don't speak on behalf of the person who has died – 'He wouldn't want you to be so sad.' How do you know? Ask yourself, is this really helping my friend to deal with the depth of their pain?

10. **Remember the anniversaries and the difficult days**
    After the funeral, most people will disappear and return to their everyday lives. But for the person who is grieving, life has changed. Birthdays, anniversaries and special days can be particularly difficult.

    Remember them. Acknowledge them. Perhaps send a kind and thoughtful note, or offer to do something lovely on that date to honour the person who has died.

11. **Don't try to fix their pain**
    It's important to remember that you can't take their pain away, however difficult it is for you, and for them, to sit with.

    What worked for others may not necessarily work for the person you're supporting. Don't give advice based on what worked for your Auntie Cath when Uncle Jim died.

    Most of the time people just want to be heard. Just being there, in the present moment, is enough. People often don't need you to do anything in particular, they just need to not be alone with their hurt. They need someone to bear witness to their pain, to show them the unbearable weight of their sorrow can be borne.

    If you say something wrong, you can just apologise, say that you didn't mean to hurt them, that knowing what to say is really difficult, and move on.

12. **Let them be sad**
    It's OK not to be OK. It's OK to be sad.

    You can hold their hand through the darkness, and guide them to the light, but only when they're ready. Just be there with hugs, a hand to hold theirs and a shoulder to cry on.

FIVE THINGS I'VE LEARNED ABOUT FRIENDSHIP SINCE LOSING MY DAD

by Hannah May

Hannah lost her dad four years ago to an aggressive, rapid cancer. She is a passionate advocate for normalising dialogue about death and loss, and is part of the team behind the Grief Network, a community for bereaved young people based in London.

1.

Some friends will hype – they will show up for the funeral, organise a group gift and text you endlessly for a week straight – and then they will lose their patience for what you are going through. Other friends will rally – quietly, slowly, genuinely. Those are the friends who will be there for the anniversaries, the milestones and all the small trigger moments in between.
Surround yourself with the latter

2.

It is OK for friendships and relationships to change, or to be lost entirely. When my dad died, I felt like my identity and sense of self shifted overnight – I didn't feel like the same person and I didn't want others to expect the same of me.

3.

It is not your job to carry the weight of other people's discomfort or expectations. If they can't sit with the discomfort to have a conversation, they're never going to understand what the discomfort feels like to carry each day. It is not up to you to teach them – your energy is better spent in other ways right now.

4.

New and meaningful friendships can be built from the most heartbreaking of circumstances. At my dad's funeral I met two of his friends and their children for the first time, and they have become like family to me. Grief has also given me the Grief Network team: a bunch of beautiful friends that just get it, and who are up for a raw and real conversation about death, loss and grief at any hour.

5.

The friendship, companionship or relationship you had with the person you lost hasn't gone anywhere – it just can't continue or evolve. My dad's taste in music, sense of humour and thirst for the seaside haven't changed, and though I miss all those things with an unbearable sadness, I can also use those things to bring him back to me when I need to.

FIVE THINGS I'VE LEARNED FROM SUPPORTING MY HUSBAND THROUGH HIS GRIEF

by Yvonne Gavan

Yvonne has been supporting her husband after the death of his 37-year-old brother.

1.

Be patient. Supporting your partner through deep loss can be very confusing. And although grief affects everyone differently, the emotional landscape that lies ahead is likely to be tumultuous. You'll be faced with blank denial, searing rage and everything in between. Be the person who doesn't expect them to be strong. Tell them it's OK.

2.

Cultivate resilience. It's very hard – In the midst of your partner's depression and pain – to feel that it's not just a little bit about you. It isn't. Be kind to yourself – get all the help you need – and don't feel guilty for wishing that things were different. Helping a partner through grief is not easy. Just keep going.

3.

Accept change. When my husband lost his brother, Euan, his sense of self was dismantled. It was as though there was a huge crack in the foundations of his being. And it was painful to watch. But I've now learned that there are both endings and beginnings in death. Through learning to live without his brother, my husband has forged a new understanding of who he is. And the fracture in his being – like in the ancient Japanese art of Kintsugi – has been filled with a beautiful seam of gold.

4.

Grief can be complex and can cause untold conflicts. Although everyone in my husband's family was left with a Euan-shaped hole after his death, the outline – the size and jagged edges – of each individual's loss was unique. Remind your partner that their broken heart is still connected to all those left behind. Tell them the story of love that still surrounds them. Gently.

5.

Stay focused on the light. Because grief is like a dark tunnel with unchartered terrain. And when you support a partner through deep loss, you navigate this tunnel with them, while holding their hand. Know that, even though the darkness will be so overwhelming that you'll keep losing your way, the light will come. Just a flicker at first, then gradually a brightness that extends to everything.

What to say when you don't know what to say

[L]

'People say shitty things because they don't know what else to say.
ANNALISE LUMLEY

Yes, it's SO difficult to know what to say. It can be awkward and uncomfortable. Don't be afraid to get it wrong and don't shy away if there are tears. Try to be there with no judgement, comparison or expectation. Don't project. Just our presence and honest intentions are often enough.

RESPONDING TO GRIEF

What not to say	What to say
I know how you feel.	I want you to know that I love you and I'm going to be here for you through this.
Time heals. You'll get over it.	I'm thinking of you.
He's in a better place/he's at peace now/he's out of pain.	This is so unfair and I'm so sorry.
God only takes the best.	I don't know what to say but I want you to know I'm here for you.
You must be so relieved.	I can just listen, or I can distract you, whatever you prefer.
My aunt's friend had cancer. She treated it with a detox diet she found on the internet.	This is so hard. But you've done hard things before and I know you can do this.
At least she had a long life.	No need to respond, but I want you to know that I'm thinking about you.
Everything happens for a reason.	I'm so sorry. It sucks that you have to go through this.
It was his time to go.	I'm so sorry for all the ways you're hurting right now. I'm hurting for you and with you.

When a partner dies

'I keep making two cups of tea. And then I remember ... I only need to make one now.'
BARBARA, WHOSE HUSBAND PAUL DIED IN MARCH 2019

A partner is someone we may have built our lives around and shared the intricacies of our daily existence with. So when they die, every single aspect of our lives will change. It's not just the big things, it's the small things, too. Ann Drysdale describes the desolate nature of this kind of loss so beautifully in her poem, 'Winter Camping', which you can read on the next page.

'Winter Camping'

One thing was always understood between us.
When you were ready to go Winter Camping
I would not be part of the adventure.
You bought equipment and wrote plans in journals,
Calling it Personal Development,
Anticipating solitude and challenge.

You never did it. Life got in the way
Until death stopped the prospect altogether.
I have not often thought about it since.

Sleeping without you was a big adventure.
A single bed, electrically warmed,
Beside the open door on to the balcony.

Birds visited. Various gastropods
Slid over the threshold and were welcome.
Cats came and went. Last night there was a storm.

I went to sleep enchanted by the wind.
It died in the small hours; the silence woke me.
I am in an extraordinary place.

Dark, starred with tiny lights across the valley,
Clouded with frozen breath. I move carefully,
Explore the limits of my warm cocoon.

Now on my left there is a precipice.
Cold fingers trace the edges of my ears.
I am alone and this is Winter Camping.

ANN DRYSDALE

FIVE THINGS I'VE LEARNED ABOUT SURVIVING THE SUDDEN DEATH OF MY HUSBAND

by Jane Kiely

Jane is a mother of two whose husband collapsed from a catastrophic brain aneurysm in November 2017. He died 24 hours later in hospital surrounded by his family and closest friends.

1.
Your mental health has to be a priority
To keep myself as balanced as possible, I eat well, write in my journal, avoid stimulants, sleep (or rest) when I can, go to counselling. I take time to do what makes me feel alive and present – and I turn down invitations if I'm feeling overwhelmed.

2.
Help is out there
Asking for, and accepting help from others is not only essential, but it has deepened mine and my children's relationships with our friends and family. Many people will not know how to help you at first; over time you'll all figure this out together, but don't fight it. Doing this alone is impossible.

3.
You have access to resources you didn't know existed
There are loads of charities that exist to help you and/or your children. Google, ask counsellors, teachers, doctors and employers. Tell them what you need help with and be open and honest. It is scary at first, but they will know the answers.

4.
Find your tribe
Find a group of people (or even one person) who is on a similar journey and talk. Empathy is hugely important, but when you're widowed at 37, there aren't usually many people in your existing friendship group who can relate to your situation. I had to find my tribe, but it was worth the search.

5.
Be kind to those closest to you
What you may find comforting right now, might be the opposite for your kids, or for the siblings and parents of your loved one. And vice versa, so look for the intention behind their actions, keep an open dialogue and explain how it makes you feel. Talk about your intentions before you act and make compromises.

FIVE THINGS I'VE LEARNED AFTER LOSING MY PARTNER IN AN UNLABELLED RELATIONSHIP

by G

'When J came back to the city, she moved in with me and became my partner in an open and unlabelled relationship. The words we used to describe our relationship changed often, but we never lost our love for each other. J died unexpectedly on 28 April 2020.'

1.

It's OK to use words to describe our relationship that we didn't settle on when you were alive. The struggle to settle on a definition impedes the process of expressing my grief. I owe no one an explanation and my words about how I describe us are mine alone now that you're gone.

2.

Other people I'm seeing might not want to hear about you. My world has stopped without you, but the rest of it keeps turning. There are so many people who love you as much as I do and they are who I can save my words for. That's OK.

3.

Instead of being angry that others have known you as deeply, playfully and intimately as I have, I can rejoice in the fact that your love has ended up right where it should be – with everyone who had the pleasure of catching your eye.

4.

I know we did right by each other in the end, because I feel I'm mourning a partner and a friend all at once. Our relationship cycled through different meanings and I miss every single thing we ever were for each other.

5.

There is no past tense of the word love. 'Til death do us part is a lie. You aren't here anymore, but I am and I love you just as deeply as when you breathed.

WHAT TO REMEMBER WHEN SUPPORTING A FRIEND WHO IS GRIEVING THE DEATH OF A PARTNER

[A]

It's well documented that bereaved people lose a proportion of their friends when a partner dies. Sometimes they just can't adjust to the new dynamic. The death of a life partner coupled with the loss of friends can make for a very lonely existence indeed.

Here's how to really show up for a friend when they need it most:

1. Perhaps they didn't do the cooking or they don't feel like making the effort now they're alone. Perhaps nothing tastes the same and they've lost their appetite. It's worth remembering that they shared mealtimes with their partner for many years and now there's a painfully empty chair at the table. *How about inviting them round for dinner? You could offer to help them make a meal or teach them how to cook a few staples. Helping out isn't about replacing their partner, or trying to fill the gaps they've left; it's about easing the transition into their new life, letting them know there can be life after death.*

2. Going to the cinema, a trip to the supermarket or going on holiday can become a solitary and lonely experience after a partner has died. *Can you arrange to take them shopping? Perhaps you can organise a night out. How can you include them in your own plans?*

3. Don't overwhelm them, but don't abandon them either. Always ensure they know they're not a burden. Give them some time and space. They need to know they can manage. They need to know they can cope and have all they need within themselves. Some people find there's an element of pride in finding out they're more than capable of doing things they've never done before.

    We worked with a lady who found life really difficult after her husband of 57 years died. She said that one of the loveliest things anyone did for her was when her neighbour, without asking, took her bins out for collection each week. She hardly knew her but it made such a difference. She felt held and cared for. *Is there something small that you can do regularly to help? How can you ensure you're being helpful and supportive, rather than overbearing?*

4. Don't always visit as a couple, and don't always go alone. Be mindful of how the person who is grieving will feel.
    Consider what you'd want and need if you were in their shoes.

5. Don't overwhelm them with endless visits and communications. It's important to offer help you can maintain. If you burn out by being there all the time and then find you can't sustain it, they'll effectively 'lose' something else important from their life, too.
    What support can you realistically provide? How can you look after yourself too?

6. Talk about their partner. Say their name. Share your stories and memories.
    Can you encourage them to do the same? Let them know it's OK to talk about their partner. It's OK to remember them.

Fran Hall is our colleague and our friend. While we were finishing this book, we were devastated to hear about the death of her husband, Steve. Even though restrictions were in place due to COVID-19, his funeral was moving and meaningful. Fran has kindly allowed us to share the poem that was read at his graveside, as well as her words on love and loss.

I HAVE COME HOME

Under a soft blanket of fallen leaves,
safe in the hush of the whispering trees
I have come home.

My time here on earth is now done,
all the noise and the clamour, the joy and the pain,
the powerful life force that drove me onwards
has slipped away into the quiet of eternity,
and I am at peace.

From now on, I will dance through your memories
threading thoughts of love through your heart.
The pain of loss will gradually ease, and the sadness will lift.
The days will be lighter, and the nights not so long,
For I am still here.

When you walk through this place, you will feel me
in the gentle touch of the breeze on your face,
in the sunlight dappling the forest floor,
in the murmur of the branches high above you,
I am all around.

I have returned to the place from whence I came,
to the elements that created me.
The earth that gave me the life I so loved
has now welcomed me back to her,
to be at one with all her beauty.

Here, under my blanket of fallen leaves
I have found my resting place.
I have come home.

FRAN HALL

'Years ago, when I was manager of this beautiful woodland burial ground, these words came to me.

My poem has, apparently, been read at many hundreds of funerals since I wrote it. I've heard it once or twice over the years, in different settings, read for people I never met, and have always felt glad when I recognised it. It is wonderful that my words have resonated with others; poetry should belong to anyone who is moved or touched by it.

And yet these words are mine, this poem is special and personal to me. I don't know where this poetry came from, it was as if the words came to me and through me for a reason. Perhaps they did. Perhaps now I understand why.

This week, these words were read in the woodland where I wrote them, as I stood at the edge of the grave that had been prepared for the body of the man that I love.

My words were read by my wonderful friend Isabel Russo, who had just delivered the most extraordinary, transformational ceremony that caught and shared his essence.

He was the love of my life, my soulmate, my partner, the man who had saved my life from a fire eight years before, on the exact same date as the day we were burying him, the man who had been my husband for just three weeks before he died from COVID-19.

As Isabel spoke the last lines, and birdsong and silence filled the stillness, we lifted the weight of the coffin and lowered it into the grave.

Everything was absolutely perfect. A circle completed in that moment. Despite everything, despite the profound loss and sadness, I felt peaceful and content.

I was surrounded by love. I had carried out this one last act together with three of our friends, Lucy, Louise and Colin, all incredible funeral directors, and all of whom had loved Steve. Together, we had fulfilled every single one of his wishes for his funeral. He had left me the greatest of gifts, the knowledge of exactly what he wanted to happen when the time came for his funeral.

Everyone who was there that day felt his presence. He was all around, he was there in the music, the lyrics, the words of the tributes, the spectacle of the motorcycles, the stunning surroundings, the sunshine and the rain, the raw power of seeing his beautiful cardboard coffin laid to rest in the grave. He was right there with us all.

I think part of his legacy is the lesson he gave us all in facing mortality. We are all going to die. Life and death are intertwined, and we cannot look away from death. If we face it full on, then we can walk through the rest of our life unafraid.

Steve Mead. My darling man. I love you.'

Written by Fran Hall in memory of Stephen Clifford Mead
19.10.1954 – 18.10.2020

FIVE THINGS I'VE LEARNED
SINCE MY PARTNER DIED

By Yasemin Hassan

'Losing a partner at 24 is something you never expect to happen to you.
You enter into a relationship, fall in love, embrace life together, make plans and
start building a future with your person. They become your best friend. When they
get sick, your world stops. Your future together is on hold. When they die, your
whole life completely changes.'

1

I never wrote anything before my partner died. I used to find it fascinating
that people could articulate words on paper. Now, out of nowhere, writing has
become my biggest comfort. I write to her about how I feel and my thoughts. It's
strangely comforting. I find it really hard to express to other people how I actually
feel. I feel guilty for how others feel when I speak the truth. When writing to my
partner on paper, there's no judgment, nothing is censored, it just flows like
word vomit and I can say whatever I want. It's a huge release.

2

Some people don't know how to deal with grief and even though it's
frustrating, I've now come to realise that it's OK. Some people just come into
your life at a particular time and show up in a way you never expected, which
at the time you really need – that is a beautiful thing.

3

They say no big changes in your first year of grief. If you feel like you want
to change your life, DO IT! I changed mine completely and so far it's working.
When she died, I felt like the life I was living wasn't fulfilling. Although it was scary
and filled me with tremendous anxiety, all I could think was that the worst has
already happened so what have I got to lose?

4

FIND YOURSELF! As corny as that sounds, it's actually true. Take the time to
discover who you are. When losing a partner, especially to an illness, you forget
who you are. Spend time alone, get to know you. Go for long walks. Have bed
days! Find what you like to do. Try and find things that make you feel closer to
your person. It provides me with comfort and helps me to get out of bed every
day. Visiting the cemetery has been the biggest form of comfort and gets me
out of the house, even if it's just for an hour.

And here is the life mantra I try to follow even if I am having a BAD BED DAY! I love, laugh and cry in AWE of her. I visit all our favourite places to be closer to her, look at the sky to think of her, lay on the beach for her, eat all of her favourite foods in her memory, listen to her favourite songs to hear her, dance with her sister for her, climb every rock with her, sing for her and embrace life because of her. And I keep my head up, in honour of her.

Her name is Talia. I'll forever talk about the person who changed and continues to change my life.

Grief lasts a lifetime

[A]

The lives of the living are dramatically altered by death. Death necessitates a total restructuring of the world as we knew it. Nothing is ever the same again when someone important to us dies. We grieve the loss of life, and the loss of the future we had imagined and planned. Grief is multi-faceted and unpredictable, and its impact is felt in all aspects of our life. It doesn't come in neat stages. There are no quick fixes or shortcuts and it can be terribly lonely.

Whatever happens, how you feel right now will change and it will keep changing. But it *does* get easier to manage and life will almost always find a way through.

We need to talk

[Λ + L]

'I believe that engaging with death is both important and overlooked. My experience tells me that death can play a role in helping us enjoy life. I also believe that focusing on death can play a part in helping us get to grips with some big challenges – like supporting older people, climate change, a broken economic system and chronic global inequality. This may not immediately make sense but if we can face up to death we can face up to anything.'
JON UNDERWOOD, THE FOUNDER OF DEATH CAFE

The more we engage with death as part of life, and life as part of death, the better our lives, and ultimately our deaths will be. But having the conversation isn't always easy. It's not something we're taught how to do. It can be awkward, embarrassing and uncomfortable. Some people might refuse to have the conversation altogether; others will be full of anxiety and fear. Talking about it won't make it happen, but avoiding it will make things much harder for everyone. In this section, we'll learn:

1. Why it's important to talk about death and dying.
2. How to gently open up a conversation about death and dying.
3. How to engage with death in interesting and thought-provoking ways.
4. How to talk to children about death and dying.
5. Questions children might ask and how to answer them.

FIVE THINGS I'VE LEARNED ABOUT TALKING ABOUT CANCER AND DEATH AS A BREAST SURGEON WITH BREAST CANCER

by Liz O'Riordan

Liz is a consultant breast surgeon who was diagnosed with stage 3 breast cancer at the age of 40.

1.

You have to talk about the elephant in the room with your loved ones. As painful as it is, get them to acknowledge that you might die sooner rather than later. Accept it. And then move on.

2.

When you talk about cancer on social media, some of your friends will die. Sometimes several die in a week. It's really really hard. And it's OK to step back and take a break.

3.

You will think crazy, irrational, illogical thoughts that many people won't understand. A friend told me he was almost pleased when his cancer came back because he could finally stop waiting for that day to come. And I got it.

4.

Get your life in order – wills, lasting power of attorney, finances. I only did that when my cancer came back but it was a huge relief knowing that everything was sorted.

5.

Thinking about your funeral doesn't have to be sad – watch Peter Kay's *Car Share* (series 1, episode 2) when Kayleigh plans her funeral music for her audience – it will make you smile.

How to talk about death and dying

[A + L]

If we can find a way to broach this subject, we may find that our anxieties and fears will reduce. By giving everyone a chance to share their concerns and worries, and listening to each other with an open heart and mind, we can all take a more empowered approach to the end of our lives. We're always working on ways to help people to have what can be a really difficult conversation. Here are some of them:

1. Open up the conversation with gentle questions. You don't have to be overt. Gently talking around the subject at first can really help. There's nothing wrong with doing a bit of stealth questioning! From experience, if you offer something of yourself it can begin the conversation. Show that you're comfortable having conversations about life and death. Set an example. 'I'm making a list of all the books I've read that I've loved to give to my children in the hope that it'll inspire them to read them too. I hope they'll pass it down to their children and their children's children too. What are your favourite books?'
2. You could try discussing your dreams for the future and your own bucket list. Share all the things you still want to achieve and express your concern that you won't have time. 'I've been thinking that I'd really love to go to Alaska. Since watching *Northern Exposure* when I was really small it's been on the list of places I want to see. I'd feel really cheated if I didn't get to go before I die. Is there anywhere in the world you still want to visit?'
3. Share your regrets. Ask about theirs. 'I really regret not being a better friend to Jay. I look back and can't believe how badly I behaved. I wish I could make things better between us. Is there anything you regret? If you could go back in time, what would you do differently?'
4. Confess the things that frighten you, even if they're not rational. 'When it's my time, I want to be cremated. After watching a scary movie when I was young, I'm terrified of being buried alive.'
5. Another way in is to talk medically and factually. By removing emotion from the topic sometimes people feel safer to begin to explore it. Thoughts and feelings will of course come into play but discussing things 'as a matter of fact' can be an excellent starting point. 'I was watching a documentary on the internet about cutting-edge treatments for people with lung cancer. Did you know that there's a new treatment being trialled in Australia? The problem is the side effects...'

6. If you listen to someone talking about being unwell or someone close to them having died, they'll often begin by telling you the basic facts of their illness or their death. Some people find it easier to begin by focusing on the why, how, when and what, rather than on the feelings attached to the story.
7. You could try opening up the conversation by talking about the music you'd like to be played at your funeral. Almost everyone we've ever met has had an idea about the music they'd like, or not like. It's a gentle and sometimes humorous way of opening up a bigger conversation. 'I can't decide on any song I'd like to be played at my funeral but I'm compiling a long list of all the things I don't want! What song would make you turn in your grave?'

THE 10 MOST REQUESTED TRACKS AT MORTLAKE CREMATORIUM IN 2020

'**My Way**' – Frank Sinatra
'**Time to Say Goodbye**' – Sarah Brightman & Andrea Bocelli
'**What a Wonderful World**' – Louis Armstrong
'**Unforgettable**' – Nat King Cole
'**Stranger on the Shore**' – Acker Bilk
'**Somewhere over the Rainbow**' – Eva Cassidy
'**Bring me Sunshine**' – Morecambe & Wise
'**Moonlight Serenade**' – Glenn Miller
'**Three Little Birds**' – Bob Marley
'**I Will Always Love You**' – Whitney Houston

Remember – these topics are too big for one conversation. You're planting seeds, watering them and watching them grow. If we have the courage to start talking about these things when there's no sign of illness to load them with the burden of sorrow, they will eventually become a normal part of our everyday way of being.

If someone really doesn't want to talk about death and dying, you can't make them. You might find it helpful to read Anna's words on the complexities of being on the same emotional page in the section about death and dying (*see* p. 93).

If you're looking to engage with death as a part of life, there are other more obvious ways to engage and open up the conversation:

1. **Go to a Death Cafe**
   A Death Cafe is a gathering of strangers who come together to talk about death while drinking tea and eating cake. It's run as a social enterprise so the gatherings are all run by volunteer hosts. They take place everywhere from front rooms to cemeteries, festivals, tea shops and local libraries.

   You can't have a Death Cafe without cake. When discussing something as unknown and uncertain as death, something as reassuringly of this world as cake is essential.

   Impressively, more than 10,000 Death Cafes have been held around the world since the movement began in our friend Jon Underwood's front room in London in 2011. That's a lot of conversations and a lot of cake.

   It's important to understand that a Death Cafe is simply a group of people meeting to talk about death. It's not bereavement support, grief counselling or group therapy.

   You can find your nearest Death Cafe by typing in your postcode on the Death Cafe website: www.deathcafe.com

2. **Host a Feast of Life, Taste of Death**
   Feast of Life, Taste of Death is one of the most delicious ways to talk about death. It takes the form of a communal meal, where people come together to share stories over food that means something to them. It's an accessible way of engaging with the difficult emotions that come up around death by breaking bread together.

   All you need is a few people (three to 12) who are willing to come together to share stories over the food that's been significant to them at some point in their lives. You could host the Feast of Life around your kitchen table at home, or you might want to hire a space such as a community hall. It can take any format, such as a candle-lit supper or even a picnic in a park.

   When we last held a Feast of Life, we sent out this message, giving our guests plenty of time to reflect upon food that had been important to them: 'What would you eat if you knew you were dying? Is there a dish that makes you feel alive? Is there something that reminds you of the best of life? What food have you been given to help you through the tough times?'

   Once the feast was laid out, we asked everyone around the table to introduce themselves and the story behind the food they'd brought along – roasted tomato soup, oranges, Caribbean takeaway, jacket potatoes with beans, cheese and coleslaw, ackee and saltfish patties, *pho*, chocolate brownies, Swedish pancakes, honey-roasted sweet potatoes and so much more.

It was an opportunity to feast on life, talk about death, share beautiful stories and connect with friends, old and new. For more information, have a look at the website: www.lifedeathwhatever.com/feast-of-life-taste-of-death

3. **Host a funeral-awareness party**

It's so much easier to arrange a funeral when someone has died if you already know about funerals. It's difficult to make empowered decisions about a funeral if you don't know very much about them.

A funeral-awareness party is a little like a Tupperware party. You invite a group of friends to come together to learn about funerals as well as to talk about what you might like for your own. It doesn't have to be gloomy. You can serve refreshments and have a good time learning about funerals and discussing what you'd like to happen at your own funeral. You could invite a modern funeral director or experienced celebrant along to share their experiences and answer your questions.

To get the conversation flowing, you might want to discuss some of the questions on p. 175–6.

4. **Go for a walk in a cemetery**

There's nothing quite like a stroll through nature to see the cycle of life and death in action. Cemeteries are often little-used yet beautiful green spaces, full of wildlife and nature. A Sunday afternoon spent walking the dog while looking at the old graves could be a way of initiating a difficult conversation.

— John's Experience

'We went for a walk in an old cemetery on the other side of town just after John received the news about his cancer returning. It's more of a wildlife reserve now. He was really reluctant to talk about what was going to happen next, so we walked in silence. In the oldest part of the cemetery, he spotted a grave for a lady called Iris who had died in 1895. He began telling me about his Aunt Iris who had died when he was a child. I asked how it had made him feel and he started talking about how no one in his family had acknowledged it and how much that had impacted their lives. He said he didn't want that for his own family.'

5. **Watch it on TV**

   When Hayley Cropper died on *Coronation Street* and was cremated in a floral cardboard coffin, more people than ever before googled 'cardboard coffin'. Her, at the time, unconventional choice, prompted a lot of conversations in front rooms all over the UK.

   When *Emmerdale*'s Lisa Dingle died in May 2019, a beautiful scene from the soap showed the funeral directors collecting her from home in a private ambulance, as her family stood around the driveway and paid their final respects. In a zoomed-out shot, the private ambulance was filmed slowly moving away, as life itself continued in the countryside surrounding her farm.

   Death and dying are much easier to engage with when we're not the ones directly affected. Watching a TV show or movie together and then talking about whatever comes up can be an easy way into a difficult conversation.

Many moons ago, bored one Sunday afternoon, I turned on the TV and *Who Will Love My Children?* was playing. It broke my heart and I cried for several hours after I'd stopped watching. I still talk about it now. It has precipitated more conversations about death and dying than anything I've read or watched since. Here are a few of our suggestions for films and TV series that may inspire a difficult conversation:

On illness – *Iris, Still Alice, The Diving Bell and The Butterfly, Bodies*
On grief – *After Life, Manchester by the Sea, Terms of Endearment, Stepmom, Who Will Love My Children?, Me and Earl and the Dying Girl, The Fault in our Stars*
On life and death – *Beaches, This Is Us, Big Fish, Fried Green Tomatoes*
On funerals – *Six Feet Under, Harold and Maude, Almost Heaven, Departures, Captain Fantastic, Still Life*

Remember, it doesn't matter how you start talking or what prompts the discussion, it just matters that you find a way to have the conversation.

FIVE THINGS YOU SHOULD KNOW WHEN TALKING ABOUT DEATH

by Tracey Bleakley

Tracey is the chief executive of Hospice UK, the national charity for hospice care. In her role, she encourages everyone to have an open and honest conversation about death.

1.

We might not like to hear it, but we are all going to die someday. Talking about it won't make it happen, but ignoring the topic makes it harder for us to make our plans, and to help others make theirs. Each year people put on hundreds of events as part of the Dying Matters campaign – each different, but each helps people have these conversations.

2.

Being willing to discuss death, and to make our plans, can be a sort of final gift to those close to us. When our time comes, they won't need to argue about the funeral, or who gets what, or anything. If you've made your plans, they will know you are getting the end-of-life care and send-off that you want.

3.

There's something quite liberating about having these conversations and getting your plans in place. Once it's done, you can get on with getting the most out of the life you have, knowing that when you die all the key practical matters will have been taken care of.

4.

About 1 per cent of the population dies each year, and each one of those deaths affects many others. If we're more comfortable talking about death, we're better able to help friends, colleagues and everyone we know who is going to be dealing with grief.

5.

Death will rarely be a happy topic of conversation, but it is an important one. The least that we owe to each other is to take part in that conversation when someone we know wants to have it. Everyone's different in how and when they approach it, and even if we aren't ready yet ourselves, we need to help our friends who are.

How to talk to children about death, dying and grief

[A]

In the UK alone, the death of one or both parents will impact around 24,000 under-16s. That means roughly one in 20 children is living with grief.

On 1 March 2018 the government announced its plans to make sex and relationship education compulsory in all secondary schools, and relationships education compulsory in all primary schools from September 2019. This is brilliant news and it paves the way for PSHE (personal, social and health education) in its entirety – including matters relating to death – to become mandatory, but we still must keep pushing until it becomes an integral part of the national curriculum. A pressing question that must be answered, too, is who is going to teach this most essential and fundamental of subjects and what are they going to say? I've long believed that the only way to begin to incite change and to truly normalise death, dying and grief is to start with primary education. The children are, after all, our future. They will shape the next generation. They will decide how they live and how they die.

During the Life. Death. Whatever. festival, we came up against a wall of ignorance and disapproval from staff, volunteers and visitors alike because of the subject matter of the exhibition and the events we were putting on. Because we were so committed to ensuring Life. Death. Whatever. made a difference and really did get people talking, we were there almost every single day so we could talk to people and engage them with the subject. Pieces of work were vetoed, children's coffins were removed and other pieces were censored or came with a disclaimer that some may find the content upsetting. This was not something we anticipated and the strength of feeling came, perhaps naively, as a shock to us. All of the complaints came from adults.

And then the children came. They jumped joyously in blackboard coffins filled with ballpit balls. They drew pictures and created memory cards for people who had died, sharing stories about them with us. They patted and cuddled therapy dogs and cats, they came to photography workshops where they created still-life set-ups with skulls and bones and other deathly accoutrements. They asked questions and they were fascinated by the answers.

In my family, we sit around and talk about what colour we're going to paint our coffins. We don't talk about it in a way that requires a big 'I'm going to sit you down now and tell you that life is finite' moment, we talk about it like it's a natural process. We all live, we all die, there's no more of a big deal to be made of it than that. But in lots of families when people die, it is talked about in whispers, kept away from children and they are not invited to go to the funeral. For lots of children, when their goldfish dies, it is replaced rather than allowing them to know the truth.

We do children a disservice by hiding the reality of life from them. We just have to acknowledge that we're not here forever and that fact doesn't have to be morbid and maudlin. My kids are not morbid and maudlin, they don't really feel any which way about it, they just know it's part of life.

How adults react and how they deal with end of life and death very much informs how their kids do. When I worked in a day centre for people living with life-limiting illness, as part of the role, I went into local schools to talk to children about end-of-life issues. They were interested, eager to learn and asked lots of questions. It wasn't a subject they shied away from or didn't want to talk about.

Death is normal but we've turned it into something else. By refusing to talk about it, we've put it on this huge pedestal and we've labelled it the most terrifying thing that can happen to anyone ever. When, actually, I've worked with a lot of people for whom it isn't those things. They've lived a good life, they've loved and they feel like they've had a really beautiful time and they're ready. When somebody dies in that way, it's sad that you're not going to see them any more but there's this real feeling that they have lived and that's the wonderful bit.

WE NEED TO TALK

Children aren't generally frightened of talking about death, dying and grief. Often, they're quite fascinated by it. If children have had personal experience of death they will sometimes take on the feelings and thoughts of the grown-ups around them. It's therefore important that adults try not to project their own fears about the subject on to children. It's essential to normalise the subject. To make it part of the everyday. Something you'd discuss over breakfast.

Children are never too young to be part of a conversation about life and death. The younger the better and the easier it is to make it all a normal part of life. There are several strategies you can use to help with this:

- Life cycles of species and of plant life are a very gentle introduction to the notion that nothing living is permanent.
- People have told me they've deliberately got pets with a short lifespan so they can begin to teach their children that nothing stays forever.
- There are some excellent children's books and films. If you don't feel confident enough to open the conversation yourself, start by reading a book or watching a film.

FILMS ABOUT DEATH FOR CHILDREN

Older children

The Fault In Our Stars by John Green – book and a film (YA PG13)

Me and Earl and the Dying Girl by Jesse Andrews – book and a film
(YA 14 years+)

Bridge to Terabithia by Katherine Paterson – book and a film
(YA PG 9 years+)

My Girl by Patricia Hermes – book and film (YA PG13)

Vicky Angel by Jacqueline Wilson – book (9 years+)

A Monster Calls by Patrick Ness – book and film (YA PG13)

Younger children

Coco – film (PG)

No Matter <u>What</u> by Debi Gliori – book (0 years+)

Death, Duck and the Tulip by Wolf Erlbruch – book (3 years+)

Sad Book by Michael Rosen – book (5 years+)

Always and Forever by Alan Durant – book (3 years+)

Goodbye Mog by Judith Kerr – book (0 years+)

Tadpole's Promise by Jeanne Willis – book (0 years+)

I Want My Hat Back by Jon Klassen – book (0 years+)

Let children ask questions. Answer them honestly using the correct terminology. Don't be afraid to say 'I don't know' if you don't. Look things up with them. Explore the topic together. Show them there's nothing to be frightened of.

When my grandfather died, the funeral director asked me which coffin I'd like him to be put in. He showed me a brochure of lots of different ones but I couldn't see one that I thought he'd like. He had this greeny-blue paint that he painted everything with: the walls of his house, the RNLI cap he found on the beach and wore every day for years, the frames around his pictures, the lamps by his bed, even his shoes when they started to look a bit mucky. He loved this paint. Or maybe he loved it because he'd been able to buy a lot of it cheaply. The colour represented him. When I thought about him I thought about this deep greeny blue and so I chose the cheapest wooden coffin with rope handles because he loved the sea and I painted his coffin his favourite colour in the garage that he'd painted all those things in over the years. My eldest daughter who was five at the time helped me paint it and as we layered up the coats of paint I told her stories about his life and what he meant to me.

When my youngest daughter was about two and her sisters were four and 14 I told them all this story and it opened up a conversation that ranged from the colour they want to paint their coffins to what they think happens when someone dies. My youngest decided she would die way after everyone else and though it made her happy that she'd outlive us, she was worried about who'd put her in her coffin if we were all already dead. She decided our puppy, who is several years younger than her, would do it! There was no sadness at all during this conversation, only laughter and inquisition and fascination. Now and again one of them will out of the blue update me on the latest colour change for their coffin or they'll ask a different question about life and death. Their questions are always met with the truth. At the moment they don't want to be buried – apparently they'd much rather be cremated than be placed in the earth. My youngest has held firm on having her coffin painted purple but right now it'll also be emblazoned with unicorns and penguins.

Sometimes I'll come home from work feeling sad. I'm honest with them about why I'm sad. It's OK to be sad. It's OK to be sad in front of your children. It's OK to tell them why you're sad. It's important to do this. They'll learn to be much more in tune with their emotions If you are. Your emotional bravery will set them in good stead. It'll teach them and show them that expressing our feelings is a good thing.

FIVE THINGS I LEARNED
WHEN MY PUPPY DIED

by Scout (aged eight)

1.

When my puppy died I was really sad so we made a funeral and my sister read a poem and we buried her under a curly bay tree. Whenever Mummy is cooking we pick a bay leaf to use and we think about her.

2.

Biscuits always help when you are sad.

3.

If you hug someone and tell them what is wrong it helps a lot.

4.

Even though I have another dog it doesn't replace the empty space that will never be filled.

5.

I feel just as bad as when she'd just died and that will never change. And just to add that people say that they are always right but they are often wrong.

FIVE THINGS I LEARNED ABOUT LIFE AND DEATH WHEN MY GREAT-GRANDMA ELLEN DIED

by Marley (aged 10)

1.

When I knew my great-grandma was dying it felt like a big dark cloud was hovering over me but it hadn't started raining yet.

2.

It took much longer for my great-grandma to die than anyone thought, including the doctors, and that made everything much harder.

3.

The very last thing she ate was ice cream. Whenever I eat ice cream I think about her.

4.

Even though my great-grandma said she felt ready to die, I wasn't quite ready to let her go.

5.

It's lovely to remember the party we had for her 90th birthday. We weren't able to go to the funeral so we planted a flower, we wrote messages to her and we went out for ice cream to honour her memory.

TALKING TO CHILDREN

No matter what question a child asks, always answer using the correct and proper words and terms. Make sure you never use euphemisms as these are confusing and misleading. Children need honesty and clarity delivered sensitively. Make sure you answer all their questions, no matter how hard it is. Don't try to distract them from the really tricky bits. Acknowledge that it's painful. There's nothing wrong with you letting them know that you're finding this immensely difficult.

What happens when someone dies?

Your response will be age-dependent. For younger children, an appropriate response would be: 'When someone dies, their body stops working. Their heart stops beating and they're no longer able to walk, talk, eat, sleep or breathe.' For older children it might be appropriate to continue with a bit more detail. Older children may have more indepth questions and it's important to answer these honestly.

It's essential to establish and confirm the permanence of death; that they cannot come back, and no one can 'fix' them:

'When someone dies they can't come back.'

'Even though they are dead, their memories will always live on in our hearts.'

Did Grandad die because I did something wrong?

You may well need to reassure a child that they haven't done anything wrong. Often, children will be concerned that they might have done something and that's why someone has died. Reassure as often as necessary. Children will frequently need you to say things several times over many different conversations. Their need for information, as well as their grief, will change as they get older and develop a different understanding of what has happened. Be prepared for them to need different and ongoing support as they progress through their lives.

Is Mummy sleeping?

Never say, 'Mummy has gone to sleep.' It's untrue and it's incredibly confusing. It might feel easier and gentler for you to allow them to think their parent fell into a long sleep but it's absolutely not the right thing to do. Always be honest. It's really hard – no one is suggesting otherwise – but it's imperative that you give children the correct information so they are able to begin to process and understand what is happening.

Do not feel like you have failed as a parent if your child needs extra support from outside the family network or from a specialist. Sometimes it's much easier to talk to someone who isn't emotionally involved. Sometimes children try to protect their living parent and don't want to upset them by telling them how sad, angry or confused they are.

If you don't have an answer to their question, because you don't know, be honest. Say, 'I don't know.' It's OK that you don't have all the answers. No one expects you to. It's much better to be upfront rather than make things up or ignore the question altogether.

Children will sometimes want lots of details. Give them the basic facts. Satisfy their curiosity. They will often stop asking questions when they feel they have enough information. Don't overwhelm them and try not to project opinion on to them. Stick with factual information. For example, it's better to say that 'Grandad died from heart disease' as opposed to 'Grandad died because he only ate fried food and he didn't do enough exercise.'

Can I see my sister again?
If a parent or sibling dies and a child asks to see them, do all you can to make this happen. Often, children need to see the reality of a situation to believe it. Conversely, never push a child to see someone if they don't want to and don't assume you know what will be best for them. Just facilitate them having time with the person who has died if they are saying it's what they want and need. Trust them. Trust their instinct and what they tell you is important to them. Encourage them to think about what would help them rather than telling them what you think would be good for them.

Where do people go when they have died?
'We don't know what happens when someone dies. Everybody believes different things. In our culture we put someone who has died into a coffin and bury them in the earth or put them into a very hot oven called a cremator. Some people believe there's a life after this one, other people believe that this life is the only one we have.'

Take time to explain what you believe happens when someone has died. If you have a particular religious or cultural belief system tell them about it, but it's always important to let children know that other people may believe different things.

Don't tell children that there's a place where all the dead people go where it's warm and lovely and they can eat ice cream all day long. It's confusing and not helpful.

Will Mummy ever come back?
'No, Mummy isn't going to come back. When people die they can't come back, no matter how much we want them to. We'll always think about Mummy and talk about her and love her but she can't come back to us. When someone dies, their bodies stop working forever.'

Who will look after me now?

When a parent or guardian dies this is often a question that they'll ask. It's essential to reassure them but it's also important not to make promises you cannot keep. Don't be tempted to say, 'I promise you I will always be here for you and that I will never go anywhere.'

You can't promise that you will never die. You will die. We all will. What you can do is promise that you will do everything in your power to look after them and be there for them. You can let them know there's a plan in place. Make a list of all the people in their life who want to take care of them and who are there to support them. Let the people on the list know!

Make sure you explain that no one will ever try to replace their parent, that no one ever could, and tell them how well loved they are and how there's a whole support network out there for them.

Talk to children about grief. They may be feeling all sorts of emotions and not understand that it's linked to their feelings about someone dying. Grief can be really confusing. Show them that it's OK to be sad. Show them that you feel sad too. Show them that it's OK to be happy as well. They need to see that there is a good life to be lived after the death of a parent.

Keep talking about their parent who has died. Tell stories. Share memories. Keep their memory alive. Lead the way. Give them permission to open up by setting an example and opening up too.

Children thrive on routine and structure. Their life has just been disrupted in the most catastrophic way and you need to give them a new structure and a new routine. Tell them who is going to pick them up from school, who is going to take them to their swimming lesson. The 'new normal' will quickly, for them at least, become just their normal. Children adapt well if they are given a structure and feel safe and held. You may feel the 'new normal' is alien to you for a very long time but don't push your feelings about it on to them, they will adjust at a different speed to you.

Listen to them. Don't shut them down. Don't shut down difficult conversations, they may need to express and explore all facets of how they are feeling and often those feelings are not pretty or easy to hear.

How do I tell a child someone has died?

Sit them down away from distractions and noise. Be gentle but be clear.
'I need to tell you that your grandad has died.'
'I'm so sorry to tell you that your grandad died today.'
'You know how we've been going to visit Grandad a lot recently because he's been unwell? Today, Grandad died.'
'Grandad died today and I am feeling really sad.'

Don't assume that they will feel the same way as you. I would never suggest saying, 'Something really sad has happened' because that may not be how they feel. Doing so can therefore be confusing and it can direct them to feel a certain way and it's important to allow them to feel how they feel. It's OK to say that you feel sad but don't make them feel they need to feel that way too.

Give them time to process your words before you say anything else. Be there to comfort them but don't overwhelm them with information. They need to have the chance to understand what you've just told them.

You could go on to say: 'Do you understand what I've just told you?' or 'Do you have any questions?'

Listen to them. Don't talk over them or overwhelm them with how you feel. Give them the space to discuss their own feelings. Don't try to have such big conversations all in one go. Expect to be talking and answering questions many times over many weeks, months and years.

Children grieve differently. Allow them to.

If a child is very young, you may need to tell them several times that someone has died and you may need to repeatedly explain that they can't and will not come back.

When someone dies, it's perfectly normal for children to feel anxious, become concerned about being separated from you, and be overly worried about their own death or the death of others important to them. They may also suffer with sleep disturbances.

Give them a clear description of how and why somebody died. Use simple but honest language. You will be helping them by telling them what happened.

Mummy is dead, does that mean I will die too?
When someone significant dies it can trigger a child to be concerned that they will die too. Explain that everyone dies but that it is very likely that they will live to a ripe old age. You can give them statistics to show that most people will die in old age.

TALKING TO CHILDREN ABOUT SERIOUS ILLNESS

The truth is always the best place to start. Always. Name the illness. Describe it as simply as you can.

'Mummy has cancer. It started in her breast and has spread to her bones. Mummy is having a treatment called chemotherapy and it might make all her hair fall out, even her eyebrows and eyelashes.'

Explain that they can't (usually) 'catch' the illness. 'It's OK to hug Mummy still. She needs lots of hugs but we might need to be a bit more gentle than usual. Mummy needs us to hug her like she's made of delicate eggshells. Mummy can't pass on her illness to you so being around her is just fine.'

Very occasionally someone will be unwell with a communicable illness. If this is the case, this needs to be addressed gently and honestly with the children too. Sometimes too, specific treatments can mean children do need to keep a temporary distance from their person.

Don't be afraid to use the correct terminology and words.

Keep children updated when there's news but allow yourselves time to process it first. You don't need to tell them straight away. It's much better for them to be given information calmly rather than when you're still reeling from the latest test results.

Don't patronise them. Don't presume to understand how they feel and don't tell them how they should be feeling. Listen to what they are telling you they're feeling. Show them it's OK for them to feel the way they do.

Make sure you have support in place for them. An experienced therapist can make a world of difference. Having a safe space away from the family where they can explore exactly how they think and feel without fear of upset or judgement will likely really help them. Don't wait until they are struggling before you put the support in place.

If they don't cry when you expect them to, if they don't respond how you imagine they will, if they behave in ways you are baffled by, allow it. Do not question them or their love for the person who is unwell. Everyone copes differently. Children cope differently. And that's OK.

FIVE THINGS I'VE LEARNED SINCE MY DAD DIED A YEAR AGO

by Hannah Mepham (aged 14)

Hannah has three cats and is her happiest when she is in the sea. In October 2018 her dad, David, died. She misses her dad and likes to continue his activism by going to lots of protests with her best friend Rhonja.

1.

It's not like the movies. Movies definitely show death and grief from a very rose-tinted perspective. And that's not to say that there won't be beautiful, melancholy, spiritually eye-opening moments, but those moments are fleeting and rare. You probably won't cry on top of a cliff while the sun sets behind you. I know it's sad – I was disappointed too.

2.

Get a cat. Let's be honest: cats are perfect. Just don't get three. They'll stress each other out and then piss everywhere. Gotta love 'em though.

3.

Everything you feel is temporary. You might not feel anything at all sometimes. It's shit but so is terminal illness. It is OK to forget that you are sad. You can be happy. You can laugh. You can not think of stuff for a while. You can drown in your sorrows. You are not obliged to be sad. Just like you are not obliged to be happy. Just remember: everything you feel or don't feel is temporary.

4.

Music cures almost everything. Put your headphones on and turn your music to full volume. Even if you don't feel happy, music can make you cry, laugh, shout, dance and sometimes you just need to feel something. If all else fails, play your music so loud it's deafening and shout the lyrics at a wall. I don't know why – it just helps.

5.

Salt water is magic. Sweat, tears or the sea. Or stand in the shower. For an hour.

FIVE THINGS THAT HELPED US TO SUPPORT TWO YOUNG CHILDREN WHEN THEIR MUM DIED

by Adam and Jade

Two years ago, Adam and Jade became Special Guardians to their niece and nephew, after their mum died.

1.
Talk about death
Talking about what death really is in an honest way was the best for us. Children can sometimes struggle with understanding the concept of 'going to sleep' and this generally doesn't help them to process their grief in a healthy way.

2.
Be honest
Answer any questions they have about death, about how they're feeling, about the person they've lost, honestly but age appropriately! Children can understand and process more than we give them credit for.

3.
Share memories
Sharing what you remember about the person who has died really helps their memory to live on. This will also make everyone smile. Avoiding talking about them doesn't help anyone.

4.
Show your emotions
Showing children that you are upset and miss the person that has died will help them realise that they are not alone in the way that they are feeling. It will help them to express their own emotions in a positive way.

5.
Don't forget to care about yourself
That child needs you, and for you to support them in the best way you can, you need to look after yourself physically and mentally. Talk to friends. Admit that you're not OK. Take a bath. Drink some wine. You're doing brilliantly.

FIVE THINGS I LEARNED FROM HAVING TO TELL MY CHILDREN THEIR DADDY HAD DIED

by Clare Haynes

Clare has two sons, aged nine and 12. Her ex-husband, their father, died due to complications following surgery to remove a brain tumour.

1.

Nothing will prepare you for having to tell your children that their daddy has died. Rehearsing what you will say is like the worst nightmare you've ever been in. You will consider if you can delay telling them. Is there any way they can have 24 more 'normal' hours before you shatter their world into a million pieces? Once you tell them their daddy has died you know that their world will be changed forever and they are going to know unimaginable pain like nothing they have ever felt before in their young lives.

2.

You will feel physically sick and want to rip out your own heart when you say the words, 'Daddy got very poorly very quickly and they couldn't keep Daddy alive, so Daddy died this morning.' Their reaction and the sound of their pain will haunt you forever.

3.

You will be permanently terrified that something will happen to you and worry about how they would cope. You hold all their memories now. What if you forget something really special and they never know that event or achievement even happened?

4.

You realise they are terrified of losing you. That you are now their whole world and their fear of losing you is huge. In the early days and months they will want to know where you are, even if you go to the toilet. They have experienced loss in its most painful form and their childhood is strewn out into what feels like a million pieces right in front of you.

5.

There will be dark days and nights. Bedtime is often the worst. When those times come you will hold them tightly and you will cry with them. Then the light creeps in and though their young lives have been shattered they will consistently amaze you with their resilience and strength and you will know that they will be OK. They will smile and belly laugh again and brighter days will come. It is on those brighter days that you will miss Daddy the most because he would be so very proud of them.

All that's left Unsaid

[A + L]

'The bitterest tears shed over graves are for words left unsaid and deeds left undone.'
HARRIET BEECHER STOWE, AMERICAN NOVELIST

Words left unspoken

Death can put us in a position where our words remain forever unspoken. Perhaps we've experienced a traumatic end to a relationship, or we've just been unable to say what we need to say the most to someone who is still around. Whatever the reasons for staying silent, the words we don't get to say can haunt us for our entire lifetime.

We invited visitors to Life. Death. Whatever. at Sutton House to anonymously leave their unspoken words on postcards that were then tied to the grand staircase. Unsaid then travelled to Winchester University, Dulwich Picture Gallery, Linden House and Redbridge Libraries, collecting unspoken words along the way. It now has a permanent home online. This is just a small selection of the thousands of Unsaid postcards from the collection.

Whatever you haven't said, you're welcome to say it here.

You taught me that love can't
exist without fear. Every night for
two months I lay on my kitchen
floor and cried.

I thought if I begged the linoleum
hard enough, you'd come back.

I'm so very glad you didn't.

#UNSAID

That day in the hospital.
We both knew. And nothing
needed to be spoken.

I miss you.

#UNSAID

I just wanted to let you know
that I still send you emails although
I know you're not here any more
and I still have an obsession for
Cigarettes After Sex. I love you.

#UNSAID

I found him Dad.
I miss you every second
of the day.

#UNSAID

I feel close to you again
now you have died.

Why did you have
to be so mean?

#UNSAID

I wish you'd told me you were going to
kill yourself. I'd have said no, and sat on
you until you decided it was easier to live.

All I did was touch your bedroom door
as if my sympathy could seep through.
I should have knocked, and asked.

I'm sorry.

#UNSAID

To Phil

You didn't lose your computer stylus – it was in the bottom of your backpack! You could park opposite the house now, the old car left there for the last 2 years has gone!

So many people came to your funeral, afterwards the musicians all played and sang. It was a lovely sunny day.

I don't know what is going to happen now.

Jackie

#UNSAID

Dad, I still can't believe you
are missing all of this.

#UNSAID

Your cooking was
fucking dreadful.

#UNSAID

It was me who pooped in
Penn Swimming Pool (in the
deep end) in 1989.

#UNSAID

I wish you had
fought for us.

#UNSAID

I wish I had told you 'NO'
and believed I had that right.

#UNSAID

Life & living

[A + L]

Life and living, death and dying. In the end it's all the same. Or is it?

If we've embraced our mortality, will we make the most of our lives? Can we change our lives by acknowledging that we'll die? If we've accepted we're going to die, how can we make the best possible use of our finite lives?

In this section, we'll encourage you to reflect on:

1. Living a life without regret.
2. How embracing death can change the way we live.
3. The essentials of self-care.
4. Kintsugi.
5. What death and dying can teach us about life and living.

FIVE THINGS I KNOW ABOUT LIVING NOW I KNOW I'M DYING

by Lucy Watts MBE

Lucy is a palliative care patient, prominent disability and health advocate, activist and consultant. As a disabled young woman, she has to overcome a wide variety of barriers, not least the low expectations of disabled people by others and the lack of accessibility, as well as living with a complex, life-limiting illness causing numerous medical needs.

1.
Quality is more important than quantity.

2.
Death is a normal part of life.

3.
Facing and embracing death can help you live a better life.

4.
Talking about dying won't make it happen.

5.
I've had the best years of my life since I've known I'm dying.

Regret

'Never regret the past. Embrace all that has made you, and never wish otherwise.'
UNSAID, 2016

We all have a tendency to regret the things we didn't do, as opposed to the things we did. When we believe we have an entire lifetime left, regrets don't seem to play so keenly on our minds, but that's not necessarily true of someone facing a life-limiting diagnosis. Can we learn a lesson about pride and humility from people who are dying? Can their regrets give us the opportunity to ensure we don't leave it too late to do the things we want and need to do?

Regrets and laments of those living with dying are entirely individual but there are many common threads: *I wish I hadn't worried so much about the things that really don't matter. I wish I'd taken more time to do the things I love with the people I love. I wish I'd told people how I felt. I wish I'd appreciated life while it was mine for the taking. I wish I hadn't taken so much for granted. I wish I hadn't wasted a single second worrying what people thought about me. I wish I'd had the chance to say sorry. I wish I'd been braver and followed my dreams. I wish I'd been kinder to myself. I wish I'd travelled and seen the world. I wish I'd taken more chances and risks. I wish I'd told her I loved her. I wish I'd been a better parent. I wish I'd been a better son. I wish I had called. I wish I hadn't been such a dick. I wish. I wish. I wish. I wish. I wish. I wish I wish I wish I wish …*

We know people are regretful. We know feelings of regret can dominate thoughts at end of life. We know the best time to address regrets is during life, when there's time to change course, to make amends, to take those chances, but we also know that something stops us doing all the things and saying all the things we really want to do and say.

Why don't we follow our passions? Take the risks we want to take? See the world? Put our hearts on the line and be honest with people about how we feel? What stops us?

I believe one thing that prevents us from living the life we want is an inherent disbelief that we are mortal and a false understanding that we have all the time in the world. If we truly acknowledge that our lives are finite, perhaps we would feel better placed to live out our entire lives taking those chances and decisions that make us truly happy.

When I'm working with people who have been given a life-limiting diagnosis, the desire to make amends frequently comes up. People often ask if it's too late to resolve things. Friends and family worry their apologies for past mistakes or actions may seem fraudulent and insincere because the person is dying. They fear it'll be seen as a selfish act and not as a genuine desire to make good or to clear their conscience. My advice every time is just to do it and say it.

What really matters is that you know your own words come from a place of love and sincerity. 'I'm sorry' is a powerful thing to say, one we don't say and mean often enough. It acknowledges someone else's upset, it bears witness to their distress. Rarely do apologies do any harm. What harm can come of saying, 'I'm sorry'? Sometimes, it's all someone needs to hear.

End-of-life doulas will help facilitate these difficult conversations. Death and dying can bring people together if we allow it. Close encounters with life's end can hold a magnifying glass up to our behaviour and present an opportunity to make amends and to let someone go with love and with peace of mind. After death, it is too late. The burden of regret can be a heavy load to carry. Don't ever let pride get in the way.

— Molly's Experience

Molly had given birth in her late teens. Her boyfriend had walked away the moment they found out she was pregnant. Molly's grandmother, Iris, had been the matriarch of the family and vocal in her opinions. They'd always been incredibly close but Molly's pregnancy had upset her grandmother's sensibilities and old-fashioned ideals. They'd fallen out and hadn't spoken for several years. Both had said things to one another that they wished they hadn't. During the last few days of her life, Iris asked to see Molly and meet her son. They visited her once the day before she died. Iris was able to see her great-grandchild for the first time. They all held hands and both women expressed their sorrow and their love. Few words were spoken but the gesture allowed both to forgive, to love, and to let go without the burning regret they'd both carried for too long.

And what about if our regret is centred around not having seen enough places, or not having experienced enough life? What can we do with the acknowledged regrets of someone who is dying? Can we make sure they have one last chance to do and say the things they want and need? The answer is yes, sometimes there is time to have 'one last…'

Will I be able to go swimming again? Can I see the sea? Can I go home and sleep in my own bed? Can I go to the movies?

We have a real duty to try to fulfil someone's last wishes. Sometimes it's enough to just plan it. Knowing that you're able to, *allowed* to, can sometimes be enough. Being given 'permission' to control what you want to do, and indeed what you will do, is incredibly important at life's end.

Part of acknowledging and embracing mortality is to understand that we do only get one chance to live the life we want and choose. Choose a life you love. Actively choose it, embrace it, love it with everything you have and when you're at the end of your glorious existence you can close your eyes and feel smug at the thought that you honoured your life, you did yourself justice. You lived well.

FIVE THINGS YOU REGRET

Here's a blank list. Write down the things you regret now. While you can, while there's time, change that list of five regrets into something else. Say the sorry you need to say. Acknowledge the hurt you caused. Ask the girl out. Book a flight to Paris. I bet good money you'll not regret doing any of those things; in fact one day, I'm sure you'll be really glad you did.

1.

2.

3.

4.

5.

AND WHAT CAN WE DO WITH THE REGRETS OF THOSE LEFT BEHIND?

Unsaid gave people the opportunity to express their sorrow and regret. It allowed unuttered thoughts and feelings to be expressed; it allowed people to offload some of the weight of their regretful load. It also gave people the occasion to see that they are not alone in their regret, that others have similar thoughts and feelings.

Could an understanding of mortality improve our lives and give greater meaning to our relationships? I really think it can.

Honour your life before the end. Do it justice. Honour the people around you and do justice to your relationships, to your life, with them.

What are you waiting for?

I wish I had gone to see you in the hospital.
I lie to myself and say I'm glad I didn't so
I will always remember you as you were, but
I don't. I wish I had told you how much you
inspire me and how much I love you.

I miss you so much x

#UNSAID

I'm sorry I couldn't help
you more, Dad.

I was so young, I didn't know
how much pain you were in.

#UNSAID

Janey,

I wish I'd said goodbye. I was
looking for the right words,
and then you were gone.

I still haven't found them.

R.

#UNSAID

If only.

#UNSAID

This could be the last time

[L]

'There's nothing worse than too late.'
CHARLES BUKOWSKI

Brilliant but wild was the best way to describe David. His unconventional lifestyle choices meant that he'd made a home for himself and his ideas in an open-minded cafe in East London. Its easygoing atmosphere was created by an eclectic collection of charity shop board games, sofas found on the street and donated books. It was grimy but charming if you didn't mind washing your own tea cup and eating cheap biscuits that had gone soft having been left out all night. It was a refuge for the waifs and strays of London: the brilliant, the broke and the brilliantly broke.

David claimed to be the manager, but he wasn't. Organisational structures and budget forecasts were of little interest to him. Someone else did that. He was the cafe's spiritual saint, charming customers and staff alike, somehow keeping the ramshackle place going with his enthusiasm.

During my early days as a newly trained funeral celebrant, I'd sit on the cafe's uncomfortable sofas, writing ceremonies, pretending I was there just to do work and not to see David. The internet never worked so my phone data was constantly drained. The music from the noisy club next door made concentrating impossible. But it was all worth it when he'd come over and put his hand on my shoulder, or whisper words of encouragement into my ear.

He had a kind of wit, cheekiness and charm that meant he could get away with pretty much anything, no matter how ridiculous. He could parachute into any situation, anywhere in the world, and not just come out unscathed, but glorious.

David danced on the streets, burst into song and spontaneously jumped aboard a mini scooter and sped around the tables when the cafe's guests were behaving a little too seriously. He blew bubbles on shoppers on Oxford Street while covered in glitter. He spent evenings with me sitting in his hideout, sculpting our feelings using the clay he kept under the futon. He created bold phallic wonders, while mine looked like blobs of overweight confusion.

It all made me cringe. I thought he was ridiculous. He was a '60s stereotype, a caricature of himself, stuck in 1966 and not 2016. He was a dreamer who needed to realise the world wasn't his for the making or the taking. I wanted to present him with a council tax bill and leave him to deal with it.

Yet I thought he was brilliant. He was the most beautiful, dangerous, unusual, fiercely intelligent and interesting boy I'd ever come across. I'd never met anyone who could make my eyes roll and my heart flip at the same time. It was quite the party trick.

I was madly in love with him.

One night at the cafe, while I was hanging out with David, I received a call from a funeral director in central London. They wanted me to put together a funeral ceremony for a brilliant young woman called Stephanie.

The week previously, Stephanie was interviewing for a job she knew she didn't want, to fund a life she was struggling to cope with. When the interviewer asked where she'd like to be in five years, she burst into tears and left the room.

Stephanie had known unhappiness. She'd spent most of the 24 years of her life experiencing anxiety and depression, which she wrote about in the form of exquisitely beautiful poetry in a diary she kept under her bed.

After the disastrous job interview, Stephanie was spending a night with her best friend. They cooked dinner together and talked about Stephanie's plans to turn her talent for writing into the future that she wanted for herself.

Stephanie didn't make it into work the next day. She never called in sick or emailed her manager with a reason. That night, she didn't turn up to her friend's birthday drinks. Her friends became concerned when they realised she hadn't been on WhatsApp since 11.23 p.m. the previous evening.

When the police broke into her rented flat in East London, they found her in her bed, cold. No one ever found out why she had died. Her death remains unexplained to this day, attributed to sudden arrhythmic death syndrome (SADS), also known as sudden adult death syndrome.

It may have been one of the sunniest days of the year, but Stephanie's funeral at an imposing crematorium in London was dark. Her family didn't want to gloss over the tragedy of her death. No one was in the mood for celebrating her life; we were there to acknowledge the devastation brought about by her death.

Her funeral was tragic, dramatic and honest. Her family and friends wore black and everyone cried openly. Their hearts were broken.

We listened to her favourite music, read extracts from the beautifully written poetry she'd only ever shared with her best friends, and listened to her friends openly weep into the mic as they talked about what a brave, bold and resilient young woman she had been.

I closed the ceremony with the truth – the words the family wanted to acknowledge her death: 'Stephanie, in the words of the people who loved you, how *unbelievably* lucky we were to have you. You were so brilliant, so brave, so talented, so loving and so *very* loved. The pain of losing you was intense but we will carry you with us always. Your light will shine when all else fades.'

I came away from Stephanie's funeral with an urgent sense that life is finite, and that I needed to make every moment count. I couldn't stop thinking about how fleeting her life had been. One moment she was there, the next moment she was dead. The brilliant Stephanie didn't have a today or a tomorrow, but I did. So right then, I knew there was a call I needed to make.

I called David. And I told him exactly how I felt.

Because of the call I made that day, David and I got together. And so began a love story that lasted just over two years.

I took the funerals I was writing to heart. I listened to the many stories about the lives that had ended with no warning, just like Stephanie's. David, too, became very aware of how fragile life can be. Especially after I met Denise, Jim's widow.

Jim was ready to sit down in his armchair and watch the evening's soaps with his wife Denise, in their semi-detached house in a quiet suburb of Essex. It had been a long day, and he wanted nothing more than a cup of tea and a biscuit. But the couple were out of milk. So Jim left Denise in the kitchen with the kettle boiling and said he'd be back in five minutes.

Jim called into the local newsagents to pick up a pint of milk. As he left the shop, he tripped over and fell down, hitting his head against the concrete. He suffered a huge bleed on his brain and died in the ambulance on the way to the local hospital.

A week later, I met Denise to discuss the arrangements for Jim's funeral.

'You have to concentrate on the good times,' Denise's friend and neighbour told her, watching her crying into a cup of tea as she sat in Jim's armchair. 'Celebrate the life that you lived together.'

'There's nothing to celebrate,' she said. 'We wasted 40 years. I can't concentrate on the good times because there weren't any really. We always thought we could sort everything out tomorrow. Now I'll never get another chance. There is no tomorrow for us.'

Inspired by Jim and Denise, I got into the habit of saying, 'This could be the last time.' David and I took it to heart – we lived for today, and ignored the reality of tomorrow.

But our relationship was complicated and unpredictable. It would be blissful and then we'd argue and wouldn't speak for many months. He finally made the decision to leave London to travel around the world, while I stayed in London to continue my work with funerals. I reluctantly said goodbye as he left for Finland, having decided we couldn't be together any more. My heart was broken.

A few months later, I received a text message out of the blue. It was a photo of a tattoo on someone's forearm. 'This could be the last time,' it read, in my handwriting. It was David, texting me from wherever he was in the world. He'd taken the exact statement I'd written in his notebook as goodbye before he departed and tattooed it, in my handwriting, on to his forearm.

His travels ended and he returned to London. One night he was lying beside me and I was stroking his arm, where my words were written. 'This could be the last time,' the tattoo read. 'But it probably won't be,' I added in black biro, as he slept.

A few months later, my phone beeped at 10.35 p.m. on a Tuesday night. It was the sister of a friend of mine, and it was unusual to hear from her. She asked if I was available to talk as it was rather urgent. I was on a night bus home and my phone was running out of battery.

'We've had some rather bad news,' she said, when we finally spoke at midnight. The line crackled. ' … had a brain haemorrhage and died this afternoon.'

'I am so sorry to hear that,' I said, then took a moment to understand what she had said. 'Sorry, who did you say had died?'

'Jon.'

The Jon she was talking about was Jon Underwood, her brother and the founder of Death Cafe. Back in 2011, Jon had invited a handful of people to gather in his front room for an open and honest conversation about death over tea and cake. Six years later, Death Cafe has become an international movement with over 5300 Death Cafes being held around the world. Death Cafe had even made it to the front page of the *New York Times*.

It was inconceivable that the man who had started Death Cafe had died. But it was true. Jon was dead. He had died at the age of 44 from acute promyelocytic leukaemia. The first sign of his illness had been when he collapsed due to a brain haemorrhage on Sunday. On Tuesday, he died in the Royal London Hospital in Whitechapel, London.

He was our colleague, our friend and a fellow revolutionary in making the worlds of death and dying better. And now he was dead.

The night I found out that Jon had died, there was only one person I wanted to see. David came to me, we ate pizza and then he held me as I cried myself to sleep. With an acute awareness that life can so abruptly be over, I wanted him to be there with me more than anything. But the truth was devastating – I knew he didn't feel the same.

I knew that I couldn't live this way and David couldn't be in my life. Loving him was reckless, irresponsible and unsustainable. I couldn't live in a constant state of anticipatory heartbreak. I knew I had to face the devastating truth: he would always be leaving, and I'd always want him to stay.

Our relationship felt like a never-ending funeral, a series of constant goodbyes that became more painful every time. I realised that if I didn't say another hello, I'd never have to go through the agony of another goodbye ever again.

One Sunday afternoon, I told him we were over and he needed to leave. I said things to him, things so awful I've wiped them from my memory because I want to forget how much I can hurt someone I love when I'm in pain. In response, David picked up his bag, walked through the door and crossed the street. I stood at the window and watched him walk into the distance.

He didn't look back. I never saw him again.

Living life for today comes with a recklessness that doesn't account for tomorrow. But living life with the awareness that life might be over tomorrow, but probably won't, transformed everything.

Partners, mortgages, careers, children, ex-husbands, friendships that cause us discomfort, situations we're not happy in – we all have a myriad of issues to deal with and life circumstances that are less than ideal.

Life is complicated. The decisions we make are complicated. How many of us really live life like we have no tomorrow, loving every moment we're alive?

The popular memes #YOLO (you only live once) and it's more nihilistic cousin #YODO (you only die once), are one and the same. They're idealistic. Easy to say, hard to put into practice and even more difficult to live with. David was my #YOLO. He was also my #YODO. He was difficult to live with, and difficult to live without.

If I'm going to die tomorrow, then oh yes, I want a slice of cake today. Probably the whole cake. But if I'm still going to be here tomorrow, and want to live a life that makes me content, then perhaps we can share a slice of cake between us and be less likely to die from heart disease tomorrow.

If I replace the idea of eating cake with my complicated relationship with David then I have to do what it takes today to be able to live a fulfilled life without him tomorrow. So far, that's included a great deal of reflection, therapy, supportive friends who have put up with my late-night calls, and tears that felt like they'd never stop flowing. I had to learn to live a life without him; I had to grieve who he was and who I was in relation to him. I had to let go of all the fun we'd had. I had to accept that I'd never see him again. I had to mourn a future that would never have him in it.

For months and months, my body ached at the thought of never seeing him again. I'd return home from funerals every evening, hoping to see him waiting at my doorstep with a bunch of flowers so I could break into the biggest smile and fall into his arms. But every time I came home and he wasn't there, I felt gratitude and relief amidst the tears. It might have been another day without him, but it was also another day away from the pain and frustration of being with him, which meant that it was another day that could lead to a better tomorrow.

Working with death is one way to be exposed to the brutal realities of what it's like to be here one moment and gone the next with absolutely no warning. It doesn't take too many experiences of extraordinary yet surprisingly ordinary deaths like Stephanie's, Jim's or Jon's for our perspective on life to shift entirely. It can be profound, transformational and empowering, while also being unsettling, frightening and uncertain.

What is death but a full stop? We live out the commas, the semicolons, the hyphens, the exclamation marks and the rest of the punctuation that makes up the sentence that is our lives, before the big black dot that is the full stop. That's the end. That's death.

Even knowing how fragile life can be, it's just not realistic to spend every day living the life that I truly want to live. I get in my way; life gets in my way. But I can live each day, making decisions that won't hurt the tomorrow I may or may not have, while also knowing that if I do die tomorrow, I won't regret how I spent today.

It's never as simple as 'live like you have no tomorrow'. It's taken a lot of tea, tears, therapy, self-love, self awareness, hard work and supportive friends to be able to cope with the realities of today, never mind tomorrow. We only live once, we only die once. The choices we make about the way we live and the way we die are complicated. But by seeing death as the inevitable end, we can make better, more empowered choices about the way we live today.

Because this might be the last time. But it probably won't be.

The essentials of self-care

[A + L]

Self-care is a difficult notion to grasp. Most of us are really bad at it. Perhaps that's because it requires acknowledging that we're not superheroes. We *all* have our vulnerabilities and weaknesses.

Self-care is saying (and meaning!), 'I am going to put myself first.' Yet we're taught over and over again that we must always put others first. To say that we need to do something for ourselves can sound like we're being selfish. But it's essential. We really can't pour from an empty cup. We can't be there for someone else if we're exhausted and drained. Self-care isn't selfish, it's an act of kindness to ourselves and to others.

A friend of Anna's is going through a really rough time. She's the mother of two young children and both her parents have been diagnosed with life-limiting conditions. She's a perfectionist with a huge sense of responsibility. She gives everything her all, all the time. She's just been promoted into the job of her dreams. It's a tricky and demanding role and she's taken some time to find her feet.

Any one of the things she's experiencing is vast. They're all very grown up, all very adult and all very overwhelming. She's struggling. Anna frequently points out that *anyone* in her situation would struggle. She must practise self-care, like all of us.

You may ask: 'What the hell is self-care anyway? What does it even mean? Why do people keep telling me I need to find ways to relax? What is "relaxing"? How on earth can anyone relax when there's so much that needs to be done?'

When the world is turning too quickly, when there aren't enough hours in the day to fit in the essentials, let alone anything that isn't truly necessary, when there's no spare money for anything other than actual daily living, what can we do to look after ourselves?

No one can carry the weight of the world on their own. No one is responsible for everything, all of the time. We are not required to carry it all. It's not all ours to carry. IT IS NOT ALL OURS TO CARRY. No one expects us to do it all.

We're enough and everything we do is enough. We can't be everything to everyone all of the time. In order to keep going, to be able to look after our families and friends, and do our jobs well, we have to put our well-being at the forefront.

When there's so much resting on our shoulders, self-care is about acknowledging that we still need to do the things that make life more bearable. Sometimes self-care is just allowing a bit of normal in.

WHAT DOES SELF-CARE MEAN TO US?

We both have intense jobs that require us to be very present for other people. It's important that we know ourselves well enough to understand what we need. For us, self-care looks something like this, but it's different for everyone:

Anna

I'm not very good at taking care of myself. It's something I need to get much better at. It's about knowing you still need to do things that make things feel a bit better. Like taking your kids to the beach and jumping in the waves even though you'll have half a mind on everything else and you're exhausted. It's about being there and being grounded with them – seeing their delight makes everything else make a bit more sense. You'll also feel like a better parent for it. When you're juggling so much it's easy to feel you're failing at everything, but the reality is you have an impossible task, you can't do it all, all the time. Do one thing really well. It's amazing how succeeding at one thing can lift us. Self-care is about knowing you need to try to get some early nights and it's about treating yourself to a quiet moment away from the chaos.

It's about letting yourself keep living your own life even while the shit is hitting the shitty fan. Watching shit TV and wallowing in a bath with too many bubbles and turning the music up too loud so all you can hear is the music rather than your over-thinking brain. Taking tiny little moments that top you back up. Not expecting too much of yourself. Saying no to stuff you know is too much. Letting someone else do something without making a fuss. Giving the kids 'breakfast for dinner' once in a while and not reprimanding yourself for it. It's about forgiving yourself, accepting you are human and letting yourself off the hook. Asking for a bit of extra love and support. Saying you feel a bit overwhelmed and need a hug/lie-in/walk/cry/swim/an hour to go for a run. Buying a crappy magazine and looking at the pictures because the words are too wordy. Not getting the train home straight away after work and taking half an hour out for you to reset and breathe and dream about far-flung adventures and sip hot chocolate. I think that's what self-care is.

'Relax' is a big word. Relaxing when you have a long list of responsibilities is one of the hardest things in the world, but by giving yourself permission to do all or any of these little things it is possible that one day you'll have a moment where you actually feel alright.

Self-care really doesn't have to be about that expensive yoga retreat or taking out a second mortgage to buy that Jo Malone candle to light when you're in a bath filled with essence of orchid oil. Self-care is making a good choice for yourself – choosing the healthy option on the menu, going for the walk you really don't feel like, meeting up with friends when you're feeling at your least sociable, cancelling plans when you can't face them, acknowledging your burden, talking and sharing the weight of your worries, watching a film.

Louise

I don't like the word 'self-care', because I think it's more about self-awareness and action. For me, it's about knowing myself well enough to make better choices for myself. It's about taking responsibility and being accountable for my actions.

I tend to rely on food as a coping mechanism so I have to watch my behaviour around it. Sometimes it's about allowing myself to enjoy a slice of cake; sometimes it's about resisting the cake and dealing with whatever's going on for me emotionally. It's about identifying patterns of unhealthy behaviour and not falling back into them.

I'm a workaholic so another part of my self-maintenance is knowing when I need to stop working and get some sleep. It's about trusting my colleagues to take the phones and be on call for a night. It's about taking an evening off to go climbing with my friend Laura, to watch the sunset over the river with my friend Julia or to eat sushi with my friend Anne. The reality of running a business means there'll always be another email, or another bill to pay. It's about knowing when enough is enough, and that it's OK to say no.

It's also important for me to remember to have fun. I try to set aside time for something I find enjoyable every single day. If I don't prioritise this, it doesn't take long for me to feel the consequences.

Everyone's self-care is different. Our idea of self-care may well be your idea of self-inflicted hell. It's about acknowledging your physical and emotional needs and honouring them.

EMERGENCY SELF-CARE:
WHAT TO DO WHEN LIFE IS UNBEARABLY HARD

Ideally, we'd treat ourselves with loving kindness every single day. But sometimes, life can be unbearably hard and we find ourselves in the midst of a self-care crisis. So when the going gets really tough, here are some things you can do to ground yourself:

Eat something
Don't just reach for the nearest hit of sugar. Choose something nourishing and nurturing, such as a handful of nuts, a banana or an energy bar.

Freshen up
Brush your teeth. Wash your face. Change your underwear. Put on some clean clothes. It makes everything feel so much better.

Freshen everything else up
Do the dishes in the sink. Do the laundry. Make the bed. Open the curtains. Let the light in.

Have a hot bath or a cold shower
A few drops of lavender oil in a hot bath helps to soothe the nervous system. A cold shower with a few drops of eucalyptus oil helps to wake us up.

Get off your phone! Stop scrolling!
Putting our phones in another room for half an hour makes a big difference to our well-being. Taking a train or bus journey without being on the phone is an opportunity to be more present in the world. It's how the world used to be, before smartphones made us always available.

Get a therapist
We can't stress the value of having an understanding therapist as a safe place to work through what's going on. It's a place to process and sometimes just to rant about what life has thrown at you.

Hang out with some different people
By getting a different perspective on our own lives, we may start to see things differently. Try hanging out with a friend you wouldn't usually see or going to lunch with a different colleague.

Go outside
Even if it's just to walk to the local shop. Breathe in some fresh air and engage with the world.

Change things around
Walk home via a different route. Move the books around on the shelf. Sort out the clothes in the wardrobe. All these small actions help us to shift our own perspective and see things differently.

Get moving
Movement helps. It gets things flowing. It doesn't need to be yoga or running a marathon, it can be as simple as going to the local cafe to have a cup of herbal tea or going for a walk in the countryside.

Avoid caffeinated drinks
If you're feeling blue, avoid caffeine. Chemical stimulation is the last thing the nervous system needs. Try something soothing that doesn't make anxiety even worse.

Drink water
Lots of it.

Find an animal to play with
If you don't have a pet, borrow one for a few hours. Failing that, watch funny cat or dog videos. Baby goats are cute, too.

Buy yourself flowers
Treat yourself kindly, like a friend who is struggling. Know what's self-love for you and give it to yourself.

Kintsugi: emotional damage and repair

[A]

One of my favourite stories as a child was about a patchwork quilt that a grand-mother sat and stitched with magical golden thread by the fire each night. It's a story that has invaded my subconscious throughout my life. We are all patch-work blankets, created and formed from our many different experiences and sewn together over a lifetime. Stitches unravel, material gets worn and torn, we fix and mend and move forwards looking and feeling slightly different but with the essence of us remaining, and with the legacy of what was lost or broken woven deep in our seams.

Everyone's grief is their own and everyone's grief is different. The one thing, however, that unites all those who grieve, no matter what or who for, is the feeling of sorrow. We are unified in sadness, yet too often we find this desolation impossible to discuss or broach. One of my favourite sayings is about being kind to whomever you meet, no matter what, because everyone you encounter is going through something you know nothing about. This reminded me of Kintsugi, the Japanese art of mending broken objects with gold.

The philosophy behind this ancient art is to take something broken and damaged and rather than hiding or trying to disguise the imperfections, emphasise the repair as part of the history and preciousness of the piece. There's no disguising the restoration, in fact the repair becomes part of the beauty of the object. The object shows its wounds, its reparation and it is almost 'reborn' to continue its life in spite of the damage. It's an acknowledgement that something that's broken can still be worthy and that no matter how damaged something is, that it can be mended and those 'fixes' can be beautiful. Not only does the repaired object become a thing of great beauty and worth, but also the act of mending – the time, effort and expense that goes into the repair – acknowledges the worthiness of the broken object. It was an important object when it was whole. Its significance remains when it's in pieces and its careful repair with a precious metal testifies to this importance. If we prize an object highly enough to fix it so delicately, elaborately and beautifully, why don't we also apply this philosophy to people?

If we fixed our imperfections with gold or something precious, if we acknowl-edged our 'damage' instead of hiding it behind the facade of coping, if we dispensed with that terribly British 'stiff upper lip', if we took the time to put ourselves, and indeed, helped others who didn't have the strength to do it themselves, back together carefully, considerately and with an overt acknowledgement that our 'ex-periences' impact greatly on us, both shaping and manipulating who we are, would we be able to be kinder to ourselves? Would we be able to be kinder to others?

What if we showed our emotional well-being the kind of empathy, understanding and attention that a Kintsugi artist shows a humble piece of broken pottery?

In times gone by, when someone died, people wore black bands and widows dressed head to toe in black not only to show respect, but also to let others know they were grieving. These traditions are few and far between nowadays and we are often told to put on a brave face. People don't discuss the death of someone close to them for fear of upset and there are so many tales of friends disappearing after someone's significant bereavement because they don't know what to say. Strangers we meet have no idea of what we are living with and going through. I wonder if we 'wore' our heartbreak as the pots wear their damage and repair, if this could make a difference to our ability to communicate and therefore to the support we receive.

'Coping' is placed on a pedestal and is revered. Conversations about people who have been recently bereaved often discuss how well they're coping, what a brave face they're maintaining and how adequately they're managing to not let it impact on their life. But not coping doesn't equate to not being brave. Showing sadness, vulnerability and breakage is not a sign of weakness. After all, who could cope well with the dying, and death of someone they love?

When my best friend died many years ago, I did not 'lose' him or misplace him from my life. He died. Nor is he 'gone'. He is very much part of me and always will be. His legacy continues in a multitude of ways and he's a part of my present and future, as he was my past. The use of euphemisms diminishes the importance and magnitude of what's happened. Sometimes in an attempt to make it sound more palatable we dilute the gravitas, and no one should try to take away anything from the magnitude of the death (and dying) of someone we love very much. It *is* life-changing and to try to reduce its impact by using 'gentler' terms feels disrespectful.

Let's show the world we are damaged but we're still beautiful. Let's begin to put ourselves back together with gold. Let's invite dialogue about our golden scars that we wear openly and with pride. Let's let people know we are a bit broken and perhaps need some help along the way. We are the product of our lives and the world would be a much lovelier place if, instead of hiding our troubles and sadness, we highlighted them and sprinkled them with gold.

FIVE THINGS I'VE DISCOVERED ABOUT LIFE AND LIVING WHILE RE-IMAGINING DEATH AND DYING

by Ivor Williams

Ivor is a designer, developing new ways of thinking about and experiencing death and dying in the 21st century.

1.

Don't let the words people use – 'hospice', 'palliative care', 'end-of-life care', 'terminal' – put you off. Try to put aside any negative feelings about those words and look to the people talking to you about it. They can help you. They really want to help you.

2.

You might be living with a loss that affects you. A loss that happened before you were even born. However, you might have the chance to come to peace with it in your own lifetime. This might be through what feels like luck, or sheer sustained effort on your part. Either way, many people may never understand why you have a sadness in you, but that's OK. You're OK.

3.

We aren't as religious as we used to be, which is fine, of course. But one big thing religion gave us is a sense of the 'larger us'. Religion had the monopoly on it for centuries, but each and every one of us – religious or not – has a deep-embedded sensation that something came before us and will come after us, too. That we are part of a constant thread of people, families, communities through time. Those religious clothes, scents and songs are just expressions of that thread through time. It's natural to think about what your life meant, when you get to the end, and how you fit into a grander scheme of things. It's the natural human spirit. I encourage you to embrace it in any way that feels right to you.

4.

Some people live a lifetime in a few short years. Others stretch it all out, decades going by. No matter how much time you have (or think you have), what do you wish you had more time for? What really brings you happiness, peace, contentment, satisfaction, purpose? What stops you from doing those things? To me, those are the only two questions you have to ask yourself.

5.

When it comes to down it, I think people are often more scared of living than they are scared of dying.

Everything we've learned about life and living from working with death and dying

[A + L]

Edna had lived next door to her friend Winnie for many years. They were saving 50p coins in a jar so they could have a joint party at the community centre to celebrate their 90th birthdays. They talked all day long, shared a love of *Eastenders* and would eat supper from the same fish and chip shop in Hackney every Friday. They made a pact: they would die at the same time so that no one was left alone.

Edna had never ordered anything from QVC but when she saw a heart-shaped casserole dish on special offer, she decided to give it a go.

When the tiny casserole dish arrived, it was too small for cooking, so Edna gave it to Winnie. 'I'm giving this to you,' she said to her. 'You've got my heart now.'

That night Edna died in her sleep from heart failure.

The following day, Winnie was sitting in her armchair holding the tiny heart-shaped casserole dish and the jar of pennies as she ate her cod and chips.

'I won't be needing these pennies now,' she explained. 'I've got a dicky heart. It won't be long now. My best friend's gone. I'll be gone soon as well.'

Working with death and dying, we hear hundreds of heartbreaking and heartwarming stories of life, love and loss, just like that of Edna and Winnie. These stories have changed our own lives, helped us work out what we value, and confirmed a few things for us about what it means to be alive.

A couple of years ago, Anna wrote a list for Clemmie Telford's 'Mother of All Lists' about what she's learned about living from working with people who are dying. We decided to come together to write a new joint list as the finale for this book.

So here it is. This is everything we have learned about life, death and everything in between.

LIFE

1. Be kind. Be really kind.
2. Walk the long way home sometimes. Take the scenic route.
3. It's not about what you do, it's about how you feel. As The Moldy Peaches sang, 'I'm in love with how you feel'.
4. Choose your battles. Before you get into an argument, think about whether it's really worth it. Does it really matter? If it does, great. If it doesn't, don't. In either case, always make up. One day you might not get the chance.
5. That old adage about never going to sleep on an argument may be impossible in real life. What is possible is to say, 'I'm really pissed off with you but I love you nonetheless'.
6. Stand up for what you believe in. Unless you're a dick, of course. If you are being a dick, stop it! Shout about what's really important. Call out the bully. Be a good person.
7. Help other people and be a voice for those who don't have their own. They'll appreciate it, even if they can't say it.
8. Do the right thing, not the easy thing. If the easy thing is the right thing, you can probably take the rest of the day off.
9. Integrity is doing the right thing for no other reason than it being the right thing to do.
10. Stick around even when times are tough. Especially when times are tough. Just be there.
11. Pay people compliments. Proper, heartfelt, genuine compliments. You know they're lovely to receive. They're also lovely to give.
12. Don't just tell people you love them, show them. Send flowers. Write letters. Bake cakes. Actions really do speak louder than words.
13. Always try. Even if you fail, it's the trying that really does count. If you do fail, fail spectacularly.
14. Take the day off sometimes. Stay in bed and watch TV.
15. Always tell and show your people how loved they are, how important they are and how invested you are in them.
16. Acknowledge everything – births, weddings, birthdays and deaths. Rituals give our lives structure and meaning.
17. 'You will find that it is necessary to let things go; simply for the reason that they are heavy.' C. JoyBell C. – author, poet and lover of cake.
18. Quitting anything – whether it's drugs, alcohol, cigarettes, caffeine, sugar or an unhealthy relationship – is hard. Do whatever you need to do until you don't need to do it any more.
19. Don't wait for tomorrow. Whatever it is, if it's possible, do it today.

20. Hugs aren't the sole property of couples. Hugs between friends, without agenda, can heal.
21. Shit happens. It's how you deal with it that's important, and how you move on.
22. If you haven't coped well with something, learn from it. Admit you were wrong then forgive yourself. We're all human.
23. The days are long but the years are short. Don't take it for granted. One day, it'll all be over.
24. Life really can be bloody unfair. We invented the whole idea of fairness to try to hide this fact.
25. No matter how impossible something feels at 3 a.m., the sun will rise again in the morning. Life does go on. Who is to say that tomorrow won't be the best day of your life?
26. Life is what you make it. We've seen young people with a life-limiting diagnosis fit more into their final six months than some octogenarians have in their whole lives. You are not too old and it is not too late.
27. You're the CEO of your own life. You report to nobody but yourself. Quit the job you hate. Don't settle for anything. Don't just let your life happen to you. Create the life you want.
28. Do what you love. That is all.

DYING

1. The thing most people are scared of is being in pain. We are much better at helping to control pain nowadays. It can take time to find the right combination of medications but they are generally really effective.
2. It's essential to have open and honest discussions with the whole healthcare team. Tell them how much something hurts. Share your worries and fears. Don't underplay what's going on. If they don't have the full picture, they can't help.
3. Never feel that you're complaining. Never feel that you're being difficult. Ask for the things you need.
4. People want to help. Let them. It makes them feel better about the world and themselves.
5. You are not a burden. YOU ARE NOT A BURDEN.
6. Dr Kate Granger created the #hellomynameis campaign before she died in 2016. Her tireless campaigning means doctors and nurses will now properly introduce themselves to their patients.
7. To all hospital staff, the person in bed seven with lung cancer is not called 'Lung cancer, bed seven'. Treat them as a person, don't treat them as a disease.

8. Medical teams take note: ask questions. Find out what matters. Ask what's tolerable. Don't assume anything. Don't loom over your patients. It's intimidating at the best of times but even more so when you're very ill and vulnerable.

9. People who are dying don't have much time, so give them yours graciously and willingly. Don't waste their time. Never waste someone's limited time.

10. Carers play a HUGE role and they need to be respected and included. Listen to them! Carers and family are not visitors, they are an essential part of the care team.

11. Medical jargon doesn't help anyone.

12. B.J. Miller is a palliative care physician and general all-round rock star of the palliative care world and we need to clone him. Watch his TED talk. Same goes for Atul Gawande. Listen to his *Reith Lectures* and read *Being Mortal*. It might just change your life.

13. Read *When Breath Becomes Air* by Paul Kalanithi. It's the story of his stage 4 lung cancer. Medics, it might just change the way you work.

14. Illness is not a battle that we can choose to win or lose. People don't die because they didn't fight hard enough. They die because their illness was an absolute motherfucker.

15. Palliative care is not end-of-life care, it's comfort care and people who are given palliative care from the point of diagnosis can have longer and more comfortable lives.

16. We need more palliative care doctors. We need more hospices and better funding for them.

17. Just because the UK is deemed to provide the best end-of-life care in the world doesn't mean we are good enough. It just means we're not as awful as the rest of the world.

18. We need the medical profession to see the students who choose to specialise in palliative and end-of-life care as heroic. Some doctors see the death of a patient as their failure to keep them alive. It's not.

19. Dying is not like it is in the movies.

20. Dignitas is nothing like it is in the movies. We loved *Me Before You* but they got the basic fundamentals of Dignitas SO wrong. Come on Hollywood, do better.

21. It's really important to make a will. It could save a lot of trouble and expense for the people who survive you.

22. By making an Advance Directive you empower your friends and family to be able to adhere to your wishes. If you don't make one, they're pretty powerless and that really sucks, for them and for you.

23. It's really important to talk to your family and friends about what you want to happen at the end of your life. And make sure you appoint a Lasting Power of Attorney, too.
24. Don't forget about your social media accounts. What would you like to happen to your online persona when you die? Some platforms, like Facebook, have legacy settings so you can decide whether your profile is deleted, or is managed by a designated person.
25. Nobody's deathbed regret is the things they did. No one has ever said: 'I wish I hadn't spent those six weeks on that beach in Thailand'.
26. Lots have people have said: 'I wish I'd spent more time with the people I love' and 'I wish I hadn't worked so hard and for such long hours.'
27. People can do the most remarkable things when they're coming to the end of their life.
28. People who are dying are still living. Treat them as such. Don't write them off because of their diagnosis.
29. Active treatments like radiotherapy and chemotherapy are really bloody tough. The endless hospital appointments often feel like a full-time job,
30. Help is often about the small things: ask people what they want. Don't assume!
31. Never assume!
32. Did you just assume something? Stop!
33. Just because Great-Aunt Bessie liked sugared almonds for her chemo snack doesn't mean cousin John will too. Ask. DO NOT ASSUME.
34. Do not invalidate someone who is ill. Help them to do the things that make them feel like themselves. If they feel up for cooking dinner, let them do it!
35. Don't patronise: 'I'm ill, I'm not stupid.'
36. Ask their advice and consult them, just like you always did.
37. You cannot 'fix' someone who is dying. Do not try.
38. People often want to leave a legacy. Helping someone leave their mark is a beautiful and significant gift.
39. Sex and intimacy can still be really important to someone when they're ill. Take the time to find out what works for them. Ask them, talk to them, be honest and open.
40. Lovers can be scared of 'hurting' someone when they're ill. If you communicate, you can reduce this risk. Try things, but accept it might not be the same. It can still be wonderful, though. Feeling sexy and desired isn't just for the healthy.
41. When a person at the end of their life is talking, the greatest gift we can give them is to listen.

DEATH

1. We are all going to die.
2. That includes you.
3. Death is the one true inevitability. There's nothing more certain in this world than our mortality.
4. Death is perfectly ordinary. When we die or someone we love dies, it becomes extraordinary.
5. Talking about sex doesn't make you pregnant; talking about death and dying won't kill you.
6. Avoiding it doesn't mean it won't happen.
7. Discussing death and dying isn't morbid, or creepy. If done right, it's life-affirming and uplifting. It's potentially even life-changing.
8. Acknowledging mortality does not make you 'a goth'.
9. No, we don't sleep in coffins and yes, we do venture out during daylight hours.
10. Kids aren't scared of death and dying if they're helped to understand it. Being told the dog went to live on a farm in the sky doesn't help. Don't project your own fears on to them.
11. Let kids ask their own questions and answer them honestly.
12. Don't use euphemisms. No one is lost and no one passed away. No one departed, took leave or slipped away. They died. Euphemisms prevent true understanding. Be straight and honest but gentle.
13. Doctors, take note: don't say to someone, 'There's nothing more I can do' because all too often that gets translated as, 'I can't help you any more, but maybe there's someone else who can.'
14. Give everyone the opportunity to say goodbye.
15. Goodbyes can be hard. They can feel impossible.
16. When someone dies, all the faultlines in family dynamics are revealed. They can easily become cracks. Tread carefully.
17. No one commits suicide. People die by suicide. It's not a crime, let's stop treating it as one.
18. Death and dying needs to be a part of our education. As early as children can possibly understand the words.
19. We cannot cure death. We can make sure people live as happy a life as possible – right up to the end.
20. We need to prepare for our deaths to help those we leave behind. We need to make death into something we can all live well with.
21. We need to plan for death and dying.
22. We need to talk about death and dying.
23. People want to talk about death and dying. They just don't know how.
24. It's not about a good death, it's about a good life with an awareness of death.
25. Let's talk about it.

FUNERALS

1. Funerals can play an important role in our grief. Don't dismiss them because you've had bad experiences in the past. You can create a funeral that works for you, whatever the circumstances.
2. If the death is expected and takes place at home or in a nursing home, take time before calling the funeral director. There's no rush. If it happens at night, consider waiting until the next morning. Light candles, play music, be with the person and give yourself time.
3. You don't need to use a funeral director in the UK. You can usually do it all yourself.
4. The person who has died can stay at home until their funeral, if that's what you want. You need to keep them cool with the windows closed and the heating off. But it's perfectly possible, legal and can be cathartic.
5. Not all funeral directors are the same. Think about what's important to you and find a funeral director who can meet your needs.
6. If a funeral director doesn't list their prices online, be wary of working with them. Funeral directors should charge, and behave, transparently.
7. Your 'local family funeral director' might be a big corporate chain in disguise. You might find that a genuinely independent funeral director can offer a more personal service at a reasonable price.
8. You can change the funeral director you're working with, even if the person who has died is already in their care.
9. It's true. In the UK, you can bury someone in your back garden.
10. Funerals don't have to be held in a church or at a crematorium.
11. You don't need to have a coffin. You could have a shroud instead.
12. You don't usually need to be embalmed, unless you're being repatriated to another country.
13. You can usually spend time with the person who has died, even if they haven't been embalmed.
14. You can usually be involved in caring for the person who has died. A good funeral director will be able to support you with this.
15. Spending time with the person who has died can be a profound and important experience.
16. A dead person is still a person.
17. It's still possible to have a beautiful and meaningful funeral, even if COVID-19-related restrictions are in place. You might have to keep it very simple and think creatively, but know that some of the most profound funerals we've seen happened when the strictest restrictions were being enforced.

18. A *Humanist* funeral is taken by an accredited celebrant from Humanists UK but a *non-religious* funeral can be taken by any celebrant. Make sure you understand the difference when you're working out the kind of funeral ceremony you'd like.

19. A good funeral honours the person who has died but is for benefit of the living.

20. We can celebrate a life without forgetting to mourn a death.

21. It's OK to cry at a funeral. If you can't cry at a funeral, when can you cry?

22. We don't need to apologise for our emotions.

23. Once you've been cremated, all that's left are bones, which are put into a machine called a cremulator and ground into fine powder, known as 'the ashes'.

24. The average fully grown adult produces about 3.6kg (8lb) of ash. That's about the size of a small shoebox.

25. You don't have to leave the flowers at the crematorium. You might want to take them home, or divide them up into smaller bunches for everyone to take away with them.

26. Funerals don't have to cost the earth. The amount of money you spend on the funeral does not equate to how much you loved the person.

27. The funeral industry is ready to change. If you're a creative, compassionate and emotionally switched-on person who might be interested in working in funerals, applications are open!

28. Working in the world of funerals can be a profound, meaningful and life-changing career choice.

29. There are new forms of body disposal being developed, but they're being met with resistance. In the UK, alkaline hydrolysis (also known as water cremation) has been delayed due to the alleged 'yuck factor'. Cremation had the same problem when it was legalised in 1902. Now cremation is the most popular choice for over 70 per cent of people in the UK.

30. We need more funeral-friendly venues as an alternative to the crematorium. If you run a venue and can safely allow funerals to take place, you'll be part of a big change towards making funerals less daunting experiences.

31. If you see a hearse, stop and take a moment. If you're at a pedestrian crossing, allow the hearse to go ahead, don't make it wait for you to cross the road. Take it as an opportunity to remember that there's a person inside the coffin and that one day, it will be you.

32. Don't wait for the funeral to say how you feel. Say it now, before it's too late.

GRIEF

1. Grief does not have five stages. It's messy and unpredictable.
2. Everyone's grief is unique.
3. Grief lasts a lifetime.
4. Grief changes but it never goes away. How you feel right now isn't how you'll always feel.
5. We all manage in different ways.
6. Never ever judge how someone else manages their own grief. Don't assume they're not grieving because they're not doing or saying the things you'd expect.
7. Don't praise bereaved people for 'coping marvellously' or 'doing well'.
8. *Think before you speak*. Things don't happen for a reason. There aren't necessarily plenty more fish in the sea. He probably isn't in a better place. They probably aren't relieved. You have no idea how anyone else feels.
9. Do not judge anyone for 'moving on' and finding a new life (or relationship) quicker than you'd expect. It's not a reflection of the depth of their love for the person who has died.
10. Never tell someone they 'should' be 'over' it by now. Never.
11. The legacy of someone you love lasts a lifetime. Be prepared to carry them in your head and heart forever.
12. When someone you know is grieving, don't be afraid to say you have no idea what to say or do. No one expects you to.
13. The depth of our grief is often directly proportional to the depth of the love we felt for the person who died.
14. Social media has changed the way we grieve. A Facebook profile might become an online memorial with friends and families sharing memories for years to come.
15. Be wary of the Facebook 'memories' feature. They always seem to pop up with a heartbreaking memory at the worst possible time. You can disable the notifications if they become too much.
16. 'Disenfranchised grief' describes the grief that society doesn't acknowledge. It doesn't make it any less painful or tricky. A home, a job, a celebrity – it's not irrelevant just because it's not a family member.
17. 'Anticipatory grief' is the grief we feel when we know someone is going to die. It can also be the fear we are going to lose something or someone – even if those feelings aren't based in reality.
18. We don't just grieve people who have died. We grieve lost love, friendships, our youth. Grief touches much more of our lives than we sometimes realise. Grief doesn't just belong to death.

19. Bereavement is what happens to us. Grief is what we feel. Mourning is what we do.
20. You never 'get over' the death of someone you love. You may learn to live with it and without their physical presence, but you'll never get over them.
21. It's OK to say their name. It's important to say their name. And to keep saying their name.
22. Tears are not weakness. It's OK to cry, and there's no limit to the tears you're allowed to shed. Cry a raincloud, if you need to.
23. It's OK if someone cries when you talk to them. You didn't do anything wrong.
24. Don't tell someone you understand what they're going through. Even if you've been through a similar situation. Every grief is different. Don't compare.
25. There are no right or wrong ways to grieve.
26. Show up after the funeral flowers have wilted. Set reminders to remember birthdays, anniversaries and important dates. Your life will quickly go back to normal; the bereaved person has a new life to forge. Be there for the long haul.
27. Make food. Delicious and healthy food that can be put in the freezer. Not just lasagne.
28. Tell stories of what the person who has died meant to you. It's lovely to know the person you loved had an impact on other people too.
29. When someone dies, the bond we shared with them doesn't die. A mother whose child has died doesn't stop being a mother.
30. Remembering and honouring the person who has died doesn't prevent moving on. It can be healing.
31. Grief really does come in waves. Calm seas, followed by huge waves that feel like they'll drown you. Try to remember the desperation you are feeling right this second will fade. It will no doubt return, then fade once again.
32. You can't rush grief. Give yourself the time you need, don't ever try to hold yourself to an arbitrary timeline. Think carefully before making life-changing decisions too soon after someone significant to you dies.
33. Treats help. Nice things help. Nice people help.
34. Never be afraid to ask for help. Never be afraid to ask for company. Friends may not want to intrude on your grief.
35. Note to friends: intrude, gently and considerately – keep intruding, frequently and with love. Being there for someone who is grieving isn't an intrusion at all. They might not be 'good company' but include them in your life. When they turn down your 999th invitation, ask your 1000th. Hold their hand. Walk their path. Help them find their new way.

IN THE END, ALL THAT REALLY MATTERS

1. Be kind.
2. Be really kind, to strangers and to the people you love. Most importantly, be kind to yourself.
3. Tomorrow might never come. Today is precious, and so are you.
4. Live your life; don't let it be something that happens to you. Grab it by the balls and enjoy it all – even the bad stuff. It's not possible to be positive all the time but by acknowledging our mortality, that gelato will taste a little bit better.
5. Acknowledge the negatives as well as the positives.
6. Whatever you're feeling, it's OK.
7. Life is finite, and it's yours for the taking. So live it. Every second of it. Moments are all we have.
8. Love with all your heart. But know when you need to walk away.
9. Be generous. Giving is definitely better than receiving.
10. Love never dies. It lives on.
11. Say sorry when you've been a dick. Say sorry when someone is hurt, even if you didn't intend to upset them. Accepting responsibility and saying sorry makes the world a better place.
12. Start to take chances on happiness. Once you have, don't stop.
13. Friends are the family we choose.
14. Don't ignore that lump, that persistent cough, that blood in your poo. Find a way to manage getting that smear. Cop a feel of your boobs regularly. Fondle your balls often and carefully enough for you to notice changes. Slather on that sun cream and get yourself a nice hat. Get your moles checked. If you sense something is awry, go and get it checked.
15. Never be afraid to ask for a second opinion. Doctors are not God. They make mistakes. If you're not comfortable or happy with your treatment, ask to see someone else.
16. Dare to dream. Don't be the typist of someone else's.
17. Sleep is a wonderful thing. Lack of sleep makes everything harder to cope with. So does not drinking enough water.
18. You cannot pour from an empty cup: when you're caring for someone, you also need to care for yourself.
19. If you know someone who is being a carer for someone who is poorly, look after them. Care for the carer.
20. No one ever really ends up where they expect. Don't be afraid to veer from the plan.
21. Don't always have a plan. Some of the best things in life happen when you have no plans at all.

22. As our clients are always telling us, 'Getting old isn't for wimps.' Make the most of your youth and health, while you still have it.
23. Don't waste your life waiting to be loved.
24. Life is a series of mini lives. Don't be afraid to move to the next chapter. Don't hold yourself in one place for too long because you're scared of what's next. Chances are there's some wonderful stuff right around the corner.
25. Set an example. If your kids see and hear you talking about difficult things they'll be better equipped to do the same.
26. Do the work on yourself. Get a therapist. Show up for your therapy appointments.
27. What's the worst that can happen? You can die? You're going to die anyway. The worst thing that can happen is that you don't get to live a full life – a life bursting full of the wonderful, the difficult, the beautiful and the bleak. The worst that can happen isn't dying; the worst that can happen is never allowing yourself to live.
28. We don't know when this will be over. The best we can hope for is to live a life with purpose and meaning.
29. Eat the gelato. Especially if it's salted caramel.
30. Wear the bikini.
31. See the world.
32. Be generous with all you have.
33. When you get the chance to make someone's life better, do it.

In the end, what really matters is knowing that we're loved, and that those around us know they're loved.

We don't know what happens next. We haven't died and lived to tell the tale. But what we do know is this: life is about love and the way we show our love. It's about the stories we live and tell. It's about our connections with each other. It's about the mark we leave imprinted on the hearts and souls of the people we love and who love us in return.

It's all a glorious, unpredictable, fragile, unstable, frightening, beautiful, wonderful and surprising mess.

Life, in the end, is all we have.

THE END.

Get involved with Life. Death. Whatever.

If you've been inspired by what you've read here, we'd love to invite you to join our online community of like-minded individuals and organisations.

The Life. Death. Whatever. website is full of inspiration, resources and guidance for whatever you're going through. You can read more about our work, find news about our events, submit your own Five Things and find details of how to get involved with Unsaid.

www.lifedeathwhatever.com

You can join us on Facebook, Instagram (lifedeathwhat) and Twitter (@lifedeathwhat) or email us at enquiries@lifedeathwhatever.com

The dictionary
of death & dying

[A + L]

A collection of the weird, wonderful and often misunderstood language used in relation to death and dying.

A IS FOR:

Advance Directives – legally binding documents (sometimes known as a 'living will') that set out someone's specific wishes for medical treatment if their health deteriorates and they're unable to make their wishes clear. It allows people to state their desire to refuse certain treatments, like CPR

Advance Statement – a document that is not legally binding, but in a similar way to a birth plan, allows you to express your preferences for care and treatment

Afterlife – the belief that someone's identity or soul continues to exist after death

Ashes – the fine, dusty, gritty grey substance that remains after a body has been cremated, comprising of large fragments of bone, which are then ground in a *cremulator*

Asleep – a euphemism for someone who is dead

Assisted/Accompanied Suicide – the act of intentionally ending a person's life to relieve suffering, also known as *euthanasia*

Autopsy – see *post-mortem*

B IS FOR:

Bearer – someone who carries the coffin, also known as a *pall-bearer*

Body, the – the term used by funeral directors to refer to the physical remains of the person who has died

C IS FOR:

Cadaver – medical term for a dead body, American

Casket – a four-sided, hinged box, usually for burial

Catafalque – a raised platform used to hold the coffin during the funeral

Celebrant – someone, usually secular, who performs a rite or ceremony such as a funeral or a wedding

Chapel of Rest – a quiet space where families and friends are able to spend time with their dead, also known as the family room

Coffin – a box used to house someone who has died, usually wider at the shoulders and narrow at the feet to fit the shape of a body

Complicated grief – a chronic and heightened grief whereby people often feel unable to manage

Coroner – an official who investigates deaths when the cause is unknown, there is reason to think the death may not be due to natural causes, or that an inquiry is needed for some other reason

Corpse – a dead body

COVID-19 – an infectious acute respiratory disease caused by SARS-CoV-2, a new coronavirus discovered in 2019

CPR – cardiopulmonary resuscitation, an emergency procedure combining chest compressions with 'mouth to mouth' artificial ventilation to 'manually preserve intact brain function' when someone goes into cardiac arrest

Cremator – the machine used for cremation

Cremulator – the machine that grinds the remnants of bone left after cremation takes place

Curtains, the – a fabric mechanism that closes around a coffin as a way of saying goodbye before a cremation takes place

D IS FOR:

Death – the end of life. Synonyms for death include demise, end, passing, passing away, passing on, expired

Death anxiety – the uncomfortable thoughts and emotions that can arise when facing the fact that we will definitely die one day

Death awareness – the state of facing life, in all its difficulties and complexities, with the awareness that one day we're all going to die

Death Cafe – a gathering of people who come together to talk about death over tea and cake

Deceased, the – the funeral profession's favourite way of describing a person who has died, replaced by 'the person who has died' or simply the person's name by progressive funeral professionals who believe that people deserve an identity after they've died

Decomposition – the process a body goes through after death as it's broken down

Dignitas – a Swiss organisation providing assisted/accompanied suicide to people living with life-limiting conditions

Direct cremation – the process of disposing of a body by cremation without a funeral service beforehand and with no one in attendance

E IS FOR:

Embalming – the process of preserving a body using chemicals, also called *hygienic treatment*

Epidemic – a disease that affects a large number of people within a community, population, or region

Euthanasia – see *assisted suicide*

F IS FOR:

Fell asleep – euphemism for died

Floral tributes – funeral director talk for the flowers presented at a funeral in honour of a person who has died

Fridge, the – where people who have died are kept cool, usually on stainless-steel trays

G IS FOR:

Good death – the idea that everyone should die well, now being replaced with the idea that a fitting or quiet death is a healthier thing to aspire towards, especially in circumstances that are outside our control

Green, the – the form that is issued by the registry office in the UK giving permission for a burial or cremation to go ahead

H IS FOR:

Hospice – a treatment model providing holistic care and emotional support for people living with life-limiting illness

Hygienic treatment – the alternative name for *embalming* used by some funeral directors, often to avoid the word and disguise the process

I IS FOR:

Inquest – a judicial inquiry to determine the cause of death

Interment – the burial of a body or ashes

K IS FOR:

Kintsugi – the Japanese art of repairing broken pottery with gold-, silver- or platinum-dusted lacquer

L IS FOR:

Life – the condition of existence, the act of being alive

Lockdown – a requirement for people to stay at home or shelter in place.

M IS FOR:

Mortician – an American term for a funeral director

Mortuary – a cold room where people who have died are stored

Mortuary technician – someone who helps with the day-to-day running of the mortuary

MRI – Magnetic Resonance Imaging, sometimes used as an alternative to a post-mortem

N IS FOR:

Nameplate – a plaque that has to go on to the coffin to identify the person who is inside

Natural burial – returning the body to the ground in the most natural way possible

New normal – a previously unfamiliar state of affairs which has become the norm

P IS FOR:

Pall-bearers – the people who carry the coffin, also known as *bearers*

Palliative care – consists of treatment, support and care for people living with life-limiting illness. Palliative care is holistic and aims to improve quality of life

Pandemic – a global outbreak of a disease, crossing international borders and usually affecting large numbers of people

Part 4 and 5 – paperwork that has to be filled in by two separate doctors in the UK before a cremation can go ahead. Part 5 was suspended at the beginning of the COVID-19 outbreak

Pathologist – a doctor who determines the cause of death

Post-mortem – the medical examination of a body after death to determine the cause of death, also known as an *autopsy*

PPE – personal protective equipment, includes items such as helmets, gloves, eye protection, high-visibility clothing, safety footwear and harnesses, as well as respiratory protective equipment, such as face masks

Pyre – large outdoor bonfire used to burn the dead in some cultures

Q IS FOR:

Quarantine – when displaying symptoms of an infectious disease, the necessity to spend a period of time in isolation to prevent transmission

R IS FOR:

Rainbow baby – a baby that is born following neonatal death, miscarriage, stillbirth or infant loss

Rest, at – a euphemism for dead

Rigor mortis – stiffening of the limbs after death caused by chemical changes in the muscles

S IS FOR:

Scanxiety – anxiety produced in anticipation of a scan, during the scan and then waiting for the results of the scan

Scattering – when ashes are released, traditionally called strewing

Shroud – a simple cotton sheet that can be used to cover and carry a person who has died; an alternative to a coffin

Skin slip – when the skin begins to peel away from the body of the person who has died, due to decomposition

Sleeping – a euphemism for dead

Stillborn – a baby who died before being born

T IS FOR:

Trocar – the item of equipment used by embalmers to puncture the main organs around the stomach in order to remove the contents

U IS FOR:

Undertaker – a person who is appointed to handle all aspects of the disposal of the dead and the funeral, also known as a funeral director

V IS FOR:

Viewing – a term used by some funeral directors to describe when people see the person who has died

W IS FOR:

Wake – traditionally the gathering after the funeral service, or sometimes the time spent with someone who has died before the funeral

Whatever – the word we use after Life. and Death. to indicate that how we deal with life says everything about how we deal with death

Will – a legally binding document in which a person states who will receive their possessions once they have died

Wreath – an arrangement of flowers for a funeral

Y IS FOR:

YOLO – you only live once

YODO – you only die once

Z IS FOR:

Zoroastrianism – an ancient Persian religion that originated 4000 years ago and is one of the oldest religions still in existence

Resources & recommended reading

[A + L]

Support, guidance and inspiration for wherever you are on your journey.

Death & dying

ZEN CAREGIVING PROJECT
A groundbreaking project in San Francisco that exists to re-imagine the end-of-life experience for both the living and people who are dying.
www.zencaregiving.org

COMPASSION IN DYING
A UK charity supporting people to know and understand their legal rights at the end of life.
www.compassionindying.org.uk

Read anything by A.A. Gill, especially his words on alcoholism, dying and the NHS. He died at Charing Cross Hospital in December 2016 and wrote beautifully about the sudden, traumatic and painful experience of lung cancer for *The Sunday Times*.

With the End in Mind by Dr Kathryn Mannix (William Collins, 2018)

A Beginner's Guide to the End: Practical Advice for Living Life and Facing Death by B.J. Miller and Shoshana Berger (Simon & Schuster, 2019)

Being Mortal by Atul Gawande (Profile Books Ltd, 2015)

Dear Life by Rachel Clarke (Little, Brown Book Group, 2020)

When Breath Becomes Air by Paul Kalanithi (Vintage, 2017)

Before I Say Goodbye by Ruth Picardie (Penguin, 1998)

Late Fragments: Everything I Want to Tell You (About This Magnificent Life) by Kate Gross (William Collins, 2015)

Advice for Future Corpses by Sallie Tisdale (Gallery Books, 2018)

Ask Me His Name: Learning to Live and Laugh Again After the Loss of My Baby by Elle Wright (Lagom, 2018)

Passed On: African American Mourning Stories by Karla FC Holloway (Duke University Press, 2002)

If you're interested in developing your knowledge of death and dying in an academic context, the University of Winchester offers a Masters degree in Death, Religion & Culture. Taught entirely online, you'll examine the ways in which death and dying are understood differently by various cultures and religious traditions, and how those understandings are played out in rituals of death, dying and bereavement. **www.winchester.ac.uk/study/postgraduate/courses/ma-death-religion-and-culture**

Grief

GOOD GRIEF TRUST

We haven't overwhelmed you with details of all the amazing charities you can turn to for support, because there are just so many. If you need help with your grief but don't know what kind of help you need or where to find it, have a look at the Good Grief Trust website. It's run for the bereaved by the bereaved. They'll be able to point you in the right direction.
www.thegoodgrieftrust.org

THE FANDANGOE KID

A print artist who addresses mental health, grief and love with brilliant and bold statements. She also runs workshops on creativity and grief.
www.fandangookid.com

REFUGE IN GRIEF

If you're looking for support with your grief, Megan Devine's website Refuge in Grief provides helpful and insightful advice that's relevant to modern life. 'Grief support that doesn't suck' is how it's been described.
www.refugeingrief.com

Griefcast (podcast) with Cariad Lloyd, available on Acast

It's Ok That You're Not Ok: Meeting Grief and Loss in a Culture That Doesn't Understand by Megan Devine (Sounds True, 2017)

Grief Works by Julia Samuel (Penguin Life, 2018)

The Dead Moms Club: A Memoir about Death, Grief, and Surviving the Mother of All Losses by Kate Spencer (Seal Press, 2017)

The Year of Magical Thinking by Joan Didion (Harper Perennial, 2006)

A Manual for Heartache by Cathy Rentzenbrink (Picador, 2017)

Funerals

GOOD FUNERAL GUIDE

A not-for-profit, independent guide to all things funeral related. The GFG go above and beyond in their commitment to improving the world of funerals, and have had a big impact on forcing the industry to behave transparently. Read their blog to stay up to date with what's happening in Funeralworld and use their directory to find a good funeral director.
www.goodfuneralguide.co.uk

GOOD FUNERAL GUILD

If you're interested in improving funerals, join the Good Funeral Guild, an initiative from the Good Funeral Guide. It's a powerful collective of like-minded people who are working to change funerals for the better.
www.goodfuneralguild.co.uk

THE NATURAL DEATH CENTRE

The Natural Death Centre has been helping people stay informed and empowered for more than 20 years. The charity's three-part handbook is a fascinating and life-changing read. It's essential for anyone who works in the world of death and dying, or is just curious about how things can be done differently.
www.naturaldeath.org.uk

FITTING TRIBUTE FUNERALS

If you're based in the USA, take a look at Amy Cunningham's pioneering funeral service, Fitting Tribute Funerals, in New York. She's running a much-needed service for people who want something inspired and inspiring in a state where the corporate approach dominates. Amy also runs The Inspired Funeral, which is an invaluable resource for everything to do with funeral ceremonies in America.
www.theinspiredfuneral.com
www.fittingtributefunerals.com

NATIONAL HOME FUNERAL ALLIANCE

A not-for-profit organisation in the USA, offering legal guidance and practical help on all aspects of doing the funeral yourself, without needing to use conventional funeral professionals.
www.homefuneralalliance.org

QUEER FUNERAL GUIDE

Ash Hayhurst is a queer trans funeral professional who has written an excellent guide to funerals for anyone who is lesbian, gay, bisexual, transgender or queer and concerned about their future funeral arrangements.

Ash says: 'The guide isn't just for LGBTQ+ people and their families, it's also for funeral professionals and anyone who works with LGBTQ+ folk. My hope is that it will help queer people to feel more empowered so that they can make the choices that are right for them. I hope it will also open up conversations between professionals about how we can help bereaved family members, and provide a space where they feel safe to be open about the whole identity of the person who has died.'
www.queerfuneralguide.co.uk

Do Funerals Matter? by William G. Hoy (Routledge, 2013)

The Good Funeral Guide by Charles Cowling (Continuum, 2010)

Funerals Your Way: A Person-Centred Approach to Planning a Funeral by Sarah Jones (independently published, 2018)

Time to Go: Practical Celebrations for the Final Milestone by Jean Francis (iUniverse, 2004)

The Dead Good Funerals Book (Dead Good Guides) by Sue Gill and John Fox (Engineers of the Imagination, 2006)

The Undertaker at Work: 1900–1950 by Brian Parsons (Strange Attractor Press, 2015)

How Great Thou Art: Fifty Years of African Caribbean Funerals in London by Paul Goodwin (Photofusion Educational Trust, 2014)

Other

Life, Lemons & Melons by Alice-May Purkiss (Blurb, 2019)

The Complete Guide to Breast Cancer: How to Feel Empowered and Take Control by Professor Trisha Greenhalgh and Dr Liz O'Riordan (Vermilion, 2018)

Somebody I Used to Know: A Memoir by Wendy Mitchell (Bloomsbury, 2018)

All the Ghosts in the Machine: The Digital Afterlife of your Personal Data by Elaine Kasket (Robinson, 2019)

The English Book of the Dead by Dave Marteau (Marcela Books, 2019)

Life Kitchen: Recipes to Revive the Joy of Taste & Flavour by Ryan Riley (Bloomsbury, 2020)

The Lost Properties of Love by Sophie Ratcliffe (William Collins, 2019)

Poetry

Essential resources for finding beautiful, modern, meaningful poetry related to love and loss.

The Book of Love & Loss, edited by R.V. Bailey and June Hall (Belgrave Press, 2014)

Staying Alive: Real Poems for Unreal Times by Neil Astley (Bloodaxe, 2002)

Being Alive: the Sequel to Staying Alive by Neil Astley (Bloodaxe, 2004)

Being Human by Neil Astley (Bloodaxe, 2011)

Love Makes a Mess of Dying by Greg Gilbert (smith|doorstop), 2019)

There Are Words: Collected Poems by Gael Turnbull (Shearsman Books, 2006)

Inventions of Farewell: A Collection of Elegies by Sandra M. Gilbert
(W. W. Norton & Company, 2001)

The Colour of Love by Jonathan Steffen (Acumen Publications, 2011)

Resources for children

WINSTON'S WISH
Winston's Wish supports children and their families after the death of a parent or sibling.
www.winstonswish.org

CHILD BEREAVEMENT UK
Child Bereavement UK supports families and educates professionals both when a baby or child of any age dies or is dying, and when a child is facing bereavement.
www.childbereavementuk.org

GRIEF ENCOUNTER
Grief Encounter supports children and their families to help alleviate the pain caused by the death of someone close to them.
www.griefencounter.org.uk

SANDS
Sands works to support anyone affected by the death of a baby, improve the care bereaved parents receive, and create a world where fewer babies die.
www.sands.org.uk

Acknowledgements

[A + L]

This book was written in honour of Jon Underwood, whose life's work has been of immense consequence to our life's work in death and dying.

We'd both like to say a huge thank you to our team at Bloomsbury – Charlotte Croft, Holly Jarrald, Zoë Blanc, Amy Greaves, Katherine Macpherson, Lizzy Ewer and Alice Graham – as well as our agent Lauren Gardner at Bell Lomax & Moreton. Thank you for believing in a book about death and dying and understanding that it's also about life and living.

Thank you to everyone who has supported Life. Death. Whatever. in so many different ways, to those who have trusted us with their unspoken words for Unsaid and to those who have allowed us to share their experiences for Five Things.

Thank you so very much to everyone who has contributed their words and stories.

This book has come to life because of the people who have shared their lives, their grief, and their deaths, with us. There are no words to describe our gratitude.

From Anna, with love

I'd like to thank everyone who has trusted me to support and walk alongside them. It has been such an honour to be a part of your lives. To the people who know some of the people who feature in these pages. These are my memories, I'm sure yours will be slightly different but I hope you feel I've conveyed the essence of the people we know and love. The book is a tribute to them.

To PBW, AHT, EOL, KF, MH, JL, DPB, FL, AW, JS, PH, VL, LT, CJD, BR, BO, KSJ, ST & BB. Your lives and your deaths have left an indelible mark.

To Louise, I count myself very lucky to work side by side with my friend. It's never easy but it's always worth it. Thank you so much.

For Lynn, there is no better teacher on earth. You are incredible. Thank you.

To Ella, for helping me to find me again. You'll never know how much it means.

To Sally, for everything you did on that day and beyond. I'll never forget it.

To Nat, I've no idea what I'd do without all our cups of coffee. Thank you, Towner.

To Jo, John (BD), Stan, Elsie and Beryl, for your endless support, for always letting us over-stay our welcome and loving us all regardless.

To Jam, Sarah C, YDH, CJ, HJB, AN, KC, MP & Charlie A.

To Sue L for your incredible proof-reading skills and so much more.

Thank you, Lois. I miss your wisdom so very much.

Thank you, Dad, for keeping a roof over our heads.

To Tom, with all my love always.

To DNRF, for showing me a whole new way of looking at the world.

For the irreplaceable Cath Dean. With love and gratitude.

To Princess 'Peebs' Bubblegum, you're the very best.

To GJS, for looking after the two smalls so I can hide away and type.

For Saima, with so much love. You are so missed.

And for Kim, where to even begin describing how much I learnt from you and how glad and grateful I am to have known you. I miss you, KSJ.

To the small army of people who helped when I was unwell. Thank you for all the meals, the fun for the girls, the smoothies, the soup, the love and the support. I'm not sure I'd be here today without you all.

One of the main reasons I wrote this book was to show my three daughters that there's nothing in life that they can't achieve. I wrote it for them: Mouse, Marley & Scout. You three are everything. This is for you.

From Louise, with appreciation

Without you, this book wouldn't have been possible:

My co-author, colleague and friend – Anna Lyons.

The people who chose Poetic Endings and in doing so, trusted us to take care of the people they love, whilst inspiring us with their ideas about how to say goodbye.

My friends and colleagues – Fran Hall, Lucy Coulbert, Natasha Bradshaw, Clare Harriott, Joanna Shears, Annika Caswell, Angie McLachlan, Natalie Charles, David Holmes, Jason Maiden, Ray Barnes, Michael Tiney, Peter Taylor, Lara Iredale, Hannah Jackson-McCamley, Ash Hayhurst, Amy Cunningham, Rosalie Kuyvenhoven, Clare Brookes, Charles Cowling, May Andrews, Andrew Hickson, Natasha Mercer, Hasina Zaman, Allistair Anderson, Dave Gordon-Shute, Jane Morgan, Isabel Russo, Toby Angel, Emma Curtis, Lee David Bengough, Indra Joyce, Jo Williamson, Carrie Thomas, Cara Mair, Carrie Weekes, Fran Glover and Rupert & Claire Callender.

The people who support me in making this important and sometimes impossible work possible – Martin Green, Matthew Green, Sandra Bromwich, Emma Bromwich, Dave Humphrey, Lauren D'mello, Lee Pennycard and the rest of the team at Green's Carriage Masters (especially Dean, Alan, Brian, Brian, Noel and Andrew), the exemplary team at Mortlake Crematorium who lead the way in setting the standards other crematoria should follow, Jamie Dundas and Laura Hicks at the Refinery, the team at Uncommon, Kea Kouvatsis at Linden House, Sue Barsky Reid, Jools Barsky and Megan Sipe-Mooney at Death Cafe, and all the members of the Good Funeral Guild, who work tirelessly to improve funerals for everyone.

Thank you for the adventures – David Blackwell.

Thank you for your love, support, encouragement and patience – Chris & Jane Hemmings, Rachel Hemmings, Dorothy Briggs, Gregory Wild-Smith, Julia Duncan, Laura Greenwood, Anne Bedi, Charlie Gavins, Shabnam Naomi Spiers, Andrew Maginley, Steve Mead, Steve Halliwell, Lis Jackson, Brigitte Bako, Sozanne Li, Olivia Belk, Cathy Negus-Fancey, Dr Lindsey Fitzharris, Lucy Coleman Talbot, Alex Collins, Annie Streater, Michael Miller, Paul Gerard, Chris Greenwood, Mary Short, Tiu de Haan, Hamilton Stansfield, Kristina Eastwood, Philip Weeks, Professor Jamie Hacker-Hughes and everyone at 1Rebel.

In loving memory of the irreplaceable Lillan Osterberg Webb.

Index

About the authors

Anna Lyons is an end-of-life doula. She supports people who are living with life-limiting illness, their family and friends. Her aim is to help people to live as good a life as possible right up until the very end. **Louise Winter** is a funeral director. Her mission is to get people to rethink funerals. She believes that a good funeral can be transformational in helping us to acknowledge and accept that someone has died.

Together they're the team behind **Life. Death. Whatever.** Their award-winning work, both together and separately, has been featured in publications around the world from the *Guardian* to *Grazia*.

Follow Life. Death. Whatever.
@lifedeathwhat
www.lifedeathwhatever.com